1917 and Beyond

Continuity, Rupture and Memory in Russian Music

edited by

Philip Ross Bullock and Pauline Fairclough

Modern Humanities Research Association
for the
UCL School of Slavonic and East European Studies
2019

Published by

The Modern Humanities Research Association
Salisbury House
Station Road
Cambridge CB1 2LA
United Kingdom
for the
UCL School of Slavonic and East European Studies

© UCL School of Slavonic and East European Studies, 2019
for selection and editorial matter; individual contributions
their contributors

The authors assert their right under the Copyright, Designs and Patents Act 1988 to be identified as the authors of this work. Parts of this work may be reproduced as permitted under legal provisions for fair dealing (or fair use) for the purposes of research, private study, criticism, or review, or when a relevant collective licensing agreement is in place. All other reproduction requires the written permission of the copyright holder who may be contacted at seer@ucl.ac.uk.

This collection also appeared as Volume 97:1 (2019) of
The Slavonic and East European Review

First published 2019

ISBN 978-1-78188-953-4

CONTENTS

Introduction — 1917 and Beyond: Continuity, Rupture and Memory in Russian Music
Philip Ross Bullock and Pauline Fairclough   1

1. Personal Friendships, Professional Manoeuvres: Edward Elgar in Russia before and after 1917
Pauline Fairclough   9

2. Revolutionaries or Delinquents: The Biopsychological Appraisals of Composers and Their Music in Early Soviet Russia
James Taylor   39

3. How Soviet Musicology became Marxist
Olga Panteleeva   73

4. The Birth of the Soviet Romance from the Spirit of Russian Modernism
Philip Ross Bullock   110

5. In Search of Russia: Sergei Rakhmaninov and the Politics of Music Memory after 1917
Rebecca Mitchell   136

6. To What End *Rusalka*? Pushkin's Folk Tragedy and Dargomyzhskii's Opera
Caryl Emerson   169

Notes on contributors   201

Cover image: 'Vladimir Lenin and Maria Ulyanova going to the Bolshoi Theater for the meeting of the 5th All-Russian Congress of Soviets', 4 July 1918 © Sputnik Images

Introduction

1917 and Beyond: Continuity, Rupture and Memory in Russian Music

PHILIP ROSS BULLOCK & PAULINE FAIRCLOUGH

LONG before the commemoration of the hundredth anniversary of the Russian Revolution in 2017, scholars of Russia and the Soviet Union had questioned the notion that 1917 might constitute some kind of single, decisive rupture, whether in historiography or history itself. In particular, historians have come to see the October Revolution as an expression of Russia's broader experience of modernity, revealing continuities between Imperial Russia and what was to become the Soviet Union, disputing narratives of exceptionalism, and proposing affinities with models of social development arguably more characteristic of Western European countries.[1] Literary scholars too had long grasped the significant connections between pre- and post-revolutionary instantiations of Russian modernism, even if these were often disputed by émigré authorities unable, or unwilling, to admit that the Soviet Union might have any claims on culture. Vladimir Nabokov, no less, offered a survey course at Cornell University in 1950 on 'The Modernist Movement in Russian Literature', which included Tolstoi, Chekhov, Blok, and even the nineteenth-century lyric poets, Fet and Tiutchev, yet pointedly avoided anything written in Soviet Union after 1917.[2] This was, though, an extreme position. More typical were those scholars who explored the continuation of the so-called 'Silver Age' well into the 1920s, or those, by contrast, who saw the roots of Soviet modernism in the

---

[1] See, for instance, David L. Hoffmann and Yanni Kotsonis (eds), *Russian Modernity: Politics, Knowledge, Practices*, Basingstoke, 2000; Daniel Beer, *Renovating Russia: The Human Sciences and the Fate of Liberal Modernity, 1880–1930*, Ithaca, NY and London, 2008; Michael David-Fox, *Crossing Borders: Modernity, Ideology, and Culture in Russia and the Soviet Union*, Pittsburgh, 2015; Mark D. Steinberg, *Proletarian Imagination: Self, Modernity, and the Search for the Sacred in Russia, 1910–1925*, Ithaca, NY and London, 2002; and Matthias Neumann and Andy Willimott (eds), *Rethinking the Russian Revolution as Historical Divide*, London, 2018.

[2] Brian Boyd, *Vladimir Nabokov: The American Years*, London, 1992, p. 171, cited in Catriona Kelly (ed.), *Utopias: Russian Modernist Texts, 1905–1940*, London, 1999, p. xix.

pre-revolutionary era or even the *fin de siècle*.³ Intellectual historians were equally alive to the impact of pre-revolutionary thought on Soviet culture, not just in the form of the precursors of the Marxist-Leninist canon, but also as represented, perhaps more surprisingly, by the complex and ambiguous legacy of Nietzsche or Russia's engagement with psychoanalysis and the theories of Freud and Jung.⁴

But what of music in this context, and how have musicologists conceived of the impact of the October Revolution? Superficially, at least, the notion of 1917 as a dramatic caesura is one that still continues to inform aspects of historical musicology. In part, this may be related to the very obvious fact that some of Russia's most prominent composers left around the time of the revolution — most notably Sergei Prokof'ev, Sergei Rakhmaninov and Igor' Stravinskii. Even if their motivations were very different, their collective stories nonetheless give the impression of a radical discontinuity. The fact that within Soviet Russia itself, it was the young Dmitrii Shostakovich who came to symbolize the cultural aspirations of the new state further corroborates this impression of a clear divide. Indeed, the whole history of twentieth-century music could be provocatively read through the binary oppositions seemingly represented by the pairing of Stravinskii and Shostakovich: Russia Abroad versus the Soviet Union; freedom versus tyranny; pure music versus musical meaning; modernism versus Socialist Realism, and so on. Such an account would, of course, be facile and reductive, yet is nonetheless often implicitly there in popular narratives, even whilst it has been comprehensively challenged in much of the academic literature. Staying with the biographical context for a moment, it is instructive to compare the story of Russian music with that represented in literary histories. Here, despite the emigration of a large number of key figures of the Silver Age, the picture is often one of a greater sense of continuity. Take, for instance, Ronald Hingley's *Nightingale Fever*, a study

---

³ Boris Gasparov, Robert P. Hughes and Irina Paperno (eds), *Cultural Mythologies of Russian Modernism: From the Golden Age to the Silver Age*, Berkeley and Los Angeles, CA and London, 1992; Irina Paperno and Joan Delaney Grossman (eds), *Creating Life: The Aesthetic Utopia of Russian Modernism*, Stanford, CA, 1994; David Bethea, *The Shape of Apocalypse in Modern Russian Fiction*, Princeton, NJ, 1989, and Victor Erlich, *Modernism and Revolution: Russian Literature in Transition*, Cambridge, MA, 1994.

⁴ Bernice Glatzer Rosenthal, *Nietzsche in Russia*, Princeton, NJ, 1986, and *New Myth, New World: From Nietzsche to Stalinism*, University Park, PA, 2002; Bernice Glatzer Rosenthal (ed.), *Nietzsche and Soviet Culture: Ally and Adversary*, Cambridge, 1994; Katherine Lahti, *The Russian Revival of the Dithyramb: A Modernist Use of Antiquity*, Evanston, IL, 2018, and Alexander Etkind, *Eros of the Impossible: The History of Psychoanalysis in Russia*, trans. Noah and Maria Rubins, Boulder, CO, 1997.

of four great modernist poets (Anna Akhmatova, Osip Mandel'shtam, Boris Pasternak and Marina Tsvetaeva).[5] To be sure, Hingley's dramatic martyrology imposes its own problems of historiography, periodization and even interpretation (which is in no way to deny the traumatic impact of history on the lives and creativity of his subjects), yet his is an account of Russian literature that reaches from the 1890s to the Stalin era and even beyond. Historical boundaries will be determined, at least to a certain extent, by the biographical outlines of the figures occupying the centre of any given narrative.

In fact, the seeming centrality of 1917 to the way that Russian music history is understood is far from ubiquitous. Studies of the Russian reception of Wagner have, like those of Nietzsche, posited some striking continuities across the revolutionary divide.[6] Skriabin too served as something of a touchstone when it came to pre- and post-revolutionary attitudes, whether to the piano repertoire, musical modernism, or to music's grander aspirations to represent the ineffable and the noumenal.[7] It is also the case that institutional studies of Russian music — for all that they amply document the enormous task of reorganizing cultural life after the trauma of the revolution and ensuing civil war — have pointed to some crucial factors that make music rather distinct from, say, literature, film or the visual arts (other than the perhaps obvious point that as a non-representational art form, music was less readily inscribed into Bolshevik policy-making than the other arts, at least in the first instance). Foremost here are established practices of international concertizing with roots in the nineteenth century, issues of technical mastery and professional competence, all of which complicated attempts to 'Bolshevize' Soviet musical organizations throughout the 1920s and even in the 1930s and 1940s, leading to some striking instances of the persistence of pre-revolutionary ideas and practices.[8] Scholarship on the

---

[5] Ronald Hingley, *Nightingale Fever: Russian Poets in Revolution*, London, 1982.

[6] Rosamund Bartlett, *Wagner and Russia*, Cambridge, 1995, and Pauline Fairclough, 'Wagner Reception in Stalinist Russia', in Luca Sala (ed.), *The Legacy of Richard Wagner*, Turnhout, 2012, pp. 309–26.

[7] Peter Deane Roberts, *Modernism in Russian Piano Music: Skriabin, Prokofiev, and their Russian Contemporaries*, 2 vols, Bloomington, IN, 1993.

[8] Pauline Fairclough, *Classics for the Masses: Shaping Soviet Musical Identity Under Lenin and Stalin*, New Haven, CT and London, 2016; Amy Nelson, *Music for the Revolution: Musicians and Power in Early Soviet Russia*, University Park, PA, 2004; Kirill Tomoff, *Creative Union: The Professional Organization of Soviet Composers, 1939–1953*, Ithaca, NY and London, 2006, and Marina Frolova-Walker and Jonathan-Walker, *Music and Soviet Power, 1917–1932*, Woodbridge, 2012.

Russian piano performance tradition is also exposing the roots of Soviet practice in turn-of-the-century intellectual and cultural life.[9] If we have only recently begun to examine these, it is perhaps because we have been too willing to subscribe to the revolutionary rhetoric of the modernists and the proletarians and too quick to believe their claims to novelty and rupture. Just as the Futurists' claims to have thrown 'Pushkin, Dostoevsky, Tolstoy, and so on, and so on, off the steamship of modernity' mask a deeper and complex engagement with the literary legacy of the past, so too do the rhetorical strategies of music's modernists demand a more careful exploration of the underlying continuities they set out to disguise or dismiss as nothing more than *perezhitki proshlogo* ('relics of the past').[10]

The most obvious aim of this group of articles is, then, to revisit the question of how we conceptualize the period boundaries that shape the writing of Russian music history, particularly, but not exclusively, with reference to the October Revolution. If much of what is argued here is to do with temporal boundaries, then its concerns are often also equally spatial, given that 1917 did not merely divide the imperial past from the Soviet present, but created both Russia Abroad and the Soviet Union (although even here, the borders could be surprisingly permeable at times). Taking inspiration from a body of scholarship which has problematized the question of how the aesthetic values of the 1920s gave way to what became Socialist Realism, as well as work which has challenged an entrenched divide between the Victorian era and modernism in English literary studies,[11] this collection ranges widely over genres (opera, symphonic music, song), combines complementary methodological approaches (reception studies, cultural memory, librettology, intellectual history) and invokes not only the October Revolution, but other widely cited turning points in Russian history (romanticism into realism, cultural revolution, the Great Patriotic War, perestroika and the post-Soviet landscape, and so on) to suggest significant continuities over the *longue durée*. Yet in calling into question the prominence of 1917 as either a terminal or inaugural moment

---

[9] Maria Razumovskaya, *Heinrich Neuhaus: A Life beyond Music*, Woodbridge, 2018.

[10] David Burlyuk, Aleksei Kruchonykh, Vladimir Mayakovsky and Velimir Khlebikov, 'A Slap in the Face of Public Taste', in Kelly (ed.), *Utopias*, pp. 120–21 (p. 120). See also, James Rann, 'A Stowaway on the Steamship of Modernity: Pushkin and the Futurists', unpublished PhD thesis, University College, London, 2013.

[11] Patrick Zuk, 'Nikolay Myaskovsky and the "Regimentation" of Soviet Composition', *Journal of Musicology*, 31, 2014, 3, pp. 354–93. In English studies, see Laura Marcus, Michèle Mendelsohn and Kirsten Shepherd-Barr (eds), *Late Victorian into Modern*, Oxford, 2016, and Kirsten Mahoney, 'The Transition to Modernism: Recent Scholarship on the Victorian/Modern Divide', *Literature Compass,* 10, 2013, 9, pp. 716–24.

in the periodization of Russian history, one must be wary of unthinkingly reinscribing other fixed points. A number of the articles here make much of the shift in cultural values that occurred towards the end of the 1920s, a period often glossed as a new form of 'cultural revolution'.[12] As Boris Groys has provocatively argued, of course, the notion of a heroic avant-garde giving way to a stultifying form of neo-classicism and conservatism is itself highly problematic, and it is important not to insist too resolutely on this slightly later period as equally, if not more decisive in the establishment of the parameters and paradigms of Soviet culture.[13] If a mantra of the 1930s was 'learn from the classics' — and the period certainly saw the widespread rehabilitation of forms and genres associated above all with the nineteenth century — then that is not the same as saying that it broke entirely with elements of modernism and the avant-garde. Indeed, as Pauline Fairclough has recently argued, the turn towards programming and writing music that was meant to be widely enjoyed was itself part of the Soviet Union's modernizing agenda, as part of the broader rejection of the older bourgeois model of elite versus popular culture.[14]

A further attendant risk in blurring the significance of moments of historical rupture is that one can find oneself not merely attending to deeper patterns of continuity, but unwittingly evoking often stereotypical ideas about mindsets, mentalities and national character which ignore individual agency, the variegated evolution of different fields and genres across time and the interplay between the *longue durée* and moment of undoubted shock and upheaval. Accordingly, several of our contributors focus, in different ways, on the central importance of personal and professional relationships and networks in shaping both practical and theoretical activity in the pre- and post-revolutionary years. Pauline Fairclough's survey of Edward Elgar's reception in Russia both before and after 1917 illustrates the crucial importance of personal relationships between composers, musicians and critics. Elgar's reputation in Russia rested on an extremely tenuous set of conditions: audiences responded to unfamiliar foreign music in the light of the familiar, and often more dazzling, music that they heard alongside it, while the upheaval of the First

---

[12] Sheila Fitzpatrick, *Cultural Revolution in Russia, 1928–1931*, Bloomington, IN, 1988, and Katerina Clark, *Petersburg: Crucible of Cultural Revolution*, Princeton, NJ, 1995.

[13] Boris Groys, *The Total Art of Stalinism: Avant-Garde, Aesthetic Dictatorship, and Beyond*, trans. Charles Rougle, Princeton, NJ, 1992.

[14] Pauline Fairclough, 'Was Soviet Music Middlebrow? Shostakovich's Fifth Symphony, Socialist Realism, and the Mass Listener in the 1930s', *Journal of Musicology*, 35, 2018, 3, pp. 336–67.

World War, then the revolution itself, put paid to the private concert series whose founders had championed the English composer. By the time Soviet Russian audiences were next offered Elgar's music, during Allied concerts, he was a remote figure of the imperial past — an international figure caught between war, revolution and changing fashions and tastes.

James Taylor and Olga Panteleeva both show how nineteenth-century scientific ideas were central to early Soviet musicological and critical narratives. Taylor's account stresses the shared vocabulary between passionately opposed groups: the 'modernist' and the 'proletarian' critics who, despite their animosity, shared multiple concerns and prejudices. Amongst these, the conviction (rooted in nineteenth-century writings not only on evolution but also on social degeneration) that environmental conditions ultimately shaped society's evolutionary progress had an extraordinary effect on Soviet critical writing. In Taylor's paradigm of music writers as 'cultural doctors', critics take on themselves the responsibility for ensuring audiences were subjected only to the 'right' kind of music, lest they develop in the 'wrong' kind of way.

Panteleeva's focus is on a more rarefied form of discourse: the development of key theoretical precepts in early Soviet musicology, as formulated in the scholarly group around Boris Asaf'ev and the Leningrad Institute of Art History in the 1920s. She tracks a process whereby the positivist, science-based elements of fin-de-siècle thought in early twentieth-century Russia go hand-in-hand with a tough, Marxist positivism. Musicologists sought 'internal laws' of music that could be identified, quantified and codified: not only the fabric of a musical work, but also its interpretation, performance and reception were all elements that could be grasped and ultimately controlled. As Panteleeva reveals, the key figure who led this early 'scientific' branch of musicology to a full-blown Marxian sociology of music that dismayed some of his former colleagues was Boris Asaf'ev. The Institute's emphasis on musicology's 'scientific' potential became suspect unless it was harnessed to a sociological platform, entirely in keeping with changing notions of the relative values of science in the cultural sphere (ultimately, all such analytical study would find itself charged under the umbrella term of 'Formalism' — an appropriate enough label, given that key theorists of Russian Formalism — Boris Tomashevskii and Iurii Tinianov among them — were themselves employed at the Institute of Art History).

Philip Ross Bullock turns to a rather differently configured topic in music history; that of genres and their evolution over time. Exploring the particular case study of art-song, Bullock argues that the broad continuities that were characteristic of the Russian romance tradition between 1900 and 1930 were downplayed or ignored completely in most Soviet-era accounts of the form. There is, perhaps, a paradox here; for all that the October Revolution can been seen as a turning point in Russian *modernity*, many Soviet commentators were profoundly hostile to artistic *modernism* itself, even though many modernist artists aligned themselves with the revolutionary project as part of their broader avant-garde aesthetics. To be sure, the art-song was perhaps the musical genre least amenable to experiment; yet as Bullock shows, composers continued to develop the repertoire throughout the 1920s in new and creative ways, and there was a striking correlation between musical developments and innovations in modernist poetry.

Each of the first four articles traces musical life within Russia itself and the often surprising legacy of elements of imperial culture within the new Soviet context. Rebecca Mitchell continues this focus by looking at the contested reputation of the music of Sergei Rakhmaninov in the Soviet Union, whilst simultaneously widening the discussion to consider parallel processes of reception and memorialization within émigré communities. Mitchell's account, which sees music as a powerful tool for the cultivation and projection of cultural memory in widely diverse contexts, attests to the ways in which Rakhmaninov and his music have been invoked to establish 'a definition of Russianness stripped of (most) political and historical baggage and celebrating an eternalized, purified image of Russian culture'. Most crucially, Mitchell's analysis of Rakhmaninov's reputation rests not so much on the work of composers, critical and other music professionals, but on the reactions of a wide range of ordinary listeners and music-lovers, illustrating how top-down attempts to shape musical canons always interact with more popular patterns of reception.

In the final essay in this special issue, Caryl Emerson widens the perspective yet further — far, indeed, beyond the revolutionary divide that structures the other contributions. Yet, by tracing debates that have surrounded both Aleksandr Pushkin's unfinished drama, *Rusalka*, and Aleksandr Dargomyzhskii's subsequent operatic adaptation of it, Emerson reminds us of the openness and contingency of all art works, as well as of their potential for reinscription and reaccentation over time and across space. Such notions are, of course, part of the roll-call of postmodernism (the names of Roland Barthes and Umberto Eco might come to mind). But they have a distinctly Russian lineage too, and one borne in part of the revolutionary moment, which gave rise both to formalist notions about the rise and fall of genres, the struggle for supremacy between different genres, and the contested, non-linear nature of literary development, as well as to Mikhail Bakhtin's resistance to closed and finite utterance and to his celebration of language and discourse as always shared, always collaborative, always exchanged.

As the title of our collection suggests, the persistence of memory itself enshrined intellectual and institutional continuities within the personal: for though musicians themselves had the rupture of 1917 thrust upon them, they did not remain passive. Indeed, we are only just beginning to realize how deeply indebted to its pre-revolutionary roots Soviet musical culture truly was, and how persistently musicians used the musical past to fortify their spaces and discourse. When older cultural values were put to revolutionary service, those values were themselves reinscribed and reinforced, so that in the end, the very notion of modernity became more controversial than that of tradition and continuity. Yet the reality of the emerging Soviet regime, with its carefully guarded borders and official suspicion of free artistic exchange, meant that for 'Russia Abroad' the rupture was starkest of all, and the dependence on memory most poignant. Our collection shows all these processes taking place in quite disparate areas of musical practice, underlining yet another aspect of the multi-headed hydra that was Soviet musical life: it was multivalent and contradictory, fuelled by processes that are often invisible to us, and far too rich to be confined within the narrow concept of 'totalitarian culture'.

1

Personal Friendships, Professional Manoeuvres: Edward Elgar in Russia before and after 1917

PAULINE FAIRCLOUGH

THANKS to a surge of interest over the last ten years or so, we know quite a lot about the performance of Russian music in late nineteenth- and early twentieth-century England: who championed it, what was performed, how it was received in the press, and who the main conduits were.[1] We know, for instance, that Petr Chaikovskii was given an honorary doctorate by Cambridge University in 1893; that his music had been regularly performed in London in the preceding decades and that both Chaikovskii and Nikolai Rimskii-Korsakov were very well known, not only in London concert circles, but in musical England generally by the end of the nineteenth century. As Philip Ross Bullock has noted, the British discovery of Russian music came hard on the heels of translations of Russian literature in the wake of the Crimean War, and tropes of what constituted 'Russianness' became tightly woven into British cultural discourse on both Russian literature and music by the end of the nineteenth century. Whether casting Russia as barbarian 'other' or praising it as a purveyor of exotic brilliance, British writings on music from the nineteenth century right up to the Soviet period generally slotted in somewhere on this spectrum of 'othering'

I am very grateful to friends and colleagues who kindly read drafts of this article and made helpful and constructive comments: Philip Ross Bullock, Caryl Emerson, John Pickard, Florian Scheding and Richard Taruskin. I also thank Patrick Zuk for generously supplying me with material on Miaskovskii.

[1] Principal sources are Philip Ross Bullock, *Rosa Newmarch and Russian Music in Late Nineteenth and Early Twentieth-Century England*, Aldershot, 2009; Gareth Thomas, 'The Impact of Russian Music in England, 1893–1929', unpublished PhD thesis, University of Birmingham, 2005, and Stephen Muir, '"About as Wild and Barbaric as could well be imagined...": The Critical Reception of Rimsky-Korsakov in Nineteenth-Century England', 93, *Music and Letters*, 4, 2012, pp. 513–42. See also, Rebecca Beasley and Philip Ross Bullock (eds), *Russia in Britain 1880–1940: From Melodrama to Modernism*, Oxford, 2013, and Elena Kuznetsova, 'Edvard Elgar i russkaia kul´tura: tochki soprikosnoveniia', in L. Kovnatskaia, M. Mishchenko and O. Chumikova, *Russko-Britanskie muzykal´nye sviazi*, St Petersburg, 2009, pp. 90–107.

Russian music, even if the tone was flattering rather than critical (it could be either depending on the critic).[2] However patchy we might regard this 'mainstreaming' of Chaikovskii, Anton Rubinshtein and Rimskii-Korsakov, Russian music was well integrated into British concert life by the end of the nineteenth century, even if there were still major belated discoveries to be made in the twentieth. For the rest of this article I will refer to 'English' rather than British music, for two reasons: 'English' was the term typically used in Russia to signify 'British', but also because, since Elgar was an English composer, the rest of our discussion is confined to English musical practice, and not to British music more broadly.

Though we know quite a lot about what English critics thought of Russian music, nothing at all is currently known of how English music was received in Russia at the same time, or even if it was heard at all. On a practical level, this is a lacuna that this article seeks partially to fill, specifically in relation to Elgar; but it also aims to show that, just as English reviews mused on the nature of 'Russianness', the Russian reception of English music also conveys a sense of how musical 'Englishness' was defined in Russian cultural circles in the early twentieth century, and would continue to be so right into the Soviet era. For while it would probably be too strong to read a kind of 'occidentalism' in Russian reviews — especially given the small sample presented here — a note of reserve is nonetheless perceptible: a sense that English music can be given a polite hearing, but was never likely to sit alongside the Austro-German, French, Italian (and, of course, Russian) greats. Tracking Elgar's reception through to the Stalin era provides a useful barometer of Russian attitudes to English music, even though the restrictions of the mature Stalin years mean that very little can be inferred simply by performance and reception history alone.

Edward Elgar was easily the most famous of English composers to be played in Russia at the beginning of the twentieth century (discounting Henry Purcell and the naturalized German composer George Frederick Handel), and this holds true all the way up to Benjamin Britten's visits in the 1960s. By the time his music was played in St Petersburg, Elgar's reputation had taken him well beyond that of a parochial talent. At the start of our chronology, in 1903, Elgar had the most promising international reputation of any British composer of his generation. Richard Strauss's remark, on hearing the oratorio, *The Dream of Gerontius* (1900), that Elgar was the 'first English progressivist' underlines the extent to which Elgar was seen

---

[2] See especially Bullock, *Rosa Newmarch*, pp. 18–37.

as something out of the ordinary (at least, for a British composer) in elite European and American musical circles; and as will be revealed, it was his early European reputation that piqued the interest of one of Russia's most extraordinary musicians and concert directors, Aleksandr Ziloti.[3] Indeed, it was this connection — forged early in Elgar's international career — that lingered as a fragmentary legacy of Elgar performance in the first twenty-five years of the Soviet regime. Following the trail of the Ziloti-Elgar relationship reveals that personal connections — reputation, assessment by peers and links with major performers — were key to Elgar's introduction to Russia, but also shows that audience and critical reception of new works was equally vital in securing a permanent repertoire position. As will be seen, Elgar's status in Russia was still unproven when the October Revolution turned Russian musical life on its head; and despite post-1917 personal connections surviving this rupture, his reputation there was too fragile to survive the combination of sweeping personnel changes and shifts in cultural fashion after the First World War.

Aleksandr Ziloti, originally a pupil of Nikolai Rubinshtein (and a composition student of Chaikovskii) began his career as a pianist, and trained with Liszt in Weimar. Upon returning to Russia in 1886 he continued to concertize internationally.[4] It is unclear when he first began to conduct professionally — probably in the 1901–02 Moscow Philharmonia season — but the first confirmed date with that orchestra was 9 February 1902, when Ziloti performed Sergei Taneev's Fourth Symphony.[5] However, his conducting was apparently not judged an unqualified success and Ziloti was not re-engaged after March 1903. Finding himself out of a job, he then moved with his family to St Petersburg, where — with the help of his wife's inherited wealth (Vera Ziloti was the daughter of the magnate and art collector Pavel Tret'iakov), and backing from business sponsors — Ziloti founded his own concert series at the Hall of the Nobility (now the Philharmonic Hall) on Nevskii Prospekt.

Ziloti's concerts were not, of course, the only private series running in the capital. The Russian Musical Society (founded 1859) was still giving regular concerts, and the Evenings of Contemporary Music (founded by the critics Viacheslav Karatygin, Val'ter Nuvel and Al'fred Nurok) had already established a reputation for progressive repertoire and ran

---

[3] See Jerrold Northrop Moore, *Edward Elgar. A Creative Life*, Oxford, 1984, p. 369.
[4] Charles F. Barber, *Lost in the Stars: The Forgotten Musical Life of Alexander Siloti*, Lanham, MD, 2002, p. 50.
[5] Ibid., p. 79.

alongside Ziloti's series until 1912.⁶ There was also the (by 1900) famously conservative 'Russian Symphony Orchestra' concert series, which was founded as a vehicle for the performance of works of the Russian National School and their associates, funded by the magnate, publisher and music-lover Mitrofan Beliaev in 1885.⁷ Besides that, the Court orchestra also gave concerts, as did the orchestra of the Sheremetev Palace, founded by Count Aleksandr Sheremetev, which gave popular symphonic (and from 1910 free) concerts. However, Ziloti's concerts did have a distinct identity: they were from the start strongly orientated towards new music, including that of the Russian National School as well as European composers, and his roster of performers was dazzlingly international. Although he was on good terms with all major Russian composers, Ziloti did not wish his series to be exclusively identified with Russian contemporary music. He made it his business to know who was up-and-coming in the music world, whether composer or performer; Russian composers who owed him their earliest big breaks included Igor′ Stravinskii, Mikhail Gnesin and Ziloti's younger cousin, Sergei Rakhmaninov. It was *de rigueur* for Conservatoire students to attend Ziloti's rehearsals; both luminaries of that institution, Aleksandr Glazunov and Rimskii-Korsakov, supported them and indeed benefited themselves from Ziloti's support.

It was in these concerts that Ziloti made the decision to champion Elgar's music, making him the first Russian musician to take any serious interest in music from Britain, and one of the first European musicians to recognize Elgar's talent. After some years the two men also became friends, since Ziloti visited England regularly both as pianist and conductor. Surviving correspondence between them is, sadly, one-sided only. When Ziloti left Russia (in secret, so as to evade arrest at the Finnish border) in late December 1919 or January 1920, he left his papers behind, and though an extraordinary number of them survive, Elgar's letters to him are not among them. But we have what may well be all of Ziloti's letters and postcards to Elgar — seven in total — preserved in the Elgar Birthplace Museum, while the St Petersburg Institute for the History of Arts has

---

⁶ See Richard Taruskin, *Stravinsky and the Russian Traditions*, 2 vols, Berkeley, CA, 1996, 1, p. 372. The group was, as Taruskin notes, affiliated to Sergei Diaghilev and the *Mir Iskusstva* circle. See also <http://silverage.ru/vechsovmuz/> [accessed 30 January 2017].

⁷ Taruskin observes that, by 1906, Beliaev's Russian Symphony concerts were not held in high regard by critics or audiences, and that for an up-and-coming composer like Igor′ Stravinskii (who obtained some early performances there thanks to the support of his teacher Nikolai Rimskii-Korsakov) there was even some stigma in being associated with the institution. See *Stravinsky and the Russian Traditions*, 1, p. 252.

preserved, among some surviving correspondence with foreign musicians, carbon copies of two letters to Elgar's publisher, Novello. And so from this point we can trace the burgeoning relationship between Ziloti and Elgar, and pinpoint where Ziloti's hopes and plans went awry, and why.[8] The following list shows the Elgar performances given in Ziloti's series between 1903–1916, with companion works:

29 November 1903, Hall of Nobility
Elgar *Cockaigne* Overture (with Bruch Violin Concerto, Bach E major Violin Concerto, Chaikovskii *Romeo and Juliet* Fantasy Overture, Glazunov *Suite from Middle Ages*)

30 October 1904, Hall of Nobility
Elgar *Enigma Variations* (with Rimskii-Korsakov Symphony No. 3, Wagner *Götterdämmerung* finale, Prelude and Liebestod from *Tristan*, Liadov Scherzo in B major)

3 December 1905, Hall of Nobility
Elgar *Introduction and Allegro* (with Wagner Wotan's Farewell and Magic Fire Music from *Götterdämmerung*, Rakhmaninov 'Fate' and 'The Gypsies', Napravnik *Don Juan*, Arenskii *Dream on the Volga* overture)

18 November 1906, Hall of Nobility
Elgar *In the South* (with Strauss *Macbeth*, Schumann Cello Concerto [Pablo Casals], Bach Brandenburg Concerto No. 1, Moore Cello Concerto [Casals])

24 January 1909, Hall of Nobility
Elgar Symphony No. 1 (with Mendelssohn *Fingal's Cave*, Liszt Piano Concerto No. 2, Stravinskii *Scherzo fantastique*, Weber *Konzertstück* for Piano and Orchestra, Liszt *Rhapsody No. 1*)

12 December 1909, Hall of Nobility
Elgar *Enigma Variations* (with Debussy *Dances for Piano and String orchestra*, *Danse Sacrée*, *Danse Profane*, Liadov *Enchanted Lake*, Chaikovskii Violin Concerto, Ravel *Rapsodie Espagnole*)

8 October 1916, Mariinskii Theatre
Elgar *Enigma Variations* and Skriabin Symphony No. 3, 'Divine Poem'[9]

At the time of Ziloti's earliest performances, Elgar was a completely unknown quantity in Russia, but he was gaining a reputation in continental

---

[8] I thank John Norris for his exceedingly generous assistance in gaining copies of all these letters from the Elgar Birthplace Museum, for checking catalogue numbers and dates for me, and for his help in gaining permission to quote from them. All of the letters referred to in this article, with the exception of those from Ziloti to Novello, are quoted with the kind permission of the Elgar Will Trust.
[9] All concert data are drawn from Barber, *Lost in the Stars*, pp. 262–337.

Europe as a promising up-and-coming composer (this despite the fact that he was already forty-two when his *Enigma Variations* (1899) and *Dream of Gerontius* (1900) achieved recognition in London and Europe).[10] By 1904, Elgar had a Covent Garden Festival dedicated to him with works conducted by Hans Richter (directing the Hallé orchestra) including *Gerontius* and *The Apostles* and he was knighted that same year.[11] The ecstatic (though anonymous) reviewer of this festival in *The Musical Times* gushed: 'Edward Elgar is a poet and a visionary, and to feel his poetry and interpret his visions it behoves the listener to make some effort to climb the spiritual heights whereon great thinkers dwell and weave their wondrous dreams.'[12]

It could be argued, however, that it was Elgar's success with *Enigma* and *Gerontius* in Europe and beyond that made the London critics regard him as a real force to be reckoned with, and Elgar's international performances were listed with pride in London music papers. In 1900 Elgar had a piece of incredible luck: the German pianist and conductor Julius Buths was in the Birmingham audience at the premiere of *Gerontius* in 1900, and was impressed by the work. He made a German translation and gave the oratorio its European premiere in Düsseldorf in December 1901, repeating it the following May. In between, he conducted the *Enigma Variations* in February 1902. As mentioned above, it was none other than Richard Strauss, with whom Buths co-directed the Lower Rhenish Music Festival, who declared Elgar the 'first English progressivist' after hearing *Gerontius* — a back-handed compliment certainly, given England's persistent label in Europe as 'Das Land ohne Musik', but one that travelled well.[13] And here another fortuitous musical meeting took place, for Buths conducted Ziloti in Rakhmaninov's Second Piano Concerto in Düsseldorf in January 1902. It would have been impossible for Ziloti to have heard Buths conduct the *Enigma Variations*, since Buths's concert took place on 7 January 1902, and Ziloti performed Taneev's Fourth Symphony in Moscow two days later. He may possibly have heard a rehearsal of the *Variations*, or heard — even from Buths directly — that it was a piece worth performing. At any rate,

---

[10] Anon., 'Edward Elgar', *The Musical Times and Singing-Class Circular*, 1 October 1900, p. 646.

[11] Anon., 'Occasional Notes', *The Musical Times and Singing-Class Circular*, 1 December 1903, p. 790.

[12] Anon., 'The Elgar Festival', *The Musical Times and Singing-Class Circular*, 1 April 1904, p. 242.

[13] The book that popularized this phrase, by Oscar A. H. Schmitz (*Das Land ohne Musik: Englische Gesellschaftesprobleme*) was published only in 1904, but it drew on ideas that were already established.

Ziloti obtained the score and performed it in his concert on 30 October 1904, soon afterwards writing triumphantly to the composer a few days later (in English, as translated by his then secretary):

> I have great pleasure in informing you that your variations, which I conducted (the first time in Russia) have had a very great success, both with the public and with the musical world; so great a success that I shall play them again next season. Mr. N. Rimsky-Korsakoff and Mr. A. Glazounoff were particularly pleased with them. I studied them very carefully (because I am quite in love with them) and the rendering was very good. I should be very much obliged if you would let me know whether you have already written, or will write, a great <u>orchestral work</u>.[14]

There is no reason to doubt Ziloti's honesty when he claimed Rimskii-Korsakov and Glazunov were impressed by the *Variations*. The critic of the foremost music journal, *Russkaia muzykal'naia gazeta* (possibly Ziloti's friend Aleksandr Ossovskii, who reviewed regularly for it, or his colleague on the paper Nikolai Findeizen), however, was more measured in his response:

> a solid, clever work, with a distinctly contemporary air, though not without a touch of scholastic heaviness. The most successful variation was number ten (a very grandiose scherzo) [...] on the basis of this performance of the work, the composer is very talented, though it is possible that, owing to the arid musical environment in England, the significance of his talent is over-rated. However, Elgar's reputation is not founded on symphonic works alone but is in fact mainly based on his oratorios *The Dream of Gerontius* and *The Apostles* which followed [*Enigma Variations*] and on which his talent can be properly judged, though as yet in Russia we have not heard them.[15]

Already in 1904 this review lays down tropes of 'Englishness' that were far from complimentary: the implication that Elgar's stature is founded on nothing more than being the best England had to offer was bad enough, but 'solid', 'clever', scholastic' and 'heavy' powerfully conveys a further meaning not directly spelled out: that of 'worthy but dull'. Undaunted,

---

[14] Elgar Birthplace Museum (hereafter, EB) 9382, dated 2/15 November 1904 (including both old and new calendar dates, as on the original letter). Underlining as in the original, which is in English.

[15] *Russkaia muzykal'naia gazeta*, No. 45, 7 November 1904, p. 1050.

Ziloti wrote to Elgar to inform him of his music's great success, and though the fact of the performance was noted (Ziloti had to pay Novello a fee for the performance rights), few translations of Russian reviews made their way to the London papers, and none that did were critical. Because German reviews of this period had been positive, it is likely that those who followed Elgar's European successes assumed that Russian critics were equally delighted with his music.[16] A notice in the London music paper, *Musical Times*, reported that the Swiss musicologist Robert Aloys Mooser had reviewed the 1904 *Enigma* performance in *Journal de St Pétersbourg* and declared that the *Variations* 'proves the existence in England of a musician endowed with temperament, possessing great technical skill' which, while not exactly a ringing endorsement, certainly compared favourably with the review in *Russkaia muzykal'naia gazeta* which — perhaps luckily — no one in England seems to have been aware of.[17] However, Mooser's carefully phrased compliment needs contextualizing. He was Ziloti's close friend, and a musician of strong opinion, highly attuned to progressive European trends and intolerant of Russian national provincialism. He probably wished to give Ziloti a reasonably positive notice, but in reality he did not rate Elgar's music highly and thought Ziloti was mistaken in his enthusiasm for it. In his memoirs he states plainly: 'it was utter folly to perform on four occasions the gloomy works of Edward Elgar. [...] an English composer who was frighteningly productive and disastrously impersonal.'[18] Mooser left Russia in 1909, so was not present to witness the full vindication of this view as far as Russian critics and audiences were concerned, but it is interesting to note his opinion of Elgar, since Mooser's European outlook made him in many ways an atypical Russian music critic. With regard to Elgar though, he seemed perfectly attuned to popular Russian musical opinion, as will be seen.

Elgar must have written a friendly reply to Ziloti, since he wrote to him again (still using his secretary to write in English) on 11 January 1905, hoping for news of the First Symphony, on which Elgar was still at work:

[16] See for example Anon., 'Occasional Notes', *The Musical Times*, vol. 46, no. 743 (1 January 1905), pp. 23–26; Anon, 'An Elgar Concert in Ostend', *The Musical Times*, vol. 49, no. 787 (1 September 1908), pp. 581–83, and 'Foreign Notes', *The Musical Times*, vol. 49, no. 789 (1 November 1908), pp. 732–34.

[17] See Anon., 'Occasional Notes', p. 26.

[18] Mary S. Woodside (ed.), *The Russian Life of R.-Aloys Mooser, Music Critic to the Tsars*, Lewiston, NY and Lampeter, 2008, p. 156.

I send you many thanks for your kind letter. I am writing to know if that Symphony you speak of is in print, or if not how soon it will be. The parts I shall not want until the early Autumn, the score, as soon as possible. It would be a good thing to have a greater work follow 'the variations' shortly; having given them, I will take anything of yours without seeing it — I ask you to give me the sole permission of giving the Symphony next winter, as my concerts take the ('first place') in the general opinion. In consequence of their having been given here, 'the variations' will be given this season in Moscow.

A year this spring I expect to be playing in England, and hope then to have the pleasure of making your acquaintance and talking things over — I should be glad to have an answer as soon as possible.
With very kind regards, sincerely yours, A. Siloti[19]

On 3 June 1906, now writing to Elgar in German (and in his own hand), Ziloti prodded the composer again about his new symphony:

Esteemed Mr. Elgar!
I am sending you a programme from which you will see that I, as your admirer, have included your Introduction and Allegro. Everyone here really likes the work, and I am even told that I am an 'Elgar specialist'. I am proud that it was I who introduced you here, and 'Gerontius' will be performed here [...].

Is the Symphony ready yet? How are things with the new Symphony? I would certainly schedule it next winter. (Do you have to write something new for orchestra before then?) Are you planning to write something else for orchestra? Everyone is talking about your variations now! Warmest greetings, your admirer A. Ziloti[20]

Though it is not certain whether he waited for Elgar's reply before sending his next postcard, Ziloti wrote again to press him for some details (this card is dated 19 July 1906):

---

[19] EB 5960. Underlining and parenthesis as in the original.
[20] EB 5961. Underlining as in the original. I thank Annika Forkert for kindly transcribing Ziloti's German handwriting in all the German-language sources included in this article, and for checking my German translations. Unfortunately, *Gerontius* was not performed in Russia, neither pre-1917, nor for the whole of the Soviet period, so far as I have been able to discover, until Evgenii Svetlanov conducted it in Moscow on 21 April 1983. I thank Levon Hakobian for this information.

Esteemed Master! Since I am now putting together my programme, I ask you to communicate to me: 1) <u>what is your new work called</u> (<u>ie</u> about which you wrote to me), 2) <u>how long is it</u>, and 3) <u>with whom is it being edited?</u> I am <u>very happy</u> to get to know a new work from you; the variations are going to be performed in summer in Pavlovsk. Warmest greetings, your admirer, A. Ziloti

ps right <u>now</u> I'm to be pitied for being a Russian.[21]

In the end, Elgar's long-awaited First Symphony would not be ready for its premiere until 1908, despite being originally planned for the 1904 Covent Garden festival; Ziloti would give the Russian premiere only in January 1909. In between harassing Elgar for his new symphony and its St Petersburg premiere, it is possible that they met on one of Ziloti's British tours. Elgar was part of a 'Birmingham Concerts Society' committee formed to organize orchestral concerts in Birmingham in the 1907–08 season, and Ziloti was engaged to conduct in the series. He also continued concertizing as a pianist in Britain during these years, appearing almost annually in venues from Edinburgh to London between 1908 and 1912; also, we know that Vera and Aleksandr Ziloti visited Elgar at his home in March 1912 during another concert tour.[22] Already a well-known pianist in London from his international concertizing days, Ziloti nurtured his English contacts and in fact his connection with Elgar and reputation in London for championing his music brought him further esteem in Britain; he had by 1913–14 already secured dates from the violist Lionel Tertis and the pianist Cyril Scott to perform in his St Petersburg series, and it was only the intervention of war that made their visit impossible.[23]

As the 11 January 1905 letter above shows, Ziloti wished to have Elgar's permission for sole performance rights in Russia for the First Symphony. On the face of it this was a strange request, and Elgar's publisher and close personal friend August Jaeger (of Novello) thought so too. As he pointed out in a letter to Elgar dated 25 August 1905, 'Siloti wants us to promise him the first performance of your apocryphal Symphony, but I had to explain that we cannot promise anything for a country whose laws do not protect

---

[21] EB 5964. Underlining as in the original. Ziloti's comment about being 'pitied for being a Russian' may well have been in reference to the tsar's dissolution of the Duma on 8 July 1906, alarmed by its growing liberalism. Nicholas II installed the monarchist and well-known right-winger Petr Stolypin as Prime Minister. Ziloti is known to have held liberal political views and supported workers' rights.

[22] See entries in Alice Elgar's diaries, 4 and 6 March 1912. EB.

[23] Ziloti's letters from Tertis and Scott have survived. See Russkii Institut Istorii Iskusstv, fond. 17, op. 1, ed. khr. 122 and 132.

our *Performing Rights*. Anyone who would be clever enough to obtain Score & parts (say through Leipzig) *before* Siloti could forestall him without our being able to prevent him'.[24] This is all fair enough, but Jaeger does not ask what for us might be the more obvious question: who else might have even wanted to perform Elgar in St Petersburg or Moscow? Ziloti might well have had an anxious eye on his colleague, the double-bass player and soon-to-be world famous conductor, Sergei Kusevitskii. Though Kusevitskii did not begin his rival series until 1909, in 1905 his career and life had taken a dramatic new turn: he divorced his first wife and married a wealthy heiress, Natal´ia Ushkova, and left Russia to study conducting with Artur Nikisch in Leipzig. This — his professional conducting training — was precisely what Ziloti had not had, and he was keenly aware of it. In 1903 he had been effectively sacked from his first professional conducting position in Moscow, aged forty. As Charles Barber speculates, 'For reasons of pride or embarrassment, he [Ziloti] took conducting lessons from no-one. Like so many gifted instrumentalists [...] he seems to have believed that those gifts were immediately and perfectly transferable to the podium. They were not and are not'.[25] Ziloti had done no more than observe Nikisch in Leipzig; he had never taken any lessons. Perhaps this lay in the back of his mind as he wrote to Elgar; or perhaps he was merely thinking of other likely conductors such as Glazunov. In any case, despite Jaeger's doubts that such an agreement could in practice be honoured, Elgar did grant Ziloti sole permission to perform his First Symphony, and Ziloti gave it its Russian premiere on 24 January 1909. Ziloti's personal touch thus bore eventual fruit.

But was this long-awaited child worth the wait so far as Ziloti was concerned? Once again, critical reviews were lukewarm. The *Russkaia muzykal´naia gazeta* critic (again probably Ossovskii or Findeizen) was polite but cautious:

> There is much that is lively, bright and pleasing in this music [...] in its overall character, Elgar's music shows the influence of Chaikovskii, Mendelssohn, Brahms, in part Wagner, all composers loved in England. There is undoubtedly the presence of a genuine — and besides that — a warm, healthy, manly talent — but that does not prevent the public here from regarding the symphony with mistrustful restraint. The name of Elgar is as yet too unfamiliar in our concert life.[26]

---

[24] EB 8754. Underlining and capitalization as in the original.
[25] Barber, *Lost in the Stars*, p. 83.
[26] Anon., *Russkaia muzykal´naia gazeta*, 1 February 1909, p. 147.

Comparing Elgar with Chaikovskii was certainly a measure of approval, certainly more so than it would have been if the comparisons had ended at Mendelssohn and Brahms, two composers who never really achieved widespread popularity in twentieth-century Russia, including in the Soviet era. And the terminology has shifted too: 'warm' and 'manly' was certainly a lot better than 'scholastic' and 'heavy'. The anonymous critic of *Muzyka i zhizn'*, however, was less positive, and even gave some indication of the audience's reaction to the symphony:

> This symphony by Elgar does not differ from the majority of [those of] contemporary Western composers in those qualities, by virtue of which it managed to be popular with our public, but nevertheless it was not without its striking features. Particularly notable for their originality were the introductory bars, with the strong giant-steps of the basses, though they significantly strained the interest of the listeners, who, by the way, cooled during the first movement and the rather lengthy adagio, but livened up in the second movement, Allegro molto.[27]

Reasons why Elgar's music failed to inspire Russian listeners could be many and various, but the companion works chosen for each concert inevitably played a significant role. If anything, they were even more critical in the premiere of the next major Elgar work, the Violin Concerto. The First Symphony was accompanied by Mendelssohn's *Fingal's Cave* — a safe opener. Elgar was next on the programme, then Liszt's Piano Concerto No. 2 played by Vasilii Sapel'nikov, a St Petersburg Conservatoire graduate and astonishing piano virtuoso who was by then resident in Europe after a brief stint as professor of piano at the Moscow Conservatoire (so Conservatoire students would have been very eager to hear him). After this came Stravinskii's new work, *Scherzo fantastique*, then another Sapel'nikov show-stopper, Weber's Konzertstück for Piano and Orchestra, and finally, Liszt's *Rhapsody No. 1* (a solo piano work). This was, in essence, Sapel'nikov's big 'back in St Petersburg' concert, and the majority of his audience would very probably have been there primarily to see him perform. Not only was he famous in Russia for his pianism, he was famous for having been (as was Ziloti) a favoured interpreter of Chaikovskii's piano concerti, having performed with the composer on a number of occasions. Elgar's symphony was perhaps overwhelmed by this dazzling display of native Russian pianism, and it is not surprising that critics

---

[27] A. P-o, *Muzyka i zhizn'*, 6 February 1909, p. 12. I have not been able to identify this critic. The journal's editors were D. E. Arkad'ev and A. L. Maslov.

focused on Sapel'nikov's playing at the expense of more detailed accounts of the new work. Tsezar' Kiui, the grouchy foe of musical modernism and one-time member of the famous *kuchka*, complained to his friend Mariia Kerzina equally of the 'terribly long symphony' and Stravinskii's 'terribly long' *Scherzo fantastique*, as though both were equally representative of the modern mainstream (or 'pseudomusic', as Kiui calls it), which they were emphatically not.[28]

Despite Ziloti's vigorous championing, then, Russian critics and audiences seemed undecided on Elgar. Was he just the best that poor old England could produce, or was he the real thing? Ziloti continued to hope that Elgar would produce another masterpiece that he could premiere in Russia. Yet even as he was trying to negotiate this coup — the summer of 1911 — he was already backing away on his earlier promise to Elgar that he would perform anything of his without even seeing it, though this was probably for financial rather than aesthetic reasons. Although it is quite clear that Ziloti sincerely considered Elgar to be an interesting composer, he also saw himself, quite naturally, as someone helping Elgar to build an international reputation. In short, he saw their relationship as mutually advantageous. And this perspective would complicate matters when Ziloti's own finances took a battering, and especially when Kusevitskii began his rival series, which vied with Ziloti's for the best artists and sole permissions to give prestigious premieres. Having asked Novello to send him the score of Elgar's Second Symphony, Ziloti reacted with dismay to the requested fee of fifteen guineas (one guinea was worth approximately one pound) which at that time was roughly equivalent to £1,650 today. And he did so in terms that made no bones about the fact that, in his view, Novello should be grateful to him for performing Elgar's music in Russia at all:

> I find your asking for 15 guineas (I do not understand whether this claim is yours or Elgar's) rather too much; the First Symphonie cost 10 guineas, and the Third will cost 20 guineas, and so the claims will go 'crescendo'! That this was asked of *me* shocked me somewhat, because I played *all* of Elgar's works, when no one wanted to know anything of him, not just in

---

[28] Taruskin, *Stravinsky and the Russian Traditions*, 1, p. 410. The 'kuchka' was the colloquial nickname for the Russian National School comprising Milii Balakirev (its founder), Nikolai Rimskii-Korsakov, Modest Musorgskii, Aleksandr Borodin and Tsezar' Kiui. By 1901 the group was defunct even though several of its members were still living. See Alexander Tumanov, *The Life and Artistry of Maria Olenina-d'Alheim*, trans. Christopher Barnes, Edmonton, AL, 2000, p. 88, where Balakirev explains that he has broken off relations with Rimskii-Korsakov and Kiui.

Russia but also in Europe. From a general perspective, one must judge the assessment of the claims from work to work, for when you ask for 10g for the First Symphony, then the Second should really cost me 5g, because it is less of a work by half. All these details have forced me not to perform the Second Symphony, and I return the score. I hope that you will not resent my cancellation and will give me preference for Elgar's next work because I have been Elgar's earliest champion here and am convinced that he will yet go on to create great works. Regarding the Violin Concerto. In Spring Ysaye told us that if it has to be paid for, he won't play it; I asked him yesterday if he would play after all (it would be desirable because the Concerto is supposed to be very beautiful); if yes, then I will tell you and pay 10g for it; Ysaye wants to play at mine on 17 January. With many thanks again for all your kindness, I remain, yours sincerely, A. Siloti.[29]

By the time Elgar's Violin Concerto was being planned for performance in Russia, Kusevitskii's concert series was in direct rivalry with Ziloti's, and Ziloti's finances were looking shaky, as his letter to Novello above makes clear. Already by 1908 his wife Vera had sold most of her jewellery to fund his concerts, the patronage of his original supporters had come to its end, and Ziloti had to find more rich backers. As Charles Barber has vividly described, Ziloti's strategy for survival as times grew harder was to throw caution to the winds. His backers needed to see dramatic results if their support was to continue. And so for the 1908–09 series he had commissioned, borrowed and booked his way to a season so outstanding that, at the end of the concert where Elgar's symphony was played, he was cheered in a prolonged standing ovation and presented with a gold wreath. That season, Artur Nikisch visited to conduct Beethoven's Eighth and Ninth Symphonies, the great cellist Pablo Casals came to play the Saint-Saens concerto, Fedor Shaliapin sang and Feliks Blumenfel'd conducted. Giving the Elgar premiere, whether or not it went down brilliantly, was a part of what made Ziloti's concerts special, and his audiences evidently realized and valued that. At least until Kusevitskii's series started, Ziloti's concerts were, as he had said to Elgar himself, *the* place to go for hearing

[29] Russkii Institut Istorii Iskusstv, fond 17, opis 1, edinitsa khranenia 6, ll. 35–37. Abbreviations and underlining as in the original, which is in German. I thank Annika Forkert for generously transcribing and translating this letter. Ziloti had a similar problem with Richard Strauss's *Salome*: Mooser had recommended he perform the 'Dance of the Seven Veils' but was told this would cost five hundred marks (a sum he could not afford). When both Strauss and the publisher made it clear the fee was non-negotiable, Ziloti withdrew all plans to perform the work. See Woodside (ed.), *The Russian Life of R.-Aloys Mooser*, p. 156, n. 6.

new music; and this remained a matter of great pride for him. His series was, however, just one more prominent Russian music venture requiring significant amounts of private investment to survive, and he was in competition with both Kusevitskii and Diaghilev who were each seeking business sponsorship at the same time. When Kusevitskii began his series in 1909, Ziloti would immediately have recognized the danger of being outbid for the biggest names and performance rights.

Ziloti's problems with Elgar's Violin Concerto began with the dedicatee, Fritz Kreisler, who had commissioned it, and with his rival Kusevitskii, who planned to perform it in his series in January 1913. Had Ziloti already worked with Kreisler, he might have been able to forestall the contract, but he had not. However, he did have good relations with the equally legendary violinist Eugène Ysaÿe. Although it was Kreisler who gave the world premiere in London, with Elgar conducting, in 1910, Ysaÿe had studied the concerto with Elgar very soon afterwards, also wishing to perform it worldwide. This could have been Ziloti's salvation. But unfortunately, relations between Ysaÿe and Elgar's publisher Novello quickly soured when terms for performing rights were discussed. In May 1911 Novello offered Ysaÿe a reduced hire rate of five pounds (approximately £520 in today's money) per performance of the Violin Concerto in Europe (four pounds if he promised to play it twenty times in one season across Europe). Ysaÿe refused and what began as a private spat between himself and Novello escalated into a public row, with Ysaÿe going to the press to accuse Novello of charging extortionate fees that damaged Elgar's chances of high quality performance, insinuating that Novello had trapped the innocent composer in a mercenary web for their own gain.

Stung by this accusation and at risk of reputational damage, Novello pointed out in a public statement that Elgar was fully cognizant of all financial arrangements and the vast bulk of any fee collected went to him directly. They also pointed out that their usual fee for the concerto was seven and a half guineas (about £800); it apparently never exceeded ten. So in reality they had reason to feel they had offered Ysaÿe a good deal. And, as they pointed out, since this was the composer's sole means of earning a living, it was not unreasonable to ask highly-paid concertizing artists to deliver a reasonable fee.[30]

---

[30] The whole argument can be seen in Anon., 'M. Ysaye and the Elgar Violin Concerto', *The Musical Times*, vol. 54, no. 839, 1 January 1913, pp. 19–20. I thank John Pickard for drawing my attention to this source. See also, Jerrold Northrop Moore, *Elgar and his Publishers: Letters of a Creative Life*, Oxford, 1987, pp. 747–60.

Ziloti was helplessly caught in the middle of this row. It looks as though he knew well that Kreisler was scheduled to perform the Elgar with Kusevitskii on 23 January 1913 and that he was desperate to steal their thunder. His proposed date — which he put directly to Novello — was 17 January — just a week before Kreisler's concert, which would have been a major coup for Ziloti and a blow for Kusevitskii. He tried to bypass the Ysaÿe-Novello row by offering to pay the maximum fee of ten guineas himself, but by then Ysaÿe was so offended and angry with Novello that he simply refused to play it, whether or not it cost him personally any money. This was an extraordinary offer from Ziloti given first, his straitened financial circumstances and second, his disappointment with the Second Symphony, fuelling the suspicion that upstaging Kusevitskii was all-important to him.

In the end, it turned out better for Ziloti that he did not manage to snatch the Russian premiere from Kusevitskii's grasp. Because Russian reactions to Elgar's concerto, which Kreisler premiered under Kusevitskii on 23 January 1913, were, so far as I have been able to find, unanimously negative, far more so than reactions to *Enigma* or to the symphony. And again, at least part of the problem was surely programming. Kusevitskii opened with Smetana, overture to *The Bartered Bride*, then went on to the Elgar, then Musorgskii, Introduction to *Khovanshchina*, 'Dawn over the Moscow River', Liadov *Baba-Iaga*, and ended with excerpts from Stravinskii's *Petrushka*. The programme note gave only the blandest biographical information about Elgar — son of an organist, began composing late, influenced by Grieg and Wagner, recently very popular in England — and stopped short of preparing the audience for the work itself, stating merely that it was composed for Fritz Kreisler. This time the critics were a lot more outspoken: the concert as a whole was judged superb, and Kreisler masterful, but none could hide their disappointment at the work he chose to perform. The critic of *Russkie vedomosti* found that the concerto 'seemed devoid of any creative flight [*polet*], but Fritz Kreisler managed to give artistic significance and interest to even the most insignificant of musical phrases'.[31] The critic of *Russkaia muzykal'naia gazeta* was once again unimpressed, and this time was blunter in his assessment:

> Every appearance by this artist-philosopher of the violin is a festival of art, but this time there was no festival. And this was the fault of the English composer Elgar... All of Kreisler's formidable powers were needed

---

[31] Anon., *Russkie vedomosti*, 1 February 1913, p. 4. This critic may have been Nikolai Kashkin, who reviewed for several papers and music journals at this time.

for such a work, lacking any creative élan [*pod″em*] and engaged in only serious thoughts, in order to leave us in anything other than a dreary mood. Kreisler was only able to offer compensation to his audience in the encores.[32]

But most critical by far was the journal *Muzyka*, a short-lived Moscow weekly, which ran from 1910–16. Its critic for this concert was 'Misantrop' — the all-too-apt pseudonym used by the composer Nikolai Miaskovskii:

> To be truthful, there is not much to say about this work: it is textually solid, its themes are lacklustre and completely without interest from the virtuosic perspective; there was one not bad, even fresh, episode in the finale, but aside from that one place, it is simply not worth playing or listening to this choleric and ponderous [*kholerichno-tiaguchii*] work.[33]

It is not surprising, after this critical onslaught, that Ziloti dropped all thoughts of performing the concerto, either with Ysaÿe or any other violinist. And he may well have been grateful to fate for preventing him from being the one to have delivered such a flop. His concerts continued through the war years in a different form until February 1917, when the conditions of revolution — strikes, marches, looting, requisitioning of buildings — made them impossible. Ziloti carried on his administrative work under extremely difficult circumstances until the end of 1919; he initially accepted the position of Director at the Mariinskii Theatre (May 1917), was arrested by the CHEKA on a charge of provocation in December (for refusing to hand over the keys of the Imperial Box, presumably to the new Commissar for Enlightenment, Anatolii Lunacharskii)[34] and when he had been released, was put under house arrest; his young son Levko was arrested and a teenaged friend arrested with him was shot (Levko Ziloti fled to Finland on his release). Finally, Ziloti was dismissed from the Mariinskii in late 1918. In either late 1919 or early 1920, with the assistance of the English musician-turned-spy, Paul Dukes, Ziloti and his wife escaped over the border to Finland and from thence made their way to England, the first of their émigré refuges, though ultimately the family would re-settle in New York.[35]

---

[32] *Russkaia muzykal′naia gazeta*, 9 February 1913, p. 164.
[33] 'Misantrop', *Muzyka*, 23 February 1913, p. 140.
[34] This episode — regarding who actually requested the keys — is unclear in Barber, *Lost in the Stars*, p. 173.
[35] See Paul Dukes, *Red Dusk and the Morrow: Adventures and Investigations in Soviet Russia*, London, 1922. Dukes does not mention Ziloti in the book, but he gives accounts of

Elgar's Soviet years
It is not possible to assert with absolute confidence that no Elgar was played in either Petrograd-Leningrad or Moscow between 1916 (the year of Ziloti's last Elgar performance) and January 1934, when the British conductor Edward Clark visited Moscow and played Elgar's 'Cockaigne' overture. The Leningrad Philharmonia archive only starts in 1921, and does not cover the interim years when Kusevitskii took over its original role as the Imperial Orchestra. By the time Kusevitskii had left Russia in 1920, Emil' Kuper was the orchestra's chief conductor, and the records begin under his tenure. In Moscow, the orchestra which, after several incarnations, became the Moscow Philharmonia, has very incomplete records until the mid-1930s and these are the orchestras with the biggest archival holdings: many other ensembles and orchestras have little or no surviving documentation at all.[36]

Neither orchestra holds evidence of Clark's trip in early 1934, because he performed with the Moscow Radio Orchestra, not the Philharmonia and the concert was broadcast only. This British musical visit was a very unusual event in Russia, for several inter-connected reasons. First of all, musical Russia was intimately connected with Europe. It had very tenuous connections with America and Britain other than both being on the touring destinations of its greatest nineteenth-century Russian performers. Therefore, even during the most culturally permissive years of the New Economic Policy and the brief 'Enlightenment' of the first half of the 1930s, visiting musicians and composers were — if you count those who had emigrated to America after 1933 — nearly all from central Europe (Fritz Stiedry, chief conductor of the Leningrad Philharmonia until 1937, among them).[37] Big names from America were not unknown: Henry Cowell visited in 1929, for example, as did the tenor Roland Hayes (1928), the violinist Ruth Posselt (1934) and the contralto Marian Anderson (1935), who were all making international tours at that time.[38] The strong Russian-Europe

---

other people he helped escape to Finland, as well as vivid descriptions of his own passages to and from the Soviet border over the same routes.

[36] See records of both Leningrad and Moscow Philharmonias in Fairclough, *Classics for the Masses: Shaping Soviet Musical Identity Under Lenin and Stalin*, New Haven, CT and London, 2016.

[37] A few British musicians did visit, as will be discussed, but they did not perform in the prestigious Philharmonia series. The English pianist John Hunt performed Ernst Křenek's Second Piano Sonata (with Beethoven op. 10 No. 3) in Moscow in early 1935, for example. See A. Konstant Smis, 'Dzhon Khant i Beveredzh Vebster', *Sovetskaia muzyka*, 1935, 4, p. 94.

[38] For a detailed discussion of this, see Fairclough *Classics for the Masses*. I use the

connection was wholly congruent not only with the personal contacts that musicians traditionally relied on for touring invitations (these being firmly rooted in Europe, many of them pre-1917) but also with the assumption that Europe provided the most fertile musical soil when it came to new music. Henry Cowell, who continued to correspond with Soviet musicians and even write for their press, was not representative of any American compositional 'school' with his shock-techniques of percussive piano writing (using whole arm clusters, for example) and so seemed more of a one-off maverick than part of an American new music aesthetic. While Béla Bartók, Alban Berg and Darius Milhaud all visited Russia to hear and perform their music, hardly any British music was performed in the most prestigious orchestral concerts in Moscow or Leningrad, nor did any British soloist perform on the Moscow or Leningrad Philharmonia stages. However, Soviet musicians were not unaware of recent trends in British music. Indeed, the Composers' Union journal (founded in 1933), *Sovetskaia muzyka*, featured an article by Michel D. Calvocoressi in January 1935 on 'English Music', in which Ralph Vaughan Williams and all the young(ish) figures on the music scene — Arthur Bliss, Arnold Bax, Herbert Howells and Gustav Holst — are accounted for. Elgar's reputation is done no favours at all by Calvocoressi's uncritical, even approving, reference to the Cambridge musicologist Edward J. Dent's opinion that 'to English ears Elgar's music is too emotional and not entirely free from vulgarity'.[39] Aside from that, no mention is made of Elgar at all. By this time Elgar, having died just the previous year, is apparently considered of no real interest in an article about contemporary British music so far as Russia was concerned.

British composers did visit Russia — Rutland Boughton was there in 1927, having joined the Communist Party of Great Britain the previous year and the communist composer Alan Bush went in 1938 and 1939 (by which time normal international musical exchange had been suspended; Bush was a fellow communist guest of the Composers' Union). But aside

---

term 'Enlightenment' after Katerina Clark's *Moscow: The Fourth Rome*, Cambridge, MA, 2011. For Henry Cowell's visit, see Elena Dubinets, 'Pervootkryvatel' novoi muzyky', *Muzykal'naia academia*, 2003, 3, pp. 196–205. Ruth Posselt's 8 December Moscow Conservatoire concert in 1935 is reviewed in *Sovetskaia muzyka*, 1934, 1, p. 75. In April 1934 Jascha Heifetz also toured in Russia for the first time since he had left for America in 1917 — his first and only return visit.

[39] M. D. Calvocoressi, 'Angliiskaia muzyka', *Sovetskaia muzyka*, 1935, 1, pp. 85–88; Dent's comment is repeated on p. 86. For a discussion of this remark, see Matthew Riley, *Edward Elgar and the Nostalgic Imagination*, Cambridge, 2009, p. 55, and Andrew Blake, *The Land Without Music: Music, Culture and Society in Twentieth-Century Britain*, Manchester, 1997, p. 22.

from the politically-motivated visits of Boughton and Bush, those of Clark (and, the following year, his friend the pianist Harriet Cohen) are of more interest to us here, because they were interlinked with another musician of the Ziloti era, one who worked with him closely and counted him as a friend: the Anglo-Russian conductor Albert Coates.

Coates was born to English parents (in England) but was educated in Russia because his father was employed there by the Russian government before the revolution. He trained under Nikisch in Leipzig and was appointed conductor of the Imperial Opera in St Petersburg in 1910. During the decade before 1917 Coates travelled regularly to and from Russia and London, and was a passionate advocate of Russian music in Britain and British music in Russia. He conducted not only orchestral concerts at the Queen's Hall in London, but was also engaged by Covent Garden Opera, principally as a Wagner conductor (this was also his speciality in St Petersburg). Like Ziloti, Coates found conditions during the civil war unbearable. He fled Russia in 1919 and returned to England, also temporarily, since after the Second World War he made his permanent home in South Africa. But because Coates remained active in London's musical life until that time, he was known to a great many figures in the capital's cultural life, including those in the BBC. Edward Clark, until his resignation from the BBC in 1936, was head of music there and had a keen interest in Russian music, as well as in Soviet politics. He was a member of the then-Bloomsbury-based Society for Cultural Relations between the Peoples of the British Commonwealth and the USSR (SCR, founded 1924) and the files of the Soviet cultural relations organization VOKS (Vsesoiuznoe obshchestvo kul´turnoi sviazi s zagranitsei) in Moscow contain some correspondence both to and from him.[40] Although letters directly relating to his visit have not been preserved so far as I have been able to discover, it is likely that VOKS and the SCR arranged it. But it is also very likely that it was facilitated by Coates, who restored professional contacts in Russia from at least as early as 1927, when he conducted Holst's 'Mars' (from *The Planets*) in Leningrad that May. The London *Daily Telegraph* reported in 1932 that Coates had been offered the position of 'Director of Leningrad and Moscow Philharmonic Societies' — a very unlikely job title, since the two organizations were completely independent of each other — but it is certain that Coates was working in Russia that year, and had been working closely with the Bol´shoi since 1930. Later in

---

[40] Gosudarstvennyi arkhiv Rossiiskoi Federatsii, fond 5283, op. 15, d. 75, l. 2; op. 3, d. 462, l. 2; op. 15, d. 12, l. 31.

1932, the *Telegraph* reported that Coates had cancelled his contract and was returning to England; but Coates still returned to conduct in Moscow and Leningrad over the next few years.[41] Therefore, if Coates had known of Clark's eagerness to visit Russia — which, given their mutual strong interest in new Russian music and Clark's powerful and influential position at the BBC seems highly likely — he was perfectly placed to facilitate it. That the two men were friends is amply illustrated by the fact that Coates made special arrangements for Clark to collect his fur coat from Berlin *en route* to Moscow. Coates wrote solicitously to Clark on 13 December 1933:

> My dear Edward
> I am writing a letter to Paula Frank, a dear old friend of mine in Berlin… who has the ticket for my *shuba* which is in storage there. I do hope, my dear Edward, that you will not go to Moscow without it. It would be dreadfully dangerous for you; January is the coldest month in the year and, by George, it can be cold. Don't forget to take my cap too; don't underrate the cold. When you come back from Russia, will you please bring the *shuba* right back to England with you, as I will want it in March for my visit to Leningrad.
>
> I was very impressed with your choice of programme, but would like to have a look at them on black and white again; would you let me have them? The Russians are not very fond of shortish pieces, they like a mouthful and it just struck me that perhaps you had too many items on each programme.
>
> I enclose a letter for you to take to Paula Frank.
> Always everything of the best to you
> Ever yours, Albert.[42]

This letter shows not only that Coates and Clark were on very friendly terms, but also, and perhaps even more importantly, that Coates was overseeing aspects of Clark's trip, including advising on his proposed programme. In the end, Clark conducted the following works: Elgar's 'Cockaigne' overture, Frederick Delius's *Brigg Fair*, John Ireland's Piano

---

[41] Anon., 'Albert Coates for Russia', *Daily Telegraph*, 30 June 1932, p. 10; 'Albert Coates and the Soviet', *Daily Telegraph*, 2 December 1932, p. 12; 'Mr Albert Coates. Concert in Soviet Workshop', *Daily Telegraph*, 18 April 1934, p. 15. He also conducted there in May and December 1934. See Iu. Vainkop, 'Kontsertnaia zhizn′ Leningrada', *Sovetskaia muzyka*, 1934, 6, p. 70, and A. Ostretsov, 'Simfonicheskie kontserty', *Sovetskaia muzyka*, 1935, 2, pp. 85–86.

[42] British Library, Add. MS. 52256, p. 86.

Concerto (performed by Maria Iudina), Constant Lambert's *Music for Orchestra* and William Walton's *Façade* suite. The concert was reviewed, in both *Sovetskaia muzyka* and (at rather more length) in the radio journal, *Govorit SSSR*, since it was a studio concert with the Moscow Radio Orchestra. The *Sovetskaia muzyka* critic was A. Konstant Smis (the pseudonym of the musicologist Konstantin Kuznetsov) but he does not even mention the Elgar work in his review (the overture 'Cockaigne'), instead concentrating entirely on the Constant Lambert and John Ireland works.[43] Evidently Kuznetsov regarded Elgar's overture as nothing more significant than an agreeable opening work, unworthy of critical reflection, probably owing to its age (composed 1901). Evgenii Braudo, the *Govorit SSSR* critic, at least gave Elgar a reasonable number of column inches; yet throughout his review he misspelled Elgar's name as 'Elgard' — a striking indication of how completely his name had vanished from Russian musical discourse. Clark performed only the overture, and Braudo does not have much to say about it: 'For its time this overture sounded bold, even expressed an unexpected melodic turn, with its own richness and beauty. Today it has lost this novelty.'[44] Perhaps Braudo's introduction to the concert was more revealing of lingering Russian attitudes to English music in general:

> The historic development of English music of the eighteenth and nineteenth centuries happened under the strong influence of German musical art, especially of the Romantic school. It is generally known that the biggest influence for English musical culture was Handel; that powerful master brought to English music a strong current of German bourgeois culture, synthesizing opera and oratorio with Italian musical techniques. In the nineteenth century almost just as great an influence on English music was Felix Mendelssohn, a composer who balanced the elements of classical and romantics schools. Nowhere in the world was Mendelssohn so often performed as in England, and this is so right up to the present time.
>
> The new English school, emerging at the start of the twentieth century, tried to break from the classical-romantic traditions and replace them with a strongly realist current. The first major master working in this direction was Edward Elgard [sic], now a venerable old man (75).[45]

---

[43] A. Konstant Smis, 'Muzykal′no-kriticheskie fragmenty', *Sovetskaia muzyka*, 1934, 3, p. 72. Konstantin Kuznetsov was a well-respected critic, musicologist and teacher who had studied philosophy at Heidelberg and had a special interest in English music.

[44] Evgenii Braudo, 'Angliiskaia muzyka na sovremennom etape dva radiovechera', *Govorit SSSR*, March 1934, p. 32.

[45] Ibid.

Indeed, the only piece Braudo summoned up any enthusiasm for at all was Walton's *Façade* suite — and even that he judged to be 'of the music-hall type'. His account of English music was not inaccurate, although very partial; but it gives a distinct impression of provincialism, dependence upon Germany (and not one of Russia's favourite Germans either — Mendelssohn was hardly ever played in orchestral concerts) and a general lack of originality and brilliance. When Harriet Cohen — Clark's friend and fellow Russian music enthusiast — made the same journey a year later to play on 31 May and 1 June 1935 (also for a radio broadcast rather than a live concert) she played Bach, Purcell, Leonid Polovinkin (a contemporary Soviet composer), Debussy, Arnold Bax and Joaquin Turina — a strikingly eclectic mix, but hardly aiming to represent British music in Russia, apart from that by Bax, her long-term lover, whose music she loyally performed all over the world.

But what of Coates — the only tangible link to pre-revolutionary Petersburg life as regards connections with Britain? Aside from his 1927 performance of 'Mars', he returned to Leningrad regularly in the early 1930s (see note 41 below for dates) and the Leningrad Philharmonia records show that he performed Elgar's *Enigma Variations* and his own *Pickwick Suite* in the 1934–35 season.[46] From 1936, foreign conductors were no longer invited and some of those already with contracts, such as Otto Klemperer and Fritz Stiedry, found they were cancelled in 1937.[47] Thus Coates's Russian career also came to an end; and no more Elgar was heard in Leningrad or Moscow, at least for the time being. But once Hitler's forces invaded the Soviet Union in June 1941 and Russia joined the Allies, everything changed yet again. In all three Moscow Philharmonia concerts organized by VOKS between 1943 and 1945, Elgar's music was played: his *Enigma Variations* in May 1943, his 'Cockaigne' overture in 1944 and 'Pomp and Circumstance March No. 3' in 1945. Reviews were blandly polite, describing all the works positively, but it was the VOKS music official, Grigorii Shneerson, who gave the fullest description of Elgar's music. Writing for *Vecherniaia Moskva*, he singled out the fourth variation ('a brilliant musical characterization of a close friend of the composer') and praises the work's 'humour and grace'.[48] Another rare event took place on 17 November 1945, this time in Leningrad (the Philharmonia having returned from their wartime exile): a concert which included Gavriil Popov's Second Symphony ('Rodina') alongside

---

[46] I have been unable to find any review of this concert, and the Philharmonia records for this season give only complete works listing, not specific concert dates.
[47] See Fairclough, *Classics for the Masses*, p. 157.
[48] Grigorii Shneerson, *Vercherniaia Moskva*, 23 May 1943.

Elgar's *Introduction and Allegro*, excerpts from Arthur Bliss's ballet suite *Chess*, Samuel Barber's *Étude* and Eli Siegmeister's *Ozark Set* — clearly intended as an Allied concert celebrating music by Soviet, British and American composers, and featuring composers whose names would soon be completely blackened in early Cold-War Soviet pronouncements on decadent Western culture.[49] After 1948, none of the music showcased in Allied concerts was heard again until after Stalin's demise.

On 21 February 1945 in Moscow, the musicologist and minor composer Igor' Belza gave an address — possibly to students rather than to musicians or the general public given that it was published by the Komitet po delam vysshei shkoly pri SSK (Soiuz Sovetskikh kompozitorov) — on 'Sovremennaia angliiskaia muzyka', a stenogram of which was published that year.[50] Belza's talk was a very basic factual account — at this stage (before the Cold War set in) polite and positive about every aspect of 'English' music (as it was always called in the Soviet press) that he mentioned. Elgar does appear, of course, and is given an approving mention for his 'deeply national' music, with no critical mention of Empire, as might have been expected if this talk had taken place in the late 1920s. Belza instead draws an uncontroversial (in Soviet terms) link between the Elgarian national sound and English folk music. The list of works he reels off is curious, and bears little relation to those Russian audiences may have heard: *King Olaf*, the Violin and Cello Concerti, the little-known *Banner of St George*, *The Kingdom*, *Coronation Ode* and, finally, the *Enigma Variations*. The fact that Belza was known for his interest in English music only underlines the extent to which this odd choice of works reveals how Soviet musicology had lost touch with it, despite the flurry of gramophone records and scores sent over by the British Council during the war.[51] Then, in Moscow, for the 1946–47 season, David Oistrakh gave a series of concerts for his 'Development of the Violin Concerto' series that, on 9 December 1946, included Elgar's Violin Concerto — so far as I am aware, the first time it had been performed in Russia since Kreisler so disappointed his audiences with the work in January 1913.[52]

---

[49] See Fairclough, *Classics for the Masses*, pp. 216–21.

[50] It was published under this title as a thin booklet by the Komitet po delam vysshei shkoly pri SSK SSSR.

[51] For details, see Fairclough, 'From Détente to Cold War: Anglo-Soviet Musical Exchanges in the Late Stalin Period', in Fairclough (ed.), *Twentieth-Century Music and Politics*, Aldershot, 2013, pp. 37–56.

[52] This concert was not reviewed in any of the major newspapers or journals so far as I have been able to establish.

And that, at least for the rest of the Stalin era, was that as far as Russia and Elgar were concerned. The next performance I have been able to verify was that given by Malcolm Sargent in May 1957, when he visited Moscow and Leningrad; he included Elgar's *Introduction and Allegro* in his second concert in Leningrad, along with Prokof´ev's *Sinfonia Concertante* (performed by Mstislav Rostropovich). It was the work's third hearing in that city since Ziloti had performed it in December 1905 (the second being the Allied concert in 1945). By that time, all memory of Ziloti's championing of Elgar had surely been forgotten by all but a few, by now very old, musicians, such as the 82-year-old pianist Aleksandr Gol´denveizer, Ziloti's old pupil at the Moscow Conservatoire. It is just possible that the possible original critic of Ziloti's first performance of Elgar's symphony, Aleksandr Ossovskii, attended or noticed the concert: he died in Leningrad two months later. In May, the month of Sargent's concert, Mikhail Gnesin, one of the composers whom Ziloti had supported as a young man, also died; Sergei Prokof´ev (another whose music Ziloti supported) had died in 1953 and Miaskovskii, who had so disliked Elgar's Violin Concerto in 1913 but who also gained support from Ziloti, had died in 1950. Shostakovich was too young to have remembered those Elgar performances; and so gradually, the generation of musicians who might have remembered slowly passed away.

Wrong music, wrong place, wrong time?
Perhaps the most striking thing about Russian Elgar reception is how vulnerable it was to political changes. After October 1917, as Russia was plunged into civil war, life for many professional musicians became so difficult that they chose to emigrate; if not immediately (as Rakhmaninov did) then gradually, over the next few years. This meant that a huge amount of experience and talent was lost, and though efforts were made to persuade that lost generation (including Ziloti) to return, they were unsuccessful in all but one famous case — that of Prokof´ev. Coates, however, was in a unique position as someone who held prestige both in London and in Russia before 1917. An Englishman by birth, his departure in 1920 did not cause him to become *persona non grata* in Russia in the way that it did for some Russian émigrés. By returning to conduct in 1927 and thereafter, Coates preserved the fragile threads of what Ziloti had achieved, even if the results were just a very few Elgar performances attracting little or no press attention. But once foreign musicians were no longer welcome after 1936–37, of course, even this tenuous link to the past was broken. As

for the Allied concerts in the mid-1940s, these were part of a much broader picture of cultural exchange that I have partly reconstructed elsewhere and it would be astonishing if Elgar had not been featured in them; but it is clear from correspondence between Soviet composers and the British Embassy during the war that Soviet musicians were more interested in discovering new British music than catching up with older works that they felt little affinity with.[53] Their awareness that Russia's musical borders had effectively closed in 1937 and may well do so again once the two nations were no longer allies meant that staying abreast of new developments in Western Europe and America was a far greater priority for them than catching up with the unfashionable music of an older generation. And when, after Stalin's death, those cultural borders were relaxed, it was Benjamin Britten who achieved recognition in Russia, not composers of the previous generation.

Perhaps the old German label of England as 'das Land ohne Musik' stuck too firmly in Russian musical memories for individual musicians to quite believe it was not true. Yet it must also be acknowledged that Elgar's chronology was not on his side in Russia, which after 1917 was a melting-pot for the most advanced avant-garde cultural movements in Europe. By the time Russian concert life was settling down in the 1920s, musicians were exploring contemporary European works, embracing modernist techniques and rejecting the comparatively staid language of the preceding generation (Russian as well as Western).[54] And even after the introduction of literary Socialist Realism in 1934 and its trickle-down effect into orchestral music, the conservative traditions of an earlier age and different culture were hardly enticing models for composers of the stature of Shostakovich and Prokof'ev, who would each come to their own productive *rapprochement* with the doctrine. For most Russians both before and after 1917, Elgar was, in short, regarded as an English domestic

---

[53] See Fairclough, *Classics for the Masses*, pp. 178–82, 'From Détente to Cold War', pp. 37–56, and also with Louise Wiggins, 'Friendship of the Musicians: Anglo-Soviet Musical Exchanges 1938–1948', in Simo Mikkonen and Pekka Suutari (eds), *Music, Art and Diplomacy: East-West Cultural Exchanges and the Cold War*, Aldershot, 2016, pp. 29–48.

[54] By the 1920s in Britain, too, Elgar's stock had fallen, to the point where some musicians expressed surprise that he had even lived so long. The journal *The Musical Times* dedicated most of its April 1934 issue to his memory; its opening editorial notes that Elgar's last important work (the Cello Concerto) had been composed in 1919, and that his continued physical existence, and appearances at the podium even struck younger British composers as somehow miraculous — as though Beethoven himself might well come on stage after him. See W. McN. (William McNaught) and H. G. (Harvey Grace), 'Edward Elgar. June 2 1837 – February 23 1934', *Musical Times*, vol. 75, 1934, pp. 305–13, esp. p. 307.

product, a provincial on the European stage, to be politely heard out when political demands required it, and no more. His music never seemed to meet the aesthetic demands of Russia's concert-going public at any point: in the 1900s he compared unfavourably with Skriabin and Stravinskii (just about meriting a comparison with Chaikovskii), while by the 1930s his music was simply regarded as irrelevant — a local curiosity from an earlier age. Had the *Enigma Variations*, Violin Concerto or First Symphony achieved instant popularity in Ziloti's concerts, they would probably have remained in Russian orchestral repertoire, just as Strauss's early tone-poems did (and indeed early Stravinskii ballets — there was never a time when *Petrushka* or *Firebird* was struck from Soviet repertoire lists). But the underwhelmed response to Ziloti's campaigning meant that this never happened, and so the moment where Elgar's music could have entered Russian orchestral repertoire passed by.

What we should make of this now is debatable. We might suspect that there was an innate snobbery in the mindset of those early twentieth-century Russian critics — a predisposition to sneer at the provincial offerings from 'das Land ohne Musik'. Ironically — given that Miaskovskii's own style was old-fashioned almost from the start — it was Miaskovskii who could most fairly be accused of that; though his disdain was fairly generously spread across nearly all new music from Europe, including that of Stravinskii.[55] There was a deep-seated defensiveness towards the hegemony of the Austro-German tradition in some sections of the early twentieth-century Russian music scene that was rooted in the Russian National School's much-vaunted distaste for the 'German' Petersburg and Moscow Conservatoires opened by Anton and Nikolai Rubinshtein, in which there was also a large dose of antisemitism.[56] But it can be found, too, in Chaikovskii's prickly attitude to European musicians whom he suspected of patronising him: writing to his brother Modest in 1877 from Vienna, he complained 'if you could only hear the offensively patronising tone in which they speak of Russian music!' Of his meeting with Liszt, he goes on to say, 'he was sickeningly polite, but all the while there was a

---

[55] See Patrick Zuk, 'Musical Modernism in the Mirror of the Myaskovsky-Prokof′ev Correspondence', in Christoph Flamm et al. (eds), *Russian Émigré Culture: Conservatism or Evolution?*, Newcastle-upon-Tyne, 2013, pp. 229–44. Prokof′ev had written in horror to Miaskovskii complaining of the 'clumsy, deadly, influence of Glazunov' in his latest work (the Fifth Symphony, 1918).

[56] See Robert Ridenour, *Nationalism, Modernism and Personal Rivalry in Nineteenth-Century Russian Music*, Ann Arbor, MI, 1981, pp. 83–85.

smile on his lips which expressed the above words pretty plainly'.[57] And Marina Frolova-Walker has charted the entire project of Russian musical nationalism from its beginnings to its Soviet incarnation, showing how the desire to promote the notion of an innate, uniquely Russian musical language — unbeholden to any European composer — was a potent force in late-nineteenth- and twentieth-century Russian musical historiography and criticism.[58] During the Soviet era itself, of course, pride in nationalism underwent a transformation, from being anathema to the Leninist internationalism of the 1920s, to being mandatory in the late 1930s and '40s — a switch that had a deep, and lasting, effect on Soviet conservatoire history teaching.[59] In both the post-1936 climate and that of the Stalinist cold war (from 1948–53), showcasing contemporary music from 'hostile' Western nations was clearly undesirable and potentially dangerous: music institutions therefore simply stopped even trying. It is hardly surprising, then, that Elgar disappears from view as he did — he was merely another European composer barred from Soviet programmes during these difficult years.

It is too easy to point to this history and infer defensive insularity as the sole preserve of Russians. For in the music world, Russia was hardly alone in mounting a defensive stance against the Austro-German canon — the English composer Ralph Vaughan Williams was no less so when he published his essays in the collection *National Music*, based on lectures he gave in Pennsylvania Bryn Mawr College in 1932, where he argued that a truly English music should be built from its folk-roots up (he had been collecting folk songs himself since the early 1900s).[60] It would be folly to conclude that Russians like Ossovskii, Miaskovskii and others were closing ranks, too anxious about their own international status to admit another outsider. Russian musical life in the pre-revolutionary era was not monolithic: ancient prejudices still remained in the critical mix (the aged *kuchkist* Tsezar' Kiui being pre-eminent among them) but Ziloti perfectly bridged the gap between Chaikovskii, Rimskii-Korsakov and Glazunov and young, ambitious internationalists like Prokof'ev and Stravinskii.

[57] Modest Tchaikovsky, *The Life and Letters of Peter Ilich Tchaikovsky*, ed. and trans. Rosa Newmarch (1907), Forest Grove, OR, 2004, p. 241.

[58] See, in particular, Marina Frolova-Walker, *Russian Music and Nationalism from Glinka to Stalin*, New Haven, CT and London, 2007.

[59] For an excellent account of this, see Marina Frolova-Walker, 'Soviet Music in Post-Soviet Musicology: The First Twenty Years and Beyond', in Frolova-Walker and Patrick Zuk (eds), *Russian Music Since 1917: Reappraisal and Rediscovery*, New York, 2017, pp. 76–102.

[60] See Ralph Vaughan Williams, *National Music*, London, 1932.

As a touring artist, he made contacts in cities across Europe, and where he encountered great musicianship and talent, he embraced it whether it came from Vienna, Paris or London. It is true that his international tours gave him privileged insights into less familiar musical cultures like that of Britain; and it is also true that Ziloti was something of a special case, both in terms of his openness to those cultures, and his unusually fine judgement when it came to choosing composers and musicians for his series. But it is nevertheless a reality that England was not able to boast of much world-class new music in those years; nor was it unreasonable for the *Russkaia muzykal'naia gazeta* critic to observe that a couple of orchestral works was an inadequate basis from which to judge whether or not Elgar was something really out of the ordinary. And if we consider Kreisler's unfortunate choice of concerto for his Russian programme, we must bear in mind what other concerti he might have offered that his Russian audience may reasonably have expected: virtuosic showcases like the Wieniawski No. 2 (a Russian favourite, having been premiered by the composer in St Petersburg in 1862) or the Beethoven, Mendelssohn or Chaikovskii concerti. Instead of playing a work that could be guaranteed to bring the house down, he chose to play a concerto no one knew, that was difficult without being showy (and so not obviously virtuosic), and which was anything but a light-hearted, sparkling show-stopper. It is unquestionably one of Elgar's greatest works, and one of the great string concerti of the last century, but it is also emotionally dense, passionate and lyrical rather than cheerful and almost a full hour long — much longer than the Wieniawski (around twenty minutes) and Mendelssohn (around thirty minutes); even the Chaikovskii is just over half an hour long. What registers most strongly in those Russian reviews of Kreisler's concert is disappointment, not xenophobic prejudice. Miaskovskii's voice was indisputably negative; but then he was negative about an awful lot of music, including that by the full roster of twentieth-century greats, starting with Mahler ('such unbelievably poor and vulgar music') and taking in Ravel ('banal'), Stravinskii ('has he lapsed into his second childhood?!'), Schoenberg ('and his litter') and Strauss ('boring and vapid').[61] Why should he have liked Elgar any better?

---

[61] For quotes, see Zuk, 'Musical Modernism in the Mirror of the Myaskovsky-Prokofev Correspondence', pp. 233 and 237. For comments on Mahler and Strauss, see Semen Shlifshtein (ed.), *N. Ia. Miaskovskii: Sobranie materialov*, 2 vols, Moscow, 1964, 1, p. 106, and Ol'ga Lamm, *Stranitsy tvorcheskoi biografii Miaskovskogo*, Moscow, 1989, p. 243. I thank Patrick Zuk for these references.

It seems fair to conclude that Elgar in Russia was a proposition doomed to failure by the forces of history. What Ziloti created was an environment for gradual familiarity and acceptance that was prevented from blossoming by war and revolution; and even Coates could not repair the damage by the time he began to conduct again in Leningrad and Moscow. Polite praise for Elgar during Allied concerts was naturally offset by keener interest in newer music, which by then Soviet audiences had been deprived of for almost a decade. Elgar's moment passed: an accident of history, a victim, perhaps, of taste and fashion; but not of prejudice.

2

Revolutionaries or Delinquents: The Biopsychological Appraisals of Composers and Their Music in Early Soviet Russia

JAMES TAYLOR

Introduction

In 1928, the Soviet musicologist Aleksandr Veprik wrote that the 'twelve-tone' technique of the Austrian composer Arnold Schoenberg (1874–1951) was the result of Germany's pre-war 'atmosphere of epigonism' which had started with Richard Wagner and his 'deeply nervous [...] idea of decomposing tonality [*razlozhenie tonal'nosti*]'.[1] Veprik, who met Schoenberg in Vienna the previous year, disapprovingly maintained that Schoenberg's influence had caused damage in Europe. He claimed that young composers like Maurice Ravel and Igor' Stravinskii had 'felt the influence of Schoenberg' and, having drawn a clear line between compositional technique and popular reception, Veprik further noted that 'atonality had a tendency to get stronger' in terms of its aesthetic influence but not in the 'consciousness of the musical masses'. In addition, he gave a detailed physical account of Schoenberg's features, which he described as: 'small, with a nervous face, with sharp gestures and big probing eyes, he gives the impression of a tormented man [...] his mannerisms convincingly suggest [...] despotism and cruelty.' For Veprik, Schoenberg's compositional language, as well as Schoenberg the man himself, epitomised an 'imitative' and 'epigonistic' threat which started from Wagner and had been 'born in retort' (*rozhdennaia v retorte*) to tonality, causing widespread 'degeneration'.[2] In this reading, Schoenberg's music was not only perceived as contagious but he himself was analysed according to his physiognomy

---

I wish to express my sincere gratitude to Pauline Fairclough, Claire Shaw, Philip Bullock and the anonymous reviewers of *The Slavonic and East European Review* for their careful reading of this article and their valuable suggestions.

[1] Aleksandr Veprik, 'Arnol'd Shenberg', *Muzyka i revoliutsiia*, 4, 1928, pp. 18–21 (p. 18).
[2] Ibid., pp. 19–21.

and personality traits, all of which were seen as conditioned by the environment in which he lived.

Numerous scholarly studies have sought to trace late-imperial and early-Soviet anxieties concerning mental and physical pathologies in the realm of public health.[3] Both medical and cultural intellectuals expressed deep concern with the 'nervousness' of Russian contemporary life, which they believed was instigated by *fin-de-siècle* urbanization and industrialization, that was causing exhaustion, fatigue, stress and weakness in working individuals. Nineteenth-century theories of degeneration, from Bénédict A. Morel's medical model to Max Nordau's cultural theorizing, which linked together hereditary predispositions with environmental influences, provided an easily adaptable framework for the empirical explanation of music's biopsychological influence.[4] As expected, music as a constituent part of that environment fed into specialized narratives about degeneration; self-appointed 'cultural doctors' sought to identify which types of music proved pathological and to explain how such delinquent individuals came to produce it.[5] Such scrutiny of individual 'deviance' already existed in Soviet-era narratives, most obviously in the writings of criminologists, which themselves drew on much earlier theories linking social, physical and racial degeneracy.[6] Louise Shelley has argued that Soviet criminologists of this period tended to focus on the personality of the offender which examined both the 'social and the psycho-physical

---

[3] For an overview, see Daniel Beer, '"Microbes of the Mind": Moral and Mental Contagion in Late Imperial Russia', *Journal of Modern History*, 79, 2007, 3, pp. 531–71; Frances L. Bernstein, 'Panic, Potency, and the Crisis of Nervousness in the 1920s', in Christina Kiaer and Eric Naiman (eds), *Everyday Life in Early Soviet Russia: Taking the Revolutionary Inside*, Bloomington and Indianapolis, IN, 2006, pp. 153–82; Jan Plamper, 'Fear: Soldiers and Emotion in Early Twentieth-Century Russian Military Psychology', *Slavic Review*, 68, 2009, 2, pp. 259–83; Irina Sirotkina, *Diagnosing Literary Genius: A Cultural History of Psychiatry in Russia, 1880–1930*, Baltimore, MD, 2002; Julie V. Brown, 'Revolution and Psychosis: The Mixing of Science and Politics in Russia Psychiatric Medicine, 1905–1913', *Russian Review*, 46, 1987, 3, pp. 283–302; Susan K. Morrissey, 'The Economy of Nerves: Health, Commercial Culture, and the Self in Late Imperial Russia', *Slavic Review*, 69, 2010, 3, pp. 645–75.

[4] On degeneration theory and its pan-European influence, see Daniel Beer, *Renovating Russia: The Human Sciences and the Fate of Liberal Modernity, 1880–1930*, London, 2008; Daniel Pick, *Faces of Degeneration: A European Disorder, 1848–1918*, Cambridge, 1989; Robert Nye, *Crime, Madness, and Politics in Modern France: The Medical Concept of National Decline*, Princeton, NJ, 1984.

[5] For a further elaboration of the term 'cultural doctors', see James Higenbottam-Taylor, 'The Cultural Doctors: Music, Health and Identity in Revolutionary Russia', unpublished PhD dissertation, University of Bristol, 2017.

[6] For these narratives in nineteenth-century Russian criminology, see Beer, *Renovating Russia*, pp. 100–18; for England, France and Italy, see Pick, *Faces of Degeneration*.

traits of the individual'.⁷ With the medical advances in physiology, genetics and endocrinology during the 1920s, Soviet criminologists investigated the hereditary transfer of psychological traits, social instincts and feelings across generations of families. As Daniel Beer has argued, 'just as the physical body of the degenerate in the pre-revolutionary period had become a distilled expression of the social order it inhabited, so now an individual's psychological predisposition could be scrutinized for information about the history of that individual's life and of the wider society he or she inhabited'.⁸ In this conceptual framework, criminologists asserted clearly that an individual's psychological complexes were embedded in their nervous systems and thus further investigation was required to explain how and why criminal tendencies persisted.

My article explores the narrative transference of these early Soviet theories of social degeneracy and its causes from the socio-scientific field to that of culture, and specifically musical culture. Early Soviet musicologists saw the musical score itself as a 'body' — the physiognomy — of healthy or defective styles, and thus identifying so-called 'deviance' within the score led to the reassessment of composers' biopsychological conditions and their socio-economic positions in former or contemporary societies.⁹ Just as Veprik had assumed with Schoenberg's music that the 'wrong' kind of music would be composed by the 'wrong' kind of person, composers could be scrutinized for signs of both physical and intellectual corruption. In this article, I illustrate how Soviet music specialists in the 1920s sought to engage in providing 'biopsychological appraisals' of composers and their music.¹⁰ By exploiting a synchronic analysis of composers'

---

⁷ Louise Shelley, 'Soviet Criminology after the Revolution', *Journal of Law and Criminology*, 70, 1979, 3, pp. 391–96 (p. 392). See also, Louise Shelley, 'Soviet Criminology: Its Birth and Demise, 1917–1936', *Slavic Review*, 38, 1979, 4, pp. 614–29.

⁸ Beer, *Renovating Russia*, p. 184.

⁹ For instance, one proletarian music specialist — Nikolai Shuvalov — argued in 1923 that 'with a detailed and exhaustive examination of samples of musical creativity in a society' it would be possible to 'judge the social conditions of life in this society and be able to check all the *unhealthy deviations* in the psyche of the social environment and discover its groupings'. Nikolai Shuvalov, 'O muzykal´nom nasledstve, o "kursakh" i izdatel´stve', *Muzykal´naia nov´*, 2, 1923, pp. 10–14 (p. 10). Shuvalov's emphasis is given in italics.

¹⁰ I have coined the term 'biopsychological appraisals' to explain how Soviet musicologists, who perceived music as an affective medium, discussed composers in terms of their biopsychological constitutions, shaped by their social environment, which would influence their behaviour and highlight the potential impact of their music on the masses. This framework links to what Daniel Beer calls the 'biologization of the social', in which criminal tendencies were seen primarily as psychological but, inherited or acquired, following the biological heredity model. Beer, *Renovating Russia*, p. 182 (pp. 182–84). Arguably this term, in many ways, also holds parallels to the genres of hagiography,

biopsychological constitutions, alongside a diachronic explanation of the environmental forces that had come to shape their psychophysiological constitutions, Soviet musicologists reasoned that it would be possible to determine whether a composer's musical output would have either a positive or a negative effect on the listening masses.

In tracing the views of music specialists, I have focused my analysis on the staple musical journals of the Soviet 1920s and their core contributors. Neil Edmunds and Amy Nelson have both identified three dominant musical factions and agendas in the 1920s: the Association of Contemporary Music (ASM), the Organization of Revolutionary Composers and Musical Activists (ORKiMD) and The Russian Association of Proletarian Musicians (RAPM), which included Prokoll — the Production Collective — based at the Moscow Conservatory by 1929.[11] Each of these groups, according to Nelson, had its own way of conceptualizing music for the new revolutionary state: ASM members remained primarily concerned with employing complex and chromatic harmonies into compositional language, and some included sounds of the machine, factories and the industrialized world; RAPM — officially established by Lev Shul′gin, David Chernomordikov and Aleksei Sergeev in June 1923 — sought to promote mass songs, rejecting musical dissonance;[12] ORKiMD — a splinter group from RAPM when Shul′gin and Sergeev left in 1924 — reiterated similar proclamations to RAPM by proposing the writing and dissemination of mass songs based on revolutionary themes.

Yet the widespread tendency to distinguish between the ASMovites (the so-called 'modernists') and the RAPMovites (the 'proletarians') as diametrically opposed in conviction (the former being considered progressive cosmopolitans and the latter being considered xenophobic

---

pathography and psychobiography writing. On pathography writing in Russia, see Irina Sirotkina, *Diagnosing Literary Genius: A Cultural History of Psychiatry in Russia, 1880–1930*, Baltimore, MD and London, 2002, pp. 1–13. For early Soviet propaganda and hagiography writing, see Nina Tumarkin, *Lenin Lives! The Lenin Cult in Soviet Russia*, Cambridge, MA, 1983; Margaret Ziolkowski, *Hagiography and Modern Russian Literature*, Princeton NJ, 1988. On psychobiography, see Louise E. Hoffman, 'Early Psychobiography, 1900–1930: Some Reconsiderations', *Biography*, 7, 1984, 4, pp. 341–51.

[11] On these various groups, see Amy Nelson, *Music for the Revolution: Musicians and Power in Early Soviet Russia*, University Park, PA, 2004, pp. 41–124. See also, Neil Edmunds, *The Soviet Proletarian Music Movement*, Bern, 2000.

[12] Aleksei Sergeev, 'Assotsiatsiia Proletarskikh Muzykantov (kompozitori, ispolniteli i pedagogi)', *Muzykal′naia nov′*, 1, 1923, 27 (p. 27). RAPM was first described as the Association of Proletarian Musicians (APM), and only later alternated between All-Russian Association of Proletarian Musicians (VAPM) and Russian Association of Proletarian Musicians (RAPM).

and anti-Western) does not hold up when considering their shared beliefs in vetting culture for the 'masses', as well as their shared vocabulary and scientific pretensions.[13] In my reading, any decisions on individual composers taken by either group were not solely governed by a nationalist criterion, but rather based on the biopsychological appraisals of composers and an examination of the particular societies in which they lived. This analysis therefore not only straddles the revolutionary divide in terms of contextualizing the discourse of music as both potentially pathological and potentially therapeutic, but also ultimately demonstrates that all factions of Soviet musicology in the 1920s were engaged in adopting biomedical terminology and integrating it into musicological discourse.

Airborne transmission: Music as pathological and therapeutic
The infectious power and influence of music over the psychological and physiological development of the masses became a key component of Soviet musicological debates in the 1920s. Indeed, it was the irregular tempi and 'convulsive' rhythms of popular music and jazz that caused the most anxiety amongst cultural specialists of the period. By 'over-exciting' the nerves, the perceived psychophysiological and emotional threat of such music, which often meshed with narratives of racial difference and sexual perversion, had emerged with a broad appeal across Soviet Russia, Europe and America.[14] Alongside narratives of popular music's pathological qualities, music — more specifically 'art music' (i.e. Western classical

---

[13] For the most recent examples of these dichotomous accounts, see Levon Hakopian, 'Shostakovich, Proletkul't and RAPM', in Pauline Fairclough (ed.), *Shostakovich Studies 2*, Cambridge, 2010, pp. 263–71 (p. 263); Elliott Antokoletz, *A History of Twentieth-Century Music in a Theoretic-Analytical Context*, New York, 2014, p. 250; Larry Sitsky, *Music of the Repressed Russian Avant-Garde, 1900–1929*, Westport, CT, 1994. For an alternative interpretation, Pauline Fairclough has shown that while both the ASMovites and RAPMovites partially divided on the dominant and contemporary trends of Western modernism, they largely embraced the works and composers of Austro-German symphonic tradition. See, Pauline Fairclough, '"Symphonies of the Free Spirit": The Austro-German Symphony in Early Soviet Russia', in Julian Horton (ed.), *The Cambridge Companion to the Symphony*, Cambridge, 2013, pp. 358–75; idem, *Classics for the Masses*, New Haven, CT and London, 2016.

[14] On the reactions to popular music and jazz in Soviet Russia in the 1920s, see S. Frederick Starr, *Red and Hot: The Fate of Jazz in the Soviet Union, 1917–1991*, New York, 1994. On popular music and affect, see David MacFadyen, *Songs for Fat People: Affect, Emotion, and Celebrity in the Russian Popular Song, 1900–1955*, Montreal and Kingston, 2002. For America and Germany, see James Kennaway, *Bad Vibrations: The History of the Idea of Music as a Cause of Disease*, Farnham and Burlington, VT, 2012, pp. 99–130. For France, see Jeffrey H. Jackson, *Making Jazz French: Music and Modern Life in Interwar Paris*, Durham, NC and London, 2003, pp. 71–103.

music, or music with an advanced technical and theoretical basis) — was discussed equally in terms of its pathological or rejuvenating capabilities. The RAPM musicologist and faction leader Lev Lebedinskii explained in 1924 that music could take control of the human nervous system, which caused a number of emotional states including a 'weakening of the will, apathy, sadness, excitement, outburst, determination, calmness, the impression of affection, tranquillity and complete peace', and thus maintained that music could have both healing and damaging effects on the individual:

> Music [...] can organize or disorganize the human nervous system and psyche, or put simply, music comes in various forms: organizing, i.e. healthy and agitating for the positive (for this we have our class view on what is good and bad); and music which is disorganizing, disrupting and corrupting the nervous system and the human psyche: such music is decadent, negative and reactionary.[15]

In a binary ideal-type formula, Lebedinskii affirmed the notion that music was either able to produce an energizing impression or corrupting impact on an individual's biopsychological constitution. Even Lenin was reportedly apprehensive about music's affective influence. Maksim Gor′kii recalled in 1924 that one evening in Moscow, Lenin was listening to Beethoven's 'Appassionata' (Piano Sonata No. 23, op. 57) and exclaimed: 'it is marvelous superhuman music [...] but I can't listen to music too often. It affects your nerves, makes you want to say stupid, nice things, and stroke the heads of people.'[16] Lenin's conception of music as over-exciting the nerves and being a potentially corrupting influence on his revolutionary consciousness demonstrated his anxiety towards music's affective power upon the individual, which might well — depending on the composers themselves — be the kind of power that would be harmful to Soviet society.

The transmission of sound and its effect on the body was, then, nothing new to musicological debate. Indeed, the discourses on music as either pathological or therapeutic had been borrowed by Soviet music specialists from an extensive array of medical, historical and cultural sources from Russia and abroad, pre-dating the Bolshevik revolution. Whilst the earliest notion of music and its effect on the health of listeners can be traced back to Pythagorean and Platonic thinking on music and cosmology in ancient

---

[15] Lev Lebedinskii, 'Beglym ognem', *Muzykal′naia nov′*, 8, 1924, pp. 13–18 (p. 13).
[16] Maxim Gorky, *Days with Lenin*, New York (reprinted by Red Star Publishers), 2014, p. 34.

Greece,[17] James Kennaway has illustrated that a systematic discourse on music as a pathological stimulant arrived towards the end of the eighteenth century, where music became perceived as a nervous stimulant like drugs or electricity. In the same way, music as a hypnotic medium came to play an important role in the emerging field of 'physiological psychology', which later came to regard the hypnotic state as an 'automatic' physical reflex.[18] Based on Franz Anton Mesmer's foundational work on 'animal magnetism' in the 1770s — the vitalist conception that music and animals held an invisible power to mesmerize patients to health — musical hypnosis later informed the work of French neurologists such as Jean-Martin Charcot, Paul Regnard, Paul Richer, Aldred Binet and Charles Féré at the Salpêtrière hospital in late nineteenth-century Paris.[19] The fear of an automated response to musical stimuli opened up the possibility of a mental contagion through music, which could threaten crowd behaviour, order and the very fabric of society.

In late imperial Russia, 'mental contagion' as a psychological tendency was often subtly linked with the idea of 'imitation' (*podrazhanie*) or 'suggestion' (*vnushenie*) and was seen to work by analogy with bacterial infection.[20] For instance, building upon the sociological research on mass psychology by French sociologists Gustav LeBon and Gabriel Tarde, Vladimir Mikhailovich Bekhterev (1857–1927), a student of Charcot, popularized the term 'suggestion' in 1898 in the meaning of a hidden psychological infection (*contagium psychicum*) from one person to another beyond conscious control. Analogous with the spread of infectious airborne biological microorganisms (*contagium vivium*), a psychological infection would occur through the transmission of words, gestures or sounds to alter human behaviour.[21] Indeed, the anxieties of music and mental

---

[17] On the ideas of music, cure and order in antiquity, see Martin West, 'Music Therapy in Antiquity', in Peregrine Horden (ed.), *Music as Medicine: The History of Music Therapy since Antiquity*, Aldershot, 2000, pp. 51–68; Jamie James, *The Music of the Spheres: Music, Science and the Natural Order of the Universe*, New York, 1993; Herbert M. Schueller, *The Idea of Music: An Introduction to Musical Aesthetics in Antiquity and the Middle Ages*, Kalamazoo, MI, 1988; Susan McClary, 'Music, the Pythagoreans, and the Body', in Susan Leigh Foster (ed.), *Choreographing History*, Bloomington, IN, 1995, pp. 82–104.

[18] James Kennaway, 'Musical Hypnosis: Sound and Selfhood from Mesmerism to Brainwashing', *Social History of Medicine*, 25, 2012, 2, pp. 1–19 (p. 2).

[19] Ibid., p. 4.

[20] Beer, *Renovating Russia*, pp. 136–38. The term 'mental contagion' was first introduced in early nineteenth-century France. See, Prosper Lucas, *De L'imitation contagieuse ou de la propagation sympathique des névroses et des monomanies*, Paris, 1833; Antoine Despine, *De la contagion morale: faits démonstrants son existence*, Marseilles, 1870. Russian terms are given by Beer.

[21] Vladimir Bekhterev, *Vnushenie i ego rol' v obshchestvennoi zhizni*, Moskva, 2014, p. 7.

contagion were ostensibly linked by the perceived elusive uncontrollability of both psychic pathogens and sound particles. Lev Tolstoi most famously expressed his psychopathological concerns with music in *The Kreutzer Sonata* (1889):

> Music acts like yawning, like laughter: I am not sleepy, but I yawn when I see someone yawning; there is nothing for me to laugh at, but I laugh when I hear people laughing. Music carries me immediately and directly into the mental condition in which the man was who composed it. My soul merges with his and together with him I pass from one condition into another, but why this happens I don't know.[22]

The unexplainable transmission of feelings through art was later developed in his book-length essay, *What Is Art?* (1897), in which Tolstoi connected the power of art to the medicalized terms 'infection' (*zarazhanie*) and 'infectiousness' (*zarazitel'nost'*).[23] Tolstoi argued that art communicated 'experience' and that 'art is that human activity which consists in one man's consciously conveying to others, by certain external signs, the feelings he has experienced, and in others being infected by those feelings and also experiencing them'.[24] The degree of infectiousness was the most important for separating 'true' art from 'counterfeit' art: 'the stronger the infection, the better the art is as art'.[25] Yet Tolstoi was evidently

---

For the French influence on his work, see Gustave Le Bon, *Psychologie des foules*, Paris, 1895; Gabriel Tarde, *L'Opinion et la Foule*, Paris, 1900, and idem, *Les Lois de L'imitation*, Paris, 1890.

[22] Ilya Vinitskii, *Ghostly Paradoxes: Modern Spiritualism and Russian Culture in the Age of Realism*, Toronto, 2009, p. 148. For the idea of infection and moral contagion in Tolstoi, see pp. 146–55.

[23] Olga Matich, *Erotic Utopia: The Decadent Imagination in Russia's Fin de Siècle*, Madison, WI, 2005, p. 29. Tolstoi was certainly familiar with psychopathological literature, in particularly Alfred Mori's article, 'The Degeneration of the Human Race: The Beginning Consequences of Idiocy', as early as 1860, and, in a diary entry in 1884, he noted that he was reading an essay entitled 'On the Study of Pathological Affects: Two Forensic Psychiatric Cases' by Russian psychiatrist Pavel I. Kovalevskii (Professor at Kharkov University). See ibid., p. 52.

[24] Leo Tolstoy, *What Is Art?*, trans. Richard Pevear and Larissa Volokhonsky, London, 1995, p. 40.

[25] Ibid., p. 120. Caryl Emerson has extensively detailed Tolstoi's aesthetics: whilst successful art could be measured on the basis of the feelings transmitted (*osobennost' chuvstva*), clarity (*iasnost'*) and artist's sincerity (*iskrennost'*), counterfeit art could be judged through 'borrowing' (*zaimstvovanie*), 'imitativeness' (*podrazhatel'nost'*), 'striking effects' (*pozrazitel'nost'*) or 'distraction' (*zanimatel'nost'*). See Caryl Emerson, 'Tolstoy's Aesthetics', in Donna Tussing Orwin (ed.), *The Cambridge Companion to Tolstoy*, Cambridge, 2002, pp. 237–51 (pp. 239–41).

concerned that music could over-excite and gravely infect a listener's biopsychological constitution. In a discussion of Wagner's impact on the listener, Tolstoi reasoned that 'if you sit in the dark in the opera and submit your brain [and] auditory nerves to the strongest possible impact of sounds calculated to produce the most irritating effect, you will probably also enter an abnormal psychological state'.[26] In drawing parallel conclusions to Max Nordau's analysis of Wagner in *Degeneration* (1892), Tolstoi perceived Wagner's music as an expression of bad infection with hypnotic tendencies to manipulate its audience. The mixture of mental contagion with musical sound reinforced the notion that certain moods or feelings, healthy or pathological, could be transferred into a listening public.

In pre-revolutionary musical life, the concern with harmonic consonance and dissonance became an important site for debates on music's psychophysiological impact on the body. There were numerous references in music journals to the idea of music transferring 'feelings' and 'experiences' alongside its mutual development with the evolution of the human psyche.[27] In many ways, this viewpoint fitted within the Soviet 'neo-Lamarckian' conception of the human organism developing and adapting towards its outer environment.[28] For example, the music critic Leonid Sabaneev wrote in 1916 that the evolution of harmony came 'subconsciously' from the shift in the 'psychological centre'; constantly playing the same music meant the body 'stopped reacting', whereas 'new irritations' were demanded by the 'psychophysiological apparatus' — the body itself.[29] Sabaneev's belief that the psyche could be substantially transformed under the pressure of new sound waves meant that the 'thirst' for new music predetermined the existence of new musical forms.[30] In

---

[26] Matich, *Erotic Utopia*, p. 48.
[27] For examples of this shift between consonance and dissonance alongside the human psyche, see Rebecca Mitchell, *Nietzsche's Orphans: Music, Metaphysics, and the Twilight of the Russian Empire*, New Haven, CT and London, 2015, pp. 25–60. On the impact of changing emotions with contemporary life, see Mark Steinberg, 'Melancholy and Modernity: Emotions and Social Life in Russia between the Revolutions', *Journal of Social History*, 41, 2008, 4, pp. 813–41.
[28] For the application of the neo-Lamarckian model in early Soviet life, see Beer, *Renovating Russia*, pp. 165–204.
[29] Leonid Sabaneev, 'Evoliutsiia gamonicheskogo sozertsaniia', *Muzykal´nyi sovremennik*, 2, 1915, pp. 18–30 (pp. 20–21).
[30] Ibid. Sabaneev is referring here to the 'theory of elasticity': solid objects will deform under pressure and their elasticity is judged according to whether the same object can return back to its original shape. While he determined that art still transferred the artist's 'feelings' and 'experiences', he maintained that the composer was still subordinated, independent of his will, to the laws of the '"inelasticity" of the psychophysiological apparatus'.

other words, the demand for new music was based upon an individual's psychophysiology and its incessant need for new sound waves. Only new dissonances could provide new moods (*nastroenie*) through music, in order to contain the same psychophysiological effects as old music had communicated in the past. In this understanding, critics claimed that musical dissonance was associated with the path of musical progress.

By linking the effects of musical dissonance with bodily reactions, Sabaneev's pre-revolutionary view correlates to the Soviet conception of the human reflex throughout the 1920s. Although cultural elites, as Irina Sirotkina states, often criticized the reflex for being too mechanistic and automaton-like, the term still appeared heavily in the lexicon across the visual arts, dance, theatre and literature, making use of Ivan Pavlov's theory of conditional reflexes, Bekhterev's 'reflexology' and Konstantin Kornilov's 'reactology'.[31] On the musical front, Lebedinskii explained in 1924 that music, through its direct appeal to the emotions, left a 'material impact', in which sound was 'received by our hearing nervous system' and this caused 'certain reflexes' to appear.[32] For Lebedinskii, music could overwhelm the nervous system and plunge the human psyche into numerous emotional states, positive or negative. In the same way, the ASM musicologist Boris Asaf´ev wrote in 1926 that while music was a 'conductor of feelings', listening to art music required more 'complex reflexes' which meant a 'more developed ear'. Based on the evolutionary hierarchies in listening, dissonance required an evolved psyche as opposed to 'everyday music' that had more of a 'direct emotional impact' because otherwise it 'may not reach the listener' at all.[33] In both cases, both Lebedinskii and Asaf´ev perceived music as being able to pass through the subconscious emotional stimuli of humans, create certain reflexes, and thus generate various emotional states. Despite their appeals to materialist philosophy, such views clearly echo the pre-revolutionary fantasies, from Nietzsche to the Russian Symbolists, about human transformation through music and the emotions.

With the notion of music's ability to transmit various moods and feelings, music came to be understood as an important part of unifying the masses in the spirit of collective health and also as a medium to communicate, through oscillating sound waves, an individual's immortal personality to the next generation. Bekhterev had been influential in exploring the idea

---

[31] Irina Sirotkina, 'The Ubiquitous Reflex and Its Critics in Post-Revolutionary Russia', *Berichte Zur Wissenschaftsgeschichte*, 32, 2009, pp. 70–81 (pp. 75–78).

[32] Lebedinskii, 'Beglym ognem', p. 13.

[33] Igor´ Glebov, 'Muzyka goroda i derevni', *Muzyka i revoliutsiia*, 3, 1926, pp. 6–8 (p. 6).

of music as cure, setting up a health commission in 1913 to address music's ability to cure physical and mental disorders.[34] Yet through his idea of *suggestion*, music could also convey the emotional energy of a personality — or psychic charge — to future generations. Already by 1916, Bekhterev was using the scientific concept of energy to explain immortality; basing his work on the principle of energy conservation, he maintained that even after death, the human personality was immortal, existing in the form of collective energy and hereditarily passing from one generation to the next.[35] He developed this idea further in his seminal work, *Collective Reflexology* (1921), in which he posited that the organs of 'touch, vision and hearing' would all play a part in uniting the masses; the latter with dead composers, mutually interacting through the transmission of sound energy:

> When an artist plays Musorgskii or Skriabin, the physical side boils down to his fingers, moving the bow across the strings of a violin [...]. Through the medium of oscillation, the sound reaches the hearing organ and excites vibration in the form of neural waves, which heads towards the auditory cortical areas. The latter sends back a wave to the peripheral and internal organs, leading to certain mimico-somatic reactions, and provokes a number of other mental reactions. It is these neural waves generated in the listeners by the same intermediary that unite the masses listening to the artist. They receive the same physical energy and charge, although the effects of the charge differentiate according to individuals who are not completely identical. However, the fact there are mimico-somatic reactions in all individuals, a common cause of unification, leads to an interaction, using the same intermediary, between themselves and with long-dead composers.[36]

Music had the potential to unite listeners with long-dead composers and, claims Bekhterev, 'music itself was an expression of certain moods, a route of infection, and the pathogen of a particular mood in others'.[37]

[34] Vladimir Bekhterev and S. Nikitin, 'Muzyka kak lechebnoe sredstvo', *Peterburgskaia gazeta*, 1913, p. 16, and 'K lecheniiu muzykoi (pis′mo v redaktsiiu)', ibid., p. 18. See also, Ekaterina Orlova, 'Research on the Influence of Music on a Person and a Society in the Works of V. M. Bekhterev: Becoming of Music Psychology in Russia', *Life Science Journal*, 11, 2014, pp. 655–57.
[35] Vladimir Bekhterev, 'Immortality from the Scientific Point of View', *Society*, 4, 3, 2006, pp. 74–80 (p. 80). First given as a speech, delivered at the St Petersburg Psychoneurological Research Institute, in February 1916 and then later published in *Vesnik znaniia* in 1918.
[36] Vladimir Bekhterev, *Kollektivnaia refleksologiia*, Petrograd, 1921, p. 110.
[37] Ibid., p. 188.

In this view, music therefore not only held the capability of unifying the masses through sound energy but equally helped transfer the ideals and personality traits of the long-dead composers through the sensory organs of those hearing their music.

Revolutionary blueprints: Scrutinizing a composer's biopsychology
In elucidating music's ability to communicate certain moods and personality traits, biopsychological appraisals of composers became an important part of denoting the suitability of their music within Soviet society. The impacts of heredity and environmental forces on fashioning a composer's biopsychology were important criteria in explaining the reasons behind a composer's creative personality. In their interaction with the post-revolutionary environment, individuals would be judged according to their ability to adapt, what Daniel Beer calls their capacity for 'revolutionary adaptation'.[38] For example, the Soviet criminologist Aleksandr Karlovich Lents (1882–1952), wrote in 1927 that psychopaths were 'individuals with an unstable nervous system who have difficulty adapting to their social environment, [...] their chief characteristic is social inadaptability'.[39] The underlying conception of degeneration, based loosely on the theory of acquired characteristics by Jean-Baptiste Lamark (1744–1829), maintained that an individual organism was in a constant struggle to adapt to its environment. Acquired environmental tendencies therefore embedded themselves into the adapting organism and were passed on to future generations via heredity. The logic follows that individuals with corrupted immune systems were seen as being unable to adapt to a given environment; they were considered incapable of competing, in the Darwinian sense, in the struggle for existence and this was presumed to provoke criminal behaviour. On the other hand, individuals who were perceived to have struggled against the prevailing forces of a pathological environment were considered 'geniuses', heroic and therefore adaptable to the post-revolutionary society.[40] In essence, biopsychological health could only be achieved through the diagnosis and cure of those factors that caused degeneration, and by identifying the transmitters of degeneration themselves.

[38] For a detailed explanation of 'Revolutionary Adaptation', see Beer, *Renovating Russia*, pp. 184–89.
[39] Aleksandr Lents, *Kriminal'nie psikhopati*, forward by V. P. Osipov, Leningrad, 1927, p. 24, cited in Beer, *Renovating Russia*, p. 185.
[40] See Irina Sirotkina, 'Mad Genius: The Idea and its Ramifications', *Intellectual News*, 10, 2002, 1, pp. 91–98; idem., 'Mental Hygiene for Geniuses: Psychiatry in the Early Soviet Years', *Journal of the History of the Neurosciences*, 16, 2007, 1–2, pp. 150–59.

Soviet music specialists, in their determination to understand an individual's biopsychology, would seek to delineate between a composer's heredity and their acquired characteristics. For example, the ASM musicologist Viktor Beliaev assessed Paul Hindemith (1895–1963) in 1924 and argued that he was primarily a 'chamber music composer' and therefore a 'carrier of an old-aged musical culture' which started from Bach, Haydn, Mozart and Beethoven and ended with Brahms, Reger and Schoenberg. It was through these German composers that Hindemith received his stylistic traits for quartet writing. Beliaev maintained that Hindemith had also 'inherited from the past' the ability to 'extract beautiful and bright sounds' from his quartet instruments.[41] In Beliaev's understanding, Hindemith had inherited 'bravery' in his compositions through his 'race', which had been cultivating a chamber style method for centuries. Yet, in addition to these inherited traits, Hindemith had 'acquired' compositional traits (i.e. complex and unsymmetrical rhythms) from the French and Russian impressionists (Stravinskii in this case), which, for Beliaev, had shaped Hindemith's 'creative personality' in a negative way.[42] Being able to experience these rhythms of the 'barbaric races' in his music, Hindemith's musical language was one of extreme 'contrasts' — a mixture of a refined musical aesthetic and primitive rhythms.[43] Asaf'ev took a similar stance in an article entitled 'Hindemith and Casella' in 1925, which argued that while Alfredo Casella was 'refined' for having 'tasted the Russo-Parisian poison' of Stravinskii, Hindemith also represented a 'paradoxical combination of rough, but full-blooded and temperamental composer breed who had received bad vaccinations [*s durnimi privivkami*]' from his environment.[44] For Asaf'ev, while Hindemith was a talented composer in his chamber music, his music overall was filled with the aesthetic 'urbanism' of the modern city, demonstrating a 'machine-like productivity' which was both 'tasteless and thick-skinned'.[45] While Asaf'ev considered Hindemith's *Kammermusik* No. 1–2 (Chamber Music, 1922–24) a healthy development, in terms of its neo-classical references to Bach and Haydn, he denigrated Hindemith's so-called attempts to infuse the machine-age

---

[41] Viktor Beliaev, 'Paul' Khindemit', *Sovremennaia muzyka*, 1, 1924, pp. 3–8 (p. 4).
[42] Ibid.
[43] Ibid., pp. 5–7.
[44] Igor' Glebov, 'Khindemit i Kazella', *Sovremennaia muzyka*, 11, 1925, pp. 11–12 (p. 11). Asaf'ev was much more positive two years later: he argued that Hindemith's music was 'full-blooded, brave, temperamental, bold, exuberant, healthy, and above all, rich with playful irony'. See Igor' Glebov, 'Elementi stilia Khindemita', *Novaia muzyka*, 2, 1927, 6, pp. 7–23 (p. 9).
[45] Ibid., p. 12.

aesthetic (for instance, in *Kleine Kammermusik*, op. 24, no. 2 [1922] for wind quintet, the fourth movement, 'Schnelle Viertel' [Fast Crochet], is replete with repetitious quaver and semi-quaver figures). The interjection of machine-like music into the traditional chamber form clearly influenced Asaf'ev's view of Hindemith. In both cases, although Hindemith allegedly possessed a 'healthy' heredity, the acquired traits from his contemporary environment were identified as damaging to his creative personality.

Sincerity in composition and biopsychological health was also a key comparative in such appraisals: there was often a connection made between a composer's health and their ability to feel emotions, which fanned anxieties about individuals carrying dual personalities.[46] According to the RAPM musicologist Iurii Keldysh, Sergei Prokof'ev (1891–1953) and his 'ideas and feelings' were conditioned in an environment of 'futurism, "urbanism" and "machinism"' — movements which stood in 'reaction' to Symbolism and Impressionism.[47] Nevertheless, Prokof'ev, who had, Keldysh alleged, 'superficially acquired' from Stravinskii only 'the external traits of his style' (in this case, the brightness and contrast of musical colours), represented a 'rough Scythian' who looked 'physically healthy' but had a 'thick-skinned psychological disposition [...] immune to emotional and aesthetic experiences'.[48] There are clear parallels here with Hindemith's biopsychological descriptors: a healthy heredity being tarnished by acquired, unemotional pathological traits. Keldysh concluded that Prokof'ev's music came across as 'buffoonery', aiming for 'physiological laughter', which served to 'mask' Prokof'ev's hostility towards the Soviet way of life. In the same manner, Konstantin Kuznetsov, writing for the ASM journal *Sovremennaia muzyka* in 1927, exclaimed that Prokof'ev had 'two faces': one face in his public profile and another in person. On the one hand, Prokof'ev's public face had the 'forehead of a thinker', he looked 'older' and 'in the lower parts of the face, there were no signs of sensuality'; on the other hand, in person, Prokof'ev had 'small, bright eyes', looked 'younger' and showed signs of 'emotional warmth, rather than buffoonery'.[49] Although both musicologists, each from the RAPM and

---

[46] On the idea of double identity in Soviet culture, see Sheila Fitzpatrick, 'Making a Self for the Times: Impersonation and Imposture in 20th-Century Russia', *Kritika*, 2, 2001, 3, pp. 469–87; Sheila Fitzpatrick, 'The Two Faces of Anastasia', in Fitzpatrick, *Tear off the Masks! Identity and Imposture in Twentieth-Century Russia*, Princeton, NJ and Oxford, 2005, pp. 102–13.

[47] Iurii Keldysh, 'Balet "Stal'noi skok" i ego avtor – Prokof'ev', *Proletarskii muzikant*, 6, 1929, pp. 12–19 (p. 12)

[48] Ibid., p. 14.

[49] Konstantin Kuznetsov, 'Zhivoi oblik Prokof'eva', *Sovremennaia muzyka*, 20, 1927, pp.

ASM wings, disagreed over whether Prokof´ev demonstrated emotional tendencies, they both linked biopsychological health, visible and invisible, with the ability to feel emotions.

Stemming from an acceptance that environmental forces shaped and inscribed an individual's biopsychology, composers from modern 'degenerate' Europe were treated rather suspiciously, whereas the French revolutionary-era Ludwig van Beethoven (1770–1827) and his immediate contemporaries (i.e. Franz Schubert and Hector Berlioz) were viewed rather more favourably. Sabaneev, writing in 1923 about Richard Strauss (1864–1949), claimed that Strauss shared a 'genetic relationship' with the German musical masters and was the 'flesh and blood of that same great sound culture which Bach, Beethoven, Mendelssohn, Brahms and Wagner created'.[50] However, although Strauss's 'genetic traits' were seen as secured, Sabaneev claimed that Strauss's 'creative psychology' depended on the political atmosphere in which he worked, which he saw as being marred by the militarism, pomp and destructive forces of the First World War. Indeed, Sabaneev asserted that these divisive forces had caused some 'internal emptiness' to appear in Strauss's compositions. On the other hand, a composer like Beethoven represented a case of both healthy heredity and favourable acquired traits from the environment. Lunacharskii wrote in 1927 that Beethoven was an 'extraordinary natural talent that was put in extremely favourable circumstances', but the success of these circumstances on contemporaries still depended upon the 'degree of biological talent'.[51] In Lunacharskii's opinion, the notion of what we might call a 'biosocial' genius meant that Beethoven's 'heartbeat was in unison' with the revolutionary masses: he 'empathised with revolution' and could correctly identify 'human society as being infected with seriously diseased traditions, constructed unreasonably and unjustly' and envisaged that its 'path of healing' was through a 'path of severe bloody struggle [with] no reconciliation, no desire to settle down and give up'.[52] Although Lunacharskii later claimed that it was laughable to suggest that Beethoven lived in favourable circumstances, especially in regards to his deafness and late-career poverty, Beethoven represented a figure of both a healthy heredity and healthy acquired characteristics from the revolutionary environment in which he lived.

251–53 (pp. 251–52).
[50] Leonid Sabaneev, 'Rikhard Straus', *K novym beregam*, 2, 1923, pp. 36–40 (p. 36).
[51] Anatolii Lunacharskii, 'Chto zhivo dlia nas v Betkhovene', *Muzyka i revoliutsiia*, 3, 1927, pp. 3–8 (p. 6).
[52] Ibid., pp. 7–8.

Even though there was a reluctance to accept that deviance was biologically encoded, music specialists still retained physical 'stigmata' as a means to explain 'atavism' in composers, based on the Italian criminologist Cesare Lombroso's theory explaining the reappearance of ancestral traits in individuals.[53] The composers Claude Debussy (1862–1918) and Arnold Schoenberg (1874–1951) received the severest scrutiny in this respect, although they received slightly different appraisals. The musicologist Anatolii Drozdov, who was a member of the Organization of Revolutionary Composers (ORKiMD) — a musical faction with close connections to RAPM[54] — wrote that Debussy's 'roots' were rather complicated. Drozdov claimed that Debussy's immediate influences were Edvard Grieg and Modest Musorgskii, alongside Debussy's closest 'relatives' — César Franck (1822–90) and Jules Massenet (1842–1912). Yet these composers were only 'acquired influences, not inherited [*vliianiia poverkhnostnye, ne po sushchestvu*]'.[55] Instead, Drozdov stated that the sources of Debussy's nature could be found in the medieval era with his revival of diatonicism, parallel chords and monody, and that this 'musical atavism underlies the "primordial" nature of Debussy'.[56] In this understanding, Debussy's inherited nature meant that he languished in a state of evolutionary primitivism which was being reflected in his revival of more primitive forms of music. In the same way, although Schoenberg was considered 'extremely talented', Aleksandr Veprik argued that Schoenberg had been trapped in the pre-war atmosphere of epigonism, a form of artistic mental contagion, which had conditioned him towards atonality.[57] Yet, alongside his environmental conditioning, the insistence of providing a visible taxonomy of deviance, detailing Schoenberg's 'small, nervous face', meant that visible, criminal defects could still be identified within the individual. Indeed, for Debussy, his inheritance perhaps proved too troubling to be solved during his lifetime, whereas Schoenberg had only been conditioned in a pathological environment and still remained salvageable. Nevertheless, both narratives imply that a composer's deviance was both embedded and traceable within their corrupted biopsychological constitution.

Despite their aversion to suggesting a correlation between physical and psychological deformities within the individual, musicologists sought

---

[53] On Lombroso in Russia, see Beer, *Renovating Russia*, pp. 100–21.

[54] For further details about ORKiMD, see Neil Edmunds, *The Soviet Proletarian Music Movement*, Bern, 2000, pp. 153–64.

[55] A more literal translation would be 'superficial influences, not essential [ones]'.

[56] Andrei Drozdov, 'Klod Debiussi', *Muzyka i revoliutsiia*, 3, 1928, pp. 19–23 (p. 23).

[57] Aleksandr Veprik, 'Arnol´d Shenberg', *Muzyka i revoliutsiia*, 4, 1928, pp. 18–21 (pp. 18–19).

to transfer readings of physical defects from the composer's body to the musical score itself. The connection between a composer's thoughts and their music was often made explicitly clear. For instance, detailing Skriabin as a 'solipsist' and 'mystic', Lebedinskii stated that 'Skriabin's music is the flesh and blood of his ideology'.[58] Likewise, Drozdov expressed the degenerate anxiety about Debussy's music that 'typical techniques and elements of his writing in revised forms have appeared in the flesh and blood of the next generation of music and continues to nurture the musical thought of the present'.[59] In this framework, a composer's musical score therefore left visible traces of a composer's ideology and constitution of thoughts.

The positivist impulse to detect physical anomalies alongside their hereditary transfer across generations of music was often reproduced in the analysis of composers' creativity. Just as criminologists identified the visible and physical deformities in individuals, music specialists often perceived the musical score as the composer's criminal 'stigmata', which could be scrutinized for traces of deviance. For example, Drozdov subsequently attempted to define Debussy's 'artistic physiognomy', detailing his most prominent compositional characteristic as 'retrospectivism' which he defined in the article as heading towards the past.[60] One characteristic trait was the 'inanimate' nature of Debussy's compositions, which appeared to 'run away from everything living'; Debussy's composition, *Des pas sur la neige* (1909–10), for example, was described as 'only the shadow of a living essence and nothing more' due to its content being about footprints in the snow.[61] Another characteristic of his compositional style was that his images and subjects were filled with 'tones of sadness' and that even the happiest of them, *L'Isle Joyeuse* (1904), was 'fraught with some mournful overtones'. His vocal works with poetry by French Symbolists Paul-Marie Verlaine (*Ariettes oubliées*, *Aquarelles*, *Fêtes galantes*) and Charles Baudelaire (*Cinq Poèmes*), and his opera *Pelléas et Mélisande* to the text by Maurice Maeterlinck, illustrated 'refined' feeling and images which were 'static and passive aesthetic contemplation', illustrating the 'tiredness of

---

[58] Lev Lebedinskii, '"Poslednii reshitel'nyi"', *Za proletarkuiu muzyku*, 5, 1931, pp. 7–12 (p. 9).

[59] Drozdov, 'Klod Debiussi', p. 20. Drozdov maintained that Debussy's influence had affected composers like Maurice Ravel (1875–1937) and Albert Roussel (1869–1937) from France; Isaac Albéniz (1860–1909) from Spain; Alfredo Casella (1883–1947) and Mario Castelnuovo-Tedesco (1895–1968) from Italy; Daniël Ruyneman (1886–1963) from Belgium; and Skriabin and Stravinskii from Russia.

[60] Ibid., pp. 20–23.

[61] Ibid., p. 20.

feelings, hypertrophy of sophistication and volitional depression, bound to reflect the artist who was nurtured in the spirit of extreme individualistic aestheticism'.[62] In this reading, a clear correlation existed between the physical (and audible) deformities of a musical score and the environmental forces that shaped an individual's biopsychology.

In the same way, by scrutinizing a composer's full body of work, from their earliest oeuvres to their last, it would be possible to map out a trajectory between their musical techniques, informed by their personality, and the environment in which the composer lived. In a sample analysis of Franz Schubert's (1797–1828) compositions, the RAPM music specialist Mikhail Bruk posited that 'some petty-bourgeois narrow-mindedness [*meshchanskaia ogranichennost´*]' had appeared in a selection of Schubert's songs.[63] On the one hand, discussing Schubert's song cycle *Die schöne Müllerin*, D. 795, Bruk argued that certain songs such as 'Das Wandern', 'Wohin?', 'Der Müller und der Bach', 'Des Müllers Blumen' and 'Des Baches Wiegenlied' were 'typically missing extensive development of musical material' and that there were 'no sharp edges, no sharp contrasts and no large internal tension' in these compositions. Bruk claimed that many of them appear musically 'primitive', which was 'the idealization of Burgher [petty-bourgeois] life'.[64] However, in another example, Bruk claimed that Schubert's *Der Erlkönig*, D. 328, based on a ballad by Goethe, was characterized as being 'filled with emotions' and containing 'contrasting musical images'.[65] Depicting the panic-stricken journey of the father on horseback through a forest, the opening motif is written in triplets (in triads, not broken chords), octaves in constant motion, marked 'fast' (crochet = 152) and builds in tension across the piece. In contrast, the middle section of each verse (see fig. 1), representing the Erl King's enticing song to the child, is musically simplistic, diatonic, in the key of C major and less challenging to perform. In this reading, Bruk praised Schubert for uniting the 'dramatic action' together and recreating the 'purposefulness of movement' throughout.[66] For Bruk, 'The Erl King' represented the pinnacle of Schubert's creativity in connecting simplistic emotions with varied musical-dramatic content.

---

[62] Ibid., p. 21.

[63] Mikhail Bruk, 'Shubert i ego pesni', *Za proletarskuiu muzyku*, 16, 1931, pp. 6–12 (p. 8).

[64] Bruk contended that the term 'Burgher' had two meanings: 1) in the literal sense, a citizen or inhabitant of a town 2) in the figurative sense, a 'Burgher' is linked to the Russian word *meshchanin* (petty-bourgeois).

[65] Ibid., pp. 9–10.

[66] Ibid.

In contrast to Schubert's earlier works, Bruk maintained that Schubert's later life circumstances, which included 'constant poverty, sickness, and recognition of his creativity only by a narrow native circle of friends', were reflected in his song cycle, *Winterreise*, D. 911, published a year after his death in 1827. The song titles from the cycle, such as 'Einsamkeit', 'Gefror'ne Tränen' and 'Der greise Kopf', were for Bruk, examples of the moment Schubert 'turned his attention inside' and away from society. Schubert's musical language also became 'more difficult' (*uslozhniaetsia*) with a 'torturous' melodic line and 'predominantly minor' with the 'attention being more focused on the internal psychological experiences'.[67] Bruk's extract as presented here, from 'Der Stürmische Morgen' from *Winterreise* (1828) is in D minor, and his melodic writing is notably more complicated and rhythmically irregular than in 'The Erl King' (see fig. 2). For Bruk, Schubert was a product of his social environment, whose 'pessimism' was reflected in his later work. Still, according to Bruk, Schubert managed to escape the later developments of 'bourgeois' art by managing to link his 'warm melodic songs' with German and Austrian folk song (*Lied*) which made them 'understood by the masses'.[68] Overall, Bruk maintained that Schubert's redeeming characteristic was his ability to connect with the psyche of the Soviet masses: his songs, on the whole, were filled with 'simple and spontaneous cheerfulness' and were, therefore, 'not alien to the most extensive and full psyche of the working classes'.[69] Nonetheless, by following the trail of a composer's full body of work, music specialists reasoned that it would be possible to identify and scrutinize the trajectory between a composer's compositional language and the environment in which they lived.

Finally, in terms of effecting revolutionary adaptation, biopsychological appraisals also emphasized how a composer's music had the ability to adapt and survive in the new post-revolutionary Soviet environment. For example, in 1927, the ASM musicologist Boris Asaf'ev wrote that Wolfgang Amadeus Mozart's (1756–91) music was 'the best at vitality' and argued that it was actually 'getting younger' (*muzyka Motsarta molodeet*), meaning that the 'sources of his music are still growing […] becoming less and less original and proprietary […] and the personal elements of his creativity are becoming less visible'.[70] Implying that Mozart's music passed through

---

[67] Ibid., p. 11.
[68] Ibid.
[69] Ibid., p. 12.
[70] Igor' Glebov, 'Mozart i sovremennost'', *Sovremennaia muzyka*, 25, 1927, pp. 55–59 (p. 56).

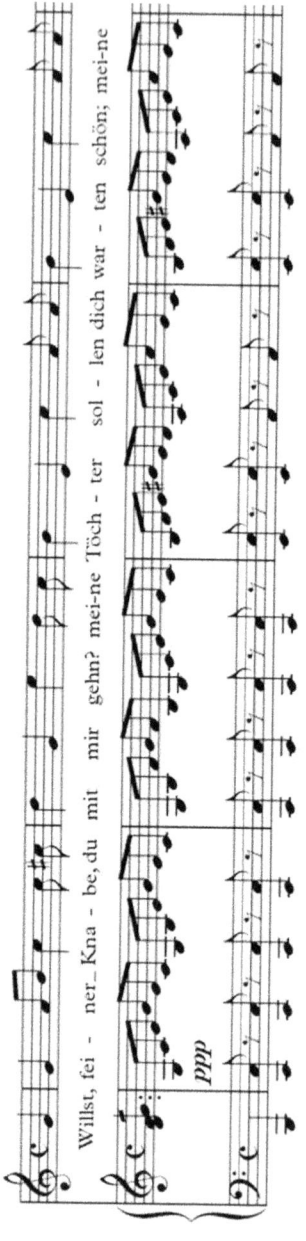

Fig. 1: Extract from Franz Schubert's *Der Erlkönig* as cited in 'Shubert i ego pesni', p. 10.

Fig. 2: Extract from 'Der Stürmische Morgen' (*Winterreise*) as cited in 'Shubert i ego pesni', p. 11.

the musical generations into a deeper human heredity, Asaf´ev posited that 'the more organically dissolved the composer is, in what is important and necessary for all people living in an era, the longer their work will live'.[71] Asaf´ev saw Mozart's music as something still able to adapt to the contemporary environment. Yet, for Asaf´ev, it was the relevance of Mozart's music as being 'custom-built for the ever-changing environment' which led him to conclude that Mozart's music should be considered 'mutable' and that 'the power of Mozart's music lies in its ability to change, in that it is fully soldered and connected to our lives but, with changing, it renews and regenerates itself'; Mozart's music 'lives' because it is 'capable of developing and, together with the life and death of generations, it mutates in them'.[72] Asaf´ev evidently perceived music as being able to perform revolutionary adaptation, healthy in its hereditary transmission through the generations of people, and adaptable as an organism in itself. Indeed, by tracing the etiologies of degeneration or health traits in a composer, music specialists could seek to explain how an individual's biopsychological make-up helped cause deleterious or healthy consequences in their musical creativity.

Class adaptation: The struggle for existence
Narratives pertaining to class adaptation became a defining feature in the writing of composers' biopsychological appraisals. With the newly ascribed class categories in the post-revolutionary era, individuals were judged according to their class positions, becoming signifiers for those who were biopsychologically damaged and unable to adapt to the new environment. Indeed, a class-based assessment of revolutionary adaptation was also tantamount to a biopsychological determination.[73] Composers who showed no real sense of struggle in their lifetimes were described as being class representatives of the bourgeoisie along with its attendant anxieties. For example, Veprik wrote in 1929 that the sudden change he perceived in Béla Bartók's (1881–1945) music of the post-war era, making it lose its infectious quality, was explained through the shift in class forces — i.e. the perceived decline of the European bourgeoisie after World War One. Veprik maintained that while progressive European composers had now turned away from atonality to put their hopes in jazz, which was 'supposed to make music healthier', these attempts had helped music lose its

---

[71] Ibid., p. 57.
[72] Ibid., p. 59.
[73] See Beer, *Renovating Russia*, p. 185n; Sheila Fitzpatrick, 'Ascribing Class: The Construction of Social Identity in Soviet Russia', *Journal of Modern History*, 65, 1993, pp. 745–70.

social significance: 'music stopped being infectious, it stopped influencing people.'[74] Whilst Veprik considered Bartók's *Allegro Barbaro* (1911) as well as his folk songs, peasant songs and Christmas carols as being 'infectious' and accessible to a mass audience due to their pronounced melodic lines, his later works (i.e. Piano Concerto No. 1, 1926) had 'dissolved' and rejected his former melodic style.[75] Veprik concluded that Bartók 'shared the fate of his class [the bourgeoisie]' and that even his 'huge talent could not save him'. Unable to adapt to the new post-revolutionary environment, Bartók joined the ranks of Schoenberg, Hindemith and Ernst Křenek who reflected 'the degeneration and death of this class'.[76] Veprik's viewpoint on this particular brand of modernism was particularly influenced by his trip to Europe in 1927, in which he was dismayed by Schoenberg's transition from a post-Romantic musical idiom to his serial technique. The rejection of melody and, as Veprik saw it, expressive content made contemporary Western music cold, emotionless and inaccessible to the masses.[77] Indeed, Veprik felt that Bartók's musical trajectory implied an uncontrollable and inadaptable biopsychological constitution.

Soviet music specialists of all factions saw class decline as a similar fate shared by the composers Aleksandr Skriabin (1872–1915) and Claude Debussy. The ASM musicologist and composer Nikolai Roslavets argued that the two composers were both clear examples of the 'full demoralization and ideological decline of Russian society' and that their ideologies arose from 'the same social preconditions'; Skriabin created 'horrible [musical] visions of sick and wounded life fantasies' and whose art reflected 'an era of decay and of an out-dated social system, built by masters on the bones of their slaves' and Debussy was the representative of 'decaying Western bourgeois culture'.[78] Klimentii Korchmarev for RAPM also contended that Skriabin's creativity developed at a time of 'spiritual decline and decay' and that Skriabin 'worked at a time when individualism already existed as a basic mood of the ruling classes'; he had failed to 'acquire' the great ideas of the time, which, according to Korchmarev, claimed that this 'explained his

---

[74] Marina Frolova-Walker and Jonathan Walker, *Music and Soviet Power 1917–1932*, Woodbridge and Rochester, NY, 2012, p. 233. For the original source, see Aleksandr Veprik, 'Tvorchestvo Bartoka i problema fol´klora', *Muzyka i revoliutsiia*, 6, 1929, pp. 22–26.

[75] Anatolii Groman penned a similar argument in *Proletarskii muzykant* following Bartók's visit to Moscow in January 1929. He noted that his earlier works received much more enthusiastic applause than his refined, less folk-oriented later works. See Fairclough, *Classics for the Masses*, p. 64.

[76] Frolova-Walker and Walker, *Music and Soviet Power*, p. 235.

[77] This view is consistent with Pauline Fairclough's analysis. See Fairclough, *Classics for the Masses*, p. 66.

[78] Nikolai Roslavets, 'Sovetskaia muzyka', *Rabis*, 43, 1927, pp. 6–8 (p. 6).

personal weakness of character'.⁷⁹ Yet, for Korchmarev, Skriabin became a 'victim of his class' and was one of the 'many valuable things sacrificed under Capitalism'. Indeed, asserts Korchmarev, Skriabin could have been saved, if he had lived a bit longer to potentially 'grasp the psychology of the winning proletariat [freed] from their sad inheritance of an outgoing era'.⁸⁰ Such narratives illustrate the notion that, despite a composer's class, the transformative potential of a healthier environment could still have a rehabilitating effect. Again, we see that both ASM and RAPM writers were keen to apply the same critical approaches to their understanding of how composers' musical ideologies were socially conditioned.

Conversely, a positive class identity carried alongside it biomedical constructions of health. The RAPM musicologist Sergei Chemodanov claimed in 1923 that Beethoven was an 'immortal genius' due to his class connection to the French revolution and, in particular, the ideology of the Third Estate.⁸¹ He wrote that with Beethoven's 'social conditioning', he represented the 'musical expression of an ideology from a certain culture, in this case the culture of the Third Estate, which was engaged in revolutionary activity in Europe at this time'.⁸² According to Chemodanov, Beethoven's compositional output relayed the ideology of the Third Estate: his third symphony ('Eroica'), dedicated to Napoleon Bonaparte, was seen to manifest 'the struggle of the heroic spirit' and through the sounds of Beethoven's funeral march, Napoleon's 'cold grave breaths' culminated in a 'living idea [with] thousands following in the footsteps of the deceased hero in the name of ideas'.⁸³ From his positive appraisal, Chemodanov swiftly concluded that Beethoven's music increased the 'vital functions of the body', making Beethoven biologically and psychologically 'close and kin to us [*blizkim i rodnym nam*]':

> This is why Beethoven is close to us. He awakes the revolutionary outburst of cheerful sounds, he moves his consciousness, revolutionizing it with

---

⁷⁹ Klimentii Korchmarev, 'Skriabin v nashi dni', *Muzykal'naia nov'*, 6–7, 1924, pp. 15–16 (p. 15).
⁸⁰ Ibid., p. 16.
⁸¹ A reference to Emmanuel-Joseph Sieyès' pamphlet, *Qu'est-ce que le tiers état?* (1789), in which he argued that three Estates exist: the First and Second Estates represented the nobility and the clergy who dominated the Third Estate — the masses. See Emmanuel-Joseph Sieyès, *Qu'est-ce que le tiers état?*, Paris, 1789, p. 120. For the Russian understanding of 'soslovie', see Sheila Fitzpatrick, 'Ascribing Class: The Construction of Social Identity in Soviet Russia', *The Journal of Modern History*, 65, 1993, 4, pp. 745–70.
⁸² Sergei Chemodanov, 'O Betkhoven i sovremennosti', *Muzykal'naia nov'*, 2, 1923, pp. 14–16 (p. 14).
⁸³ Ibid., p. 15.

great social ideas, and increases the vital functions of the body, infusing in his orgiastic joy. And this makes Beethoven, with all his social conditioning of the old culture, truly eternal and immortal, always needed and infinitely close and related to us — the contemporaries and participants of the greatest revolutionary movement.[84]

The term *rodnoi* — 'kin' — here gives the meaning of a familial or blood relationship.[85] Beethoven's positive musical impact, in terms of increasing the 'vital functions of the body' and imparting the emotions of 'orgiastic joy', is expressed as a clear testament to the effect of his music on an individual's biopsychological constitution.

Depictions of composers as having physically and mentally suffered, both as victims of societal forces and of capitalist exploitation, were also an important part of manifesting their heroic and against-all-the-odds struggle for existence.[86] As Pauline Fairclough has shown, in early Soviet music journals these narratives particularly feature around Beethoven and his closest contemporaries.[87] Beethoven, along with Joseph Haydn (1732–1809) and even Richard Wagner (1813–83), was presented as a struggling victim of capitalist economics and forced to compose out of the necessity of sustenance. Again, Sergei Chemodanov wrote:

> Even such great artists as Haydn, Beethoven and Wagner could not protect themselves [...]. Haydn wrote minuets for christenings, weddings and German Burgher balls, Beethoven on his own ironic recognition (in a letter to one of his friends) often was forced to compose *Noten in Nöthen* ['Notes in Need']; 'it is very sad when you have to write for a piece of bread' said Beethoven bitterly. Wagner also composed on request, [artists], whether fully subservient or in a more refined form, worked under the auspices of different kinds of patronage.[88]

---

[84] Ibid., p. 16.

[85] For the definition of *rodnoi*, see Margaret Paxson, *Solovyovo: The Story of Memory in a Russian Village*, Bloomington and Indianapolis, IN, 2005, p. 53; Victoria E. Bonnell, *Iconography of Power: Soviet Political Posters under Lenin and Stalin*, Berkeley, CA, 1997, pp. 164–65.

[86] On the heroism of the New Soviet Person, Lilya Kaganovsky has argued that 'the world of the Stalinist novel and Stalinist film is filled with damaged male bodies. Their sacrifices to the Soviet cause make them worthy of elevation to the status of "hero"'. Lilya Kaganovsky, *How the Soviet Man Was Unmade: Cultural Fantasy and Male Subjectivity under Stalin*, Pittsburgh, PA, 2008, p. 3.

[87] Pauline Fairclough has written extensively on how musical commentators presented certain composers as victims of capitalist exploitation and their struggles against the prevailing ideologies of the time. See Fairclough, *Classics for the Masses*, pp. 12–100.

[88] Sergei Chemodanov, 'Muzykal′no-khudozhestvennye perspektivi v proletarskom

Chemodanov effectively concluded that composers' individuality was stifled by the power of capital, drawn away from their profession to 'chase the slice of bread', whereas a proletarian state would eradicate this economic dependency.[89] Yet suffering was still considered beneficial: Roslavets (ASM) claimed that Schubert's impoverished family background allowed him to 'grasp a little bit of active, honest thought' and was something which allowed him as a composer to 'boldly break the established classical canons before him' and 'move art forward'.[90] In the same way, Drozdov (ORKiMD) argued that Hector Berlioz's (1803–69) whole life was a 'battle with hostile forces' which despite his 'persistence and perseverance' he was not always successful due to 'constant poverty'.[91] Although Berlioz lived 'alone, without friends and without hope […] he never changed his slogan […] his creativity did not reflect any reactionary or mystical decadence, as happened with Liszt and Wagner'.[92] Indeed, a composer's biopsychological resilience to a pathological environment represented a symbolic metaphor of their struggle for existence.

Within this narrative of struggle, Beethoven's deafness featured as a reason behind his heroic portrayal. One narrative affirmed that Beethoven had caused his own deafness in rejection of the bourgeois environment while another contended that he overcame his deafness as a display of courage. For instance, the RAPM music specialist Mikhail Ivanov-Boretskii posited that Beethoven's alienation from a wider audience was a plausible explanation of his deafness. According to Ivanov-Boretskii, after the Napoleonic wars (1803–15), an 'acute break in public sentiment' began which 'crushed political reaction' and made 'Beethoven less and less understood by the public [which] strove for peace and the enjoyment of life'. This alienation from the audience affected Beethoven in the purely 'material sense' of poverty and subsequently 'forced Beethoven to withdraw into himself in majestic isolation; an isolation which finally contributed to his deafness'.[93] On the other hand, the Soviet theatre and music critic Emmanuil Beskin, writing in 1927 for the journal of the art workers' union Rabis, argued that it was entirely conceivable that Beethoven had suicidal thoughts about his deafness, but instead with 'great energy and stamina came into a titanic battle with the physical suffering and overcame them.

gosudarstve', *Muzykal'naia nov'*, 4, 1924, pp. 11–15 (pp. 11–12).
[89] Ibid., p. 12.
[90] Nikolai Roslavets, '100 let so dnia smerti Frantsa Shuberta', *Rabis*, 25, 1928, p. 4.
[91] Andrei Drozdov, 'Gektor Berlioz', *Muzyka i revoliutsiia*, 1, 1929, pp. 20–25 (p. 21).
[92] Ibid., p. 22.
[93] Mikhail Ivanov-Boretskii, 'Betkhoven', *Muzykal'naia nov'*, 10, 1924, pp. 31–33 (p. 32).

[...] in his compositions we see this fighting between "to be" or "not to be", always ending in the victory of "to be", monumentally chanting the joy of life through all difficulties and through all its obstacles'.[94] Beskin's view here coincides with broader Soviet conceptions of deafness, which were torn between understanding deafness as a symptom of unculturedness that flourished under capitalism, and viewing it as an impetus to the Soviet 'overcoming' of personal hardships.[95] In viewing Beethoven as striving to overcome his so-called 'defect', Beskin concluded that it was Beethoven's 'supply of optimism' and his 'heroic' music that made such a sharp contrast with the 'degenerative drug' of Skriabin's music.[96] In this reading, Beethoven's optimism in struggling to overcome his physical afflictions was a trait which could potentially be transfused through his compositions and used as regenerative medication. The trait of struggle (or 'overcoming'), so closely linked to the notion of class, was an important feature in the biopsychological appraisals of composers.

'Beethovenizing' the masses: The transmission of personality
Having scrutinized the biopsychological predispositions of composers and their social environment, music specialists would seek to explain how a composer's personality affected their musical aesthetic, illustrating which moods or traits could be transferred through their music. The transmission and inculcation of positive traits — discipline, courage and sobriety — into the Soviet masses fed into narratives about the development of the New Soviet Person.[97] Thus, with an understanding of the inherited or acquired traits in forming the personality, a narrative pertaining to the connection between an individual's personality and their creativity could be produced. Returning to Hindemith, Beliaev maintained that his 'composer-personality' (*kompozitorskaia lichnost'*), based on an analysis of his inherited and acquired influences, was strikingly distinctive among his fellow modernists, and that his 'easy attitude [*legkost' otnosheniia*] affects his compositions and their appearance'.[98] For Beliaev, Hindemith's personality meant that: 'He does not express his creative ideas as adequately

[94] Emmanuil Beskin, 'Betkhoven k stoletiiu so dnia smerti', *Rabis*, 11, 1927, p. 3.
[95] On the Soviet understanding of deafness, see Claire Shaw, *Deaf in the USSR: Marginality, Community, and Soviet Identity, 1917-1991*, Ithaca, NY, 2017.
[96] Beskin, 'Betkhoven k stoletiiu so dnia smerti', p. 3.
[97] Vadim Volkov, 'The Concept of *Kulturnost'*: Notes on the Stalinist Civilising Process', in Sheila Fitzpatrick (ed.), *Stalinism: New Directions*, London, 2000, pp. 210-30; David L. Hoffman, *Stalinist Values: The Cultural Norms of Soviet Modernity 1917-1941*, Ithaca, NY and London, 2003.
[98] Beliaev, 'Paul' Khindemit', pp. 5-6.

as he could. He leaves too much to decode and to the understanding of the performer [...] other composers would not be able to interpret it.'[99] The improvisational nature of Hindemith's creativity was also perceived as a point of contention, having stated that 'it sometimes causes pretty significant roughness [*nerovnost'*] in his work [...] unintelligible [...] not always interesting, and sometimes even rude and tasteless'.[100] In Beliaev's appraisal, although Hindemith's compositions left visible defects that could be identified, his personality, inherited and shaped by the environment, could be scrutinized to explain why such deformities persisted in his compositional aesthetic. Asaf'ev agreed with Beliaev in that, musically speaking, Hindemith's personality generated themes and rhythms that were perceived as 'convulsive' and employed 'nervous spasms instead of broad development [...] with a touch of eroticism'.[101] Asaf'ev concluded that Hindemith's music was far from being 'accessible to the majority of people and their experiences' and that he was 'very inhospitable and very tasteless'.[102] Both accounts suggest that Hindemith's supposedly corrupted biopsychology meant that his music epitomised nervousness and thus made his music inaccessible to the masses.

The resonance behind employing a discourse of convulsive rhythms was to unite the composer's biopsychological constitution with the pathological capabilities of their music on the human body. In other words, irregular rhythms were seen to symbolize degeneration within the composer and also denote music's pathological influence. Maksim Gor'kii most famously claimed in 1928 that listening to the 'insane cacophony' of the foxtrot led to 'involuntary' (*nevol'no*) imaginations of 'sexual madmen' being conducted by a 'stallion-like man swinging his enormous phallus'; it was foxtrot rhythm, he maintained, that helped to spread homosexuality 'epidemically' and caused 'degeneration'.[103] Lunacharskii also wrote in 1929 about popular music's psychophysiological effect on the organism. Invoking the Pavlovian dog analogy, he argued that the 'fast pace' of the foxtrot made people 'twitch like puppets on strings' and that tango was 'syncopal music' [read: fainting music] which 'mesmerizes, soothes with erotic hushabies, and lowers your entire nervous activity'.[104] The

---

[99] Ibid., p. 7.
[100] Ibid.
[101] Igor' Glebov, 'Khindemit i Kazella', *Sovremennaia muzyka*, 11, 1925, pp. 11–12 (p. 11).
[102] Ibid., p. 12.
[103] Maksim Gor'kii, 'O muzyke tolstykh', *Pravda* (18 April 1928), p. 2.
[104] Anatolii Lunacharskii, 'Sotsial'nie istoki muzykal'nogo iskusstva', *Proletarskii muzykant*, 4, 1929, pp. 12–20 (pp. 18–19).

rhythms of popular music and their harmful psychophysiological effects on the nervous system provided an easy traceable framework back to an individual's biopsychology.

Within the psychophysiological concern of music's affective influence, biopsychological inoculations against musical styles were seen as social prophylaxis.[105] This 'inoculatory logic' was particularly prevalent throughout the 1920s, especially after the Civil War, in which the Soviet authorities described corrupted anti-Soviet elements in the Civil War as 'a dangerous epidemic' and sought to remove those 'harmful elements' through 'a systematic "filtering" of unreliable elements from the population'.[106] On the musical front, Lebedinskii (RAPM) declared that 'the enemy aims to inoculate [read: inject] dandyism, stupidity, petty-bourgeois beneficence and decadence through song' and therefore events based around mass singing were conceived as 'politically important'.[107] Beethoven, on the contrary, was seen to provide inoculation in safeguarding future generations of composers. In a 1927 report entitled, 'At the Committee for the Preparation of the Beethoven Festivities', one music specialist wrote that Beethoven currently had limited 'influence on young composers', but that Beethoven's music was 'close and related to the Proletarian fighters for socialism' and that the aim for the state and music society should be 'to inoculate [*privit'*] the young, adaptive, even susceptible organisms of new music culture with Beethoven'.[108] The fear of unhealthy inoculations was an evident anxiety in nurturing the New Soviet Person. In essence, 'healthy' composers were clearly paramount in music specialists' narratives about the production of healthy musical styles.

In the collective eyes of Soviet musicologists, Beethoven represented a figure of bravery and heroism, personality traits that were considered necessary for transmission within Soviet society.[109] Mikhail Ivanov-Boretskii (for RAPM) wrote in 1924 that Beethoven's connections to the

---

[105] Jacob Emery has illustrated that Tolstoi regularly exploited the inoculation metaphor in art. Jacob Emery, 'Art Is Inoculation: The Infectious Imagination of Leo Tolstoy', *Russian Review*, 70, 2011, 4, pp. 627–45 (pp. 634–39).

[106] Peter Holquist, 'State Violence as Technique: The Logic of Violence in Soviet Totalitarianism', in David L. Hoffmann (ed.), *Stalinism: The Essential Readings*, Oxford, 2003, pp. 129–56 (p. 141). See also, Eric Naiman, *Sex in Public: The Incarnation of Early Soviet Ideology*, Princeton, NJ, 1997, p. 263, and Katerina Clark, *Petersburg: Crucible of Cultural Revolution*, Cambridge, MA, 1995, pp. 204–12.

[107] Lev Lebedinskii, 'O shansonetke, "voennoi muzyke" i aviamarshe', *Za proletarskuiu muzyku*, 3, 1931, pp. 2–12 (p. 12).

[108] Anon, 'V komitete po podgotovke Betkhovenskikh torzhestv', *Muzykal'noe obrazovanie*, 1–2, 1927, pp. 167–69 (p. 168).

[109] On Beethoven's Soviet image, see Nelson, *Music for the Revolution*, pp. 187–90.

French revolution meant that his creativity was 'the manifestation of a psyche of a new person' and therefore 'the psyche of Beethoven's creativity must be considered brave and calling for battle'.[110] For Ivanov-Boretskii, it was Beethoven's 'strength, courage, call to battle and revolutionary spirit' that were the aspects of Beethoven's creativity that provided him with 'vitality'.[111] Mozart also received a favourable appraisal: Asaf´ev maintained that it was the 'universalism' of Mozart's compositional style that made him acceptable to the new environment because it was based in simplicity — it was a simplicity based on the 'full and immediate comprehension of life and the simple emotional truth of expression' and that 'we can now go back to life [...] which is sober, clear, hard-working and ingenious'.[112] These characteristic traits were clear expressions of the Soviet discourse on 'culturedness' (*kul'turnost'*), where the Soviet authorities sought to inculcate new norms and values of 'bodily hygiene, domestic order [...] labour efficiency [and] appreciation of high culture' within Soviet individuals.[113] Both Ivanov-Boretskii and Asaf´ev claimed that Mozart's music instilled positive traits that would be conducive to transforming the Soviet masses towards a sober and hard-working lifestyle.

Having identified personality traits beneficial to the masses, music critics claimed that concert performers played an important role in transferring these characteristic qualities through their performances. Indeed, following the biopsychological framework, Lunacharskii argued in 1926 that 'the victory of the revolution must either awaken musicians or give birth [*porodit'*] to new musicians of Beethoven's type'.[114] For Lunacharskii, performers must learn to play and interpret Beethoven as the masses now demanded 'monumental strength of performance' that would be 'congenial to their own fighting vitality':

> We do not need musicians who would Chopin-ize or Debussy-ize Beethoven himself. We either need crystal clear, honest, tranquil and powerful performers, who would, like in a clear mirror, give us an accomplished performance; or the type of performer who is tendentious, passionate, refracting everything through their own prism for imposing their own stamp, which would Beethoven-ize [*betkhovenizirovat'*] us and Bach, on the one hand, and Debussy on the other, but who also brings them closer to us, signposting everything in them that is courageous and

[110] Mikhail Ivanov-Boretskii, 'Betkhoven', *Muzykal'naia nov'*, 10, 1924, pp. 31–33 (p. 32).
[111] Ibid., p. 33.
[112] Glebov, 'Mozart i sovremennost'', p. 59.
[113] Hoffman, *Stalinist Values*, p. 16.
[114] Anatolii Lunacharskii, 'Velikie sestri', *Muzyka i revoliutsiia*, 1, 1926, pp. 14–19 (p. 18).

living, forcing these aspects to dominate over scholastic and extremely refined styles.[115]

In essence, the role of the performer should either strive to reflect an 'honest' accomplished performance or bring out the courageous and living qualities in compositions to bring dead composers closer to the masses. Roslavets agreed in 1927 regarding the new Soviet performer: modern Soviet artists were now characterized in terms of their performing style as something 'special' and that 'courage, strength, rhythmic and dynamic precision, healthy logical phrasing [and] the clear planning of performing tasks: these are the characteristic features of the performing style of Soviet musicians'.[116] The role of the Soviet performer was therefore based on performing works with courage and strength, in the hope of 'Beethovenizing' the masses.

In terms of Beethoven's closest contemporaries — Berlioz and Schubert — there appears to be some evidence of a hierarchy existing with Beethoven at the top and Berlioz and Schubert as his subsidiaries.[117] For example, Drozdov argued that the 'ideological closeness of Berlioz's creativity to our contemporary consciousness, our social order [*stroi*] and way of life [*byt*], which has determined the content of his compositions, is saturated with elements of heroism and dramatic effect [...] monumental scale [...] huge dynamics'. Yet, for Drozdov, Berlioz was most closely related to Beethoven, who brought out the 'heroic character' in his creativity. He concluded that the absence of Berlioz in mass concert hall programmes was a 'huge void' and the lack of this composer who is 'so close to us ideologically and historically' is a 'disadvantage for us [and for] our musical progress'.[118] Berlioz's ideologically heroic and consistent character had been implanted into his compositions, which was considered necessary for transmission within contemporary society.[119] With regards to Schubert, Asaf'ev wrote

---

[115] Ibid.

[116] Nikolai Roslavets, 'Sovetskaia muzyka', *Rabis*, 43, 1927, pp. 6–8 (p. 8).

[117] Pauline Fairclough has shown that composers like Hector Berlioz, Franz Schubert — and the late Romantics — Franz Liszt, Robert Schumann, Richard Wagner, Gustav Mahler and Richard Strauss were seen as more problematic than Beethoven's predecessors (Bach, Haydn and Mozart) in terms of marketing them to the public. Fairclough, *Classics for the Masses*, pp. 26–38.

[118] Drozdov, 'Gektor Berlioz', p. 25.

[119] Berlioz's 'Funeral and Triumphal' Symphony (1840), commemorating those who died in the 1830 revolution, was performed often throughout the Soviet 1920s along with regular performances of his *Symphonie Fantastique* (1830). See Fairclough, *Classics for the Masses*, pp. 34–35.

in 1927 that his characteristic trait was 'emotional openness (sensitivity and susceptibility of the nervous system) to meet the diversity of life experiences' and that Schubert was not egotistical because 'thanks to his instinct of selection and his ability to concentrate universal emotional states in sounds, he transfers them in intonations to many people. [...] like Mozart, Schubert belonged to everything — the environment, people and nature — rather than himself'.[120] Asaf′ev concluded that despite Schubert's 'historical distance', his music offered a 'lot of good and valuable things about the emotional experience of such a vibrant era'.[121] Schubert's characteristic traits allowed him to send positive and selfless 'emotional states' through musical intonations to the masses.

Not everyone agreed with this interpretation of Schubert: Mikhail Pekelis wrote that he was not like Beethoven because 'active energy, overcoming obstacles and fighting and achieving were absent in Schubert's creativity' and he did not have the 'strictness and severity of some emotions typical of Beethoven's effective fighting'.[122] Although Pekelis admitted that Schubert became 'self-aware' in leaving the feudal nobility, his compositional creativity was 'lacking an element of struggle'.[123] Similarly, Bruk in 1931 depicted Schubert as having fought against the dominant trend of Romanticism, making it possible to feel 'Schubert's psychological wholeness in music, [absence of] terminally-sick refinement and nervousness, which has characterized works by Chopin, Schumann and — taking the later romantics — Liszt and Wagner'.[124] Yet, for Bruk, Schubert's music still contained 'unnatural characteristics [...] and moments of depression and disappointment'.[125] In the battle of transmitting moods and feeling through music, Schubert could not compete with Beethoven in terms of his creative personality. Indeed, part of the reason for Soviet critics' preference for Beethoven rather than Schubert could also be associated with an early form of Stalinist monumentalism. Masterworks like Beethoven's Ninth Symphony were considered vital throughout the Soviet 1920s, and when pitted against smaller-scale pieces, like Schubert's songs, Schubert's music could

---

[120] Igor′ Glebov, 'Shubert i sovremennost′', *Sovremennaia muzyka*, 26, 1927, pp. 76–78 (p. 77). For an extensive discussion on the term 'intonation' in Russian/Soviet musicological thought, see Gordon D. McQuere, 'Boris Asafiev and *Musical Form as a Process*', in Gordon D. McQuere (ed.), *Russian Theoretical Thought in Music*, Rochester, NY, 2009, pp. 217–52.
[121] Ibid., p. 78.
[122] Mikhail Pekelis, 'Frants Shubert', *Muzyka i revoliutsiia*, 10, 1928, pp. 7–15 (p. 11).
[123] Ibid., p. 15.
[124] Bruk, 'Shubert i ego pesni', pp. 7–8.
[125] Ibid., p. 12.

never achieve the status given to Beethoven.[126] In essence, the tendency towards Soviet monumentalism, shown in epic films, novels and large-scale architecture, was also celebrated and reflected through *musical* monuments of the past.

Yet even when Soviet music specialists disagreed on particular composers, they were still bound by the same discursive framework of diagnosing healthy or dangerous tendencies and their impact upon the masses. In a uniquely positive analysis of Schoenberg in 1923, Roslavets argued that Schoenberg's psychological predisposition illuminated a 'natural revolutionary, healthy and vigorous, a disciplined man of intellect and iron will, with a psyche and constitution of thoughts the polar opposite of Impressionism' and concluded that Schoenberg, having dominated over Albert Giraud's refined impressionist poetry in *Pierrot Lunaire* (1912), was 'strong' because everything he created would be 'close and understood by us [...] it is the living embodiment of our thoughts, feelings and aspirations'.[127] Although RAPM musicologists tended to reject claims that Schoenberg and atonality were progressive and comprehensible, they still exploited a biomedical discourse to illustrate music's effect on the individual biopsychology. The RAPM writer Grigorii Liubomirskii argued that atonal music was 'unsuitable' for the untrained working masses and, by using it as a pedagogical approach, it would be impossible to 'nurture a healthy generation of musicians'.[128] In a similar article on atonal music, another RAPM musicologist (initials A. A.) claimed that anything which lies outside the logic of repeating a melodic line and diatonic harmony is 'a typical bourgeois perversion of art, resulting in degeneration and gluttonous brain obesity'.[129] In their respective evaluations, both Schoenberg and his twelve-tone compositional language were perceived as being representative of 'bourgeois perversion' and could therefore negatively impact the individual. Nevertheless, in all accounts, there existed a clear consensus about music's ability to affect the masses, either positively or negatively. Biopsychological appraisals merely helped provide an adequate explanation for the persistence of either healthy or pathological music in Soviet society.

---

[126] For an extensive study on music and monumentalism in nineteenth-century Germany, see Alexander Rehding, *Music and Monumentalism: Commemoration and Wonderment in Nineteenth-Century Germany*, New York and Oxford, 2009.

[127] Nikolai Roslavets, '"Lunnyi P'ero" A. Shenberga', *K novym beregam*, 3, 1923, pp. 28–33 (p. 32).

[128] Grigorii Liubomirskii, 'Atonal'naia muzyka', *Muzykal'naia nov'*, 6–7, 1924, p. 12 (p. 12).

[129] A. A., 'Atonal'naia muzyka', *Muzykal'naia nov'*, 9, 1924, pp. 12–13 (p. 12).

Conclusion

In their musicological accounts of composers, Soviet music specialists of the 1920s sought to diagnose which composers' compositional output had either a healthy or harmful effect on the masses. Both before and after 1917, the understanding of music and its psychophysiological impact on the body was both a cause for concern and celebration amongst musicologists. On the one hand, music could provide therapeutic effects in individuals, inculcating various positive moods or preparing the human biopsychology for heroic deeds. On the other hand, music as a pathological source of degeneration — narratives that were primarily associated with the rhythms of popular music and jazz — was perceived to cause neurasthenia, the weakening of an individual's nervous system. Yet to apprehend how and why such music came into existence, a composer's creative personality — their biopsychological constitution — had to be inspected for the definitive answers. In drawing up such appraisals, music specialists turned to the language and frameworks of the biomedical sciences to provide an empirical explanation for the threats posed by certain composers. Exploiting positivistic techniques established in the pre-revolutionary narratives of medicine and criminology, musicologists believed that a composer's personality provided an explanation behind the persistence of deviance shown in their musical aesthetic and, vice versa, the musical score provided the visible stigmata of that personality.

By being able to analyse a composer's convictions or personality traits (or even ascribe traits to composers), it became possible to predict the quality of their music's impact upon the listening masses. This process became particularly pertinent to the cultural elite's civilizing mission of the New Soviet Person; in a bid to transform the individual and society, music had to be applied with precision. For example, with regards to the appraisals of Austro-German symphonic composers, Beethoven was often set up as the model for emulation: he was biopsychologically stable, able to adapt to the new revolutionary environment and suppress his individuality for the sake of the collective; he was brave, heroic, and a class-conscious member of the Third Estate. By contrast, less socially engaged composers like Debussy were, on the whole, deemed socially unfit: biopsychologically static, atavistic, depressed and tired, and a class representative of the bourgeoisie. Indeed, while the reason behind such rhetoric was primarily ideological (i.e. the classics were far less problematic than the 'contaminated' Western contemporary composers and their music), at times, it was a power play between opposing musical factions to secure their favourite composers (such as in the case of Roslavets vs. RAPM on Schoenberg). Nevertheless, through incorporating discourses from the biomedical sciences into musicological appraisals, music specialists from all factions were able to adequately construct and express accounts, both positively and negatively, of a composer's personality, compositional output and, most importantly, their transferable traits to the masses. It was through this dedicated process that Soviet music specialists were able to determine composers' fitness levels and voice opinion on whether to include them into early Soviet music culture.

3

How Soviet Musicology became Marxist

OLGA PANTELEEVA

Music held a special place in the culture of the Russian Silver Age. A world-view that Rebecca Mitchell called 'musical metaphysics', which saw music's transcendent meaning as central to the intellectual and spiritual development of Russian society, permeated artistic and philosophical circles in the *fin de siècle*.[1] The idea that music was able to reach beyond the mundane and tap into truer and higher planes of existence remained as relevant for Symbolism as it had been for Romanticism. As the art least bound by representation of earthly reality and least accessible to the rational mind, music offered a direct path *a realibus ad realiora* — from reality toward a higher reality — and the possibility of attaining this higher reality through creative activity.[2]

Barely a decade after the October Revolution, a solidly materialistic approach supplanted this discourse, awash in idealist and religious philosophies. The newly institutionalized Russian musicology boasted a fully-fledged research paradigm that approached music like any other phenomenon of the social and natural world which could and ought to be comprehended rationally. By the end of the Cultural Revolution (1928–32), this academic paradigm had become decidedly Marxist.[3]

Sections of this article were presented at the annual meeting of the American Musicological Society, Louisville, 2015, and the annual conference of the Royal Musical Association, Birmingham, 2015, where it received helpful feedback from panel members and the audience. I owe special thanks to Pauline Fairclough, Vadim Keylin and Anicia Timberlake, for reading and commenting on several drafts of this article, and the anonymous SEER reviewers for their constructive criticisms.

[1] Rebecca Mitchell, *Nietzsche's Orphans: Music, Metaphysics, and the Twilight of the Russian Empire*, New Haven, CT, 2015.
[2] 'A realibus ad realiora' is an expression coined by the poet Viacheslav Ivanov to capture the thrust central to Symbolism.
[3] In this article I am using the term Marxism to denote early Soviet interpretations of Marxism, which later came to be known as Marxism-Leninism. Archival documents from the 1920s, however, are consistent in using the term Marxism, not Marxism-Leninism.

In what follows I ask two questions: Why did musicologists enthusiastically embrace Marxism as a valid research framework in the years of NEP, even before they were pressured to do so by Narkompros? And why was this flourishing musicological paradigm then truncated in the late 1920s, despite its advocates having willingly adopted a Marxist outlook? To answer these questions, I trace intellectual continuities across the year 1917, further challenging perceptions of that year as a purported 'zero hour' of Soviet culture. Many early Soviet musicological precepts were actually realizations of ideas that scholars had internalized during their pre-revolutionary training. To demonstrate this, I first analyse the intellectual genealogies that bridged the revolutionary divide, and then examine the rise and fall of the first Soviet research institutes, in which musicology was practised as an officially recognized academic discipline. I organize my analysis around three related claims.

First, I argue that the channels through which ideas travelled from the pre-revolutionary to the early Soviet periods were more heterogeneous than has previously been discussed in the literature. Rather than focusing on well-known names, I analyse the diffuse press discourse where these precepts were often articulated more clearly than in the writings of professional musicians and critics. Tracing different transmission paths, I challenge the remnants of the reductive Cold War version of the history of Russian music criticism that still influences our modern understanding of Soviet Marxist thought.

Second, I foreground a trend in Russian music discourse at the turn of the century that, compared to musical metaphysics, has received less attention in the critical literature.[4] Rooted in the positivist philosophy that gripped the humanities in the mid-nineteenth century, this trend could be called 'science envy': the idea that the study of music should aspire to be as rigorous as the natural sciences, and should strive to discover objective laws governing music's structure and historical development. Showing that scientistic discourse on music abounded both before and after 1917, I argue that what made Marxist frameworks appealing to Soviet musicologists was the convergence between the positivist imperative to find laws of music and Soviet Marxist determinism.

Third, I demonstrate how the meaning of studying music 'scientifically' shifted during the late 1920s toward a greater emphasis on Marxism and

---

[4] For a recent example that does engage with this trend, see James Higenbottam-Taylor, 'The Cultural Doctors: Music, Health and Identity in Revolutionary Russia', unpublished PhD dissertation, University of Bristol, 2017.

sociology, dispensing with a natural-scientific focus. This move coincided with the policies of the Cultural Revolution which were designed to promote greater social mobility, and which resulted in an overhaul of staff and administration at the institutes. Together, these two developments were responsible for the demise of the early Soviet musicological paradigm.

This narrative runs alongside, not contrary to, the accounts of pre-revolutionary Russian culture as steeped in musical metaphysics. In doing so, it acknowledges the 'double consciousness' of the epoch.[5] There was no clear boundary between these sets of convictions. In actuality, these ideas coexisted, sometimes in the minds of the same individuals, and were indeed to a great extent two sides of the same coin: both were concerned with the search for universals, be they rationally discoverable scientific laws or intuitively communicated divine revelations. However, some writers clearly identified with one of these two positions and issued militant statements against each other in the name of scientific progress or in passionate defence of music's ineffability.

By the end of the 1920s the scales tipped decidedly towards the former. The rapid process of Sovietization wrestled an art considered by many to be quintessentially transcendent into a materialist framework. Without understanding the positivist side of *fin-de-siècle* writing on music we miss an important line of continuity between late imperial and early Soviet Russia represented within music-scientific discourse. This line of continuity lies at the heart of the creative, international and interdisciplinary musicological paradigm of the 1920s that remains unprecedented — a great 'what could have been' of Russian musicology. Most importantly, the story of how Russian musicology became Marxist opens a window on more than strictly disciplinary affairs. It shows the institutional and interpersonal processes through which humanities knowledge was produced in the increasingly repressive Soviet state.

The Cold War invention of 'Russian thought on music'
The expression 'thought on music' (*mysl' o muzyke*) was used by Soviet musicologists as an umbrella term for any verbal discourse on music, be it critical, philosophic or academic. Today, the term is still used, but scholars are mindful of its origins. For instance, in her monograph on the Soviet appropriation of the art music canon, Marina Raku puts the term in scare quotes to convey an unspoken awareness that 'thought on music' entails

---

[5] Michael Saler, 'Introduction', in id. (ed.), *The Fin-de-Siècle World*, New York, 2015, pp. 1–8 (p. 3).

not just the intellectual history of writing on music but rather its Soviet representation.[6] This master narrative was artificially constructed during the Cold War and has been challenged since,[7] but still survives both in Russia and in the West.

The term *mysl' o muzyke* was popularized in Iulii Kremlev's massive monograph of the same name, *Russian Thought on Music*, the three volumes of which — tackling historical periods from 1825–60, 1861–80 and 1881–94 — were published in 1954 and 1960.[8] Individual chapters of this work were dedicated to those writers who, according to Kremlev, espoused progressive views. All of them could easily be listed here: Vladimir Odoevskii, Nikolai Mel'gunov, Aleksandr Serov, Vladimir Stasov, Tsezar' Kiui, the rest of the *moguchaia kuchka*,[9] German Larosh, Petr Chaikovskii, Anton Rubinshtein and Sergei Taneev. The introductory and concluding chapters did consider many 'lesser' critics and paid a compulsory tribute to Dobroliubov, Chernyshevskii and Belinskii. But even these chapters frequently featured key figures such as Serov and Stasov. In 1980, an eponymous sequel to Kremlev's study that accounted for the period from 1985 to 1917 adopted the same cast of characters. The author, musicologist Aleksandr Stupel', added sections on several more writers, ending with Nikolai Miaskovskii, Boris Asaf'ev and Anatolii Lunacharskii.[10] And so, the evolutionary progression of Russian thought on music from Odoevskii to Asaf'ev was complete. This oversimplified, lopsided genealogy elevated some writers above measure, allowing their voices to resound over the intellectual landscape while silencing the majority of other voices of the vibrant *fin-de-siècle* discourse on music.

---

[6] Marina Raku, *Muzykal'naia klassika v mifotvorchestve sovetskoi epokhi*, Moscow, 2014, pp. 135 and 188.

[7] See, for instance, Olga Manulkina, '"Foreign" versus "Russian" in Soviet and Post-Soviet Musicology and Music Education', in Marina Frolova-Walker and Patrick Zuk (eds), *Russian Music since 1917: Reappraisal and Rediscovery*, Oxford, 2017; Marina Raku, 'Sotsial'noe konstruirovanie "sovetskogo muzykovedeniia": rozhdenie metoda', *Novoe literaturnoe obozrenie*, 137, 2016, 1, pp. 39–57; Elina Viljanen, 'The Problem of the Modern and Tradition: Early Soviet Musical Culture and the Musicological Theory of Boris Asafiev (1884–1949)', unpublished PhD dissertation, University of Helsinki, 2017; Marina Frolova-Walker and Jonathan Walker, *Music and Soviet Power: 1917–1932*, Woodbridge and Rochester, NY, 2012.

[8] Iulii Kremlev, *Russkaia mysl' o muzyke; ocherki istorii russkoi muzykal'noi kritiki i estetiki v XIX veke*, Leningrad, 1954.

[9] Composers Modest Musorgskii, Nikolai Rimskii-Korsakov, Milii Balakirev and Aleksandr Borodin.

[10] Aleksandr Stupel', *Russkaia mysl' o muzyke, 1895–1917: ocherk istorii russkoi muzykal'noi kritiki*, Leningrad, 1980.

Kremlev wrote this study in the immediate aftermath of the so-called 'musicologists' affair' of 1949. Like composers during the anti-formalist campaign of 1948, musicologists were chastised for paying excessive attention to 'formalist' Western music while neglecting Socialist Realist aesthetics. A month before the publication of the infamous resolution, 'On Muradeli's Opera "The Great Friendship"', Andrei Zhdanov gave a speech at the Conference of Workers of Soviet Music that became a precursor to the infamous *Pravda* article.[11] In that speech he quoted at length from Stasov and Serov, citing them as models of ideologically correct writing on music.[12] The campaign against musicologists referenced Zhdanov's speech both directly and implicitly. Scholars were reprimanded for neglecting the legacy of foundational Russian thinkers on music such as Odoevskii, Serov, Stasov, Chaikovskii, Rimskii-Korsakov and Asaf'ev, as well as for relying on the works of German musicologists.[13] A flurry of studies on these music critics appeared in the following years.[14] Lining up neatly into a carefully constructed indigenous genealogy, these writers became the main cast of Kremlev's story.

As Ol´ga Manulkina has demonstrated, the effects of the 'musicologists' affair' were immediately disastrous for Soviet music scholarship and could be felt for decades after that, indeed, until the present day. These consequences included a shrinking range of topics that were safe to study, plummeting numbers of specialists in Western music, severed ties with the international academic community and a general decline in the prestige of historical musicology as opposed to the ostensibly more 'autonomous' field of music theory.[15] Kremlev's origin story of Soviet musicology, too, proved to be so deeply seated that it made it without major revisions into the ten-volume *History of Russian Music* (1983–2004) — a textbook that is currently widely used in music history courses in Russian conservatories.[16]

---

[11] The resolution was published in *Pravda* on 10 February 1948; Zhdanov gave his speech in mid-January 1948.

[12] *Soveshchanie deiatelei sovetskoi muzyki v TsK VKP(b)*, Moscow, 1948, pp. 137–39 and 142–44.

[13] Tikhon Khrennikov, 'Protiv kosmopolitizma i formalizma v muzykal´noi kritike i muzykovedenii', *Sovetskoe iskusstvo*, 19 February 1949, p. 2; Anonymous, 'Reshitel´no ochistit´ sovetskoe muzykovedenie ot burzhuaznykh kosmopolitov', *Sovetskoe iskusstvo*, 26 February 1949, p. 1.

[14] See the series, 'Russkaia klassicheskaia muzykal´naia kritika', published by Muzgiz.

[15] Manulkina, '"Foreign" versus "Russian"'.

[16] Iurii Keldysh, Ol´ga Levasheva and Aleksei Kandinskii, *Istoriia russkoi muzyki*, 10 vols, Moscow, 1983–2004. The section on the early Soviet musicology in volume 10B, written by Levon Hakobian and Roman Berchenko is exceptional because it provides a thorough and thoughtful overview of writing on music at the turn of the twentieth century. However,

It remains a basic template in histories of Russian music produced in Europe and North America as well.[17]

This neat progression suppressed the many Western authors who had had formidable influence on Russian musicologists, and along with them anyone else who could not be plausibly portrayed as a progenitor of Socialist Realism. These silenced voices were as diverse and resistant of categorization as Borges's famous list of animals — they were symbolist, metaphysical, positivist, religious; they were translated from European languages, belonged to those who emigrated, advocated scientific inquiry, et cetera. In this article I follow the development of one of these previously neglected intellectual trends that was of particular importance to the Soviet musicology of the 1920s, starting in the last decade of the nineteenth century.

Scientific rhetoric as gatekeeping

Basking in the reflected glory of the sciences, the humanities in both Russia and in the West in the nineteenth century aspired to study art and society with natural-scientific methods. Musicology was no exception. Whenever musicologists gained a foothold in larger academic circles, be it a newly created professorial position or a department, it was because their work was recognized as academically respectable, i.e. methodologically rigorous and objective.

Relying on Johann Friedrich Herbart's theory of aesthetics, scholars at the University of Vienna favoured empirical approaches which, when applied to a work of art, could uncover its objective characteristics. When the famous music critic Eduard Hanslick applied for a lectureship in music history and aesthetics in 1856, he shrewdly aligned himself with this pervasive 'Herbartization' of the Austrian humanities. Hanslick's treatise, *On the Musically Beautiful* (*Vom Musikalisch-Schönen*, 1854), claimed that

the genealogies it constructs ultimately prove not very helpful for understanding of the institutionalized musicology of the 1920s. The authors focus on those branches of music scholarship that comprise musicological faculties at present-day Russian conservatories, while the research institutes of the 1920s were explicitly modelled in opposition to the conservatories and their utilitarian understanding of music history and theory.

[17] For instance, Frances Maes's *A History of Russian Music* duly mentions the usual suspects (see chs 3 and 4). Even Richard Taruskin, whose *Stravinsky and the Russian Traditions* does more than justice to heterogeneous intellectual genealogies of Russian musicians, does not venture far from the canonical cast of characters when describing Russian nineteenth-century debates on music in his *Oxford History of Western Music*. Francis Maes, *A History of Russian Music: From Kamarinskaya to Babi Yar*, Berkeley, CA, 2002; Richard Taruskin, *The Oxford History of Western Music. Vol. 3: The Nineteenth Century*, New York, NY, 2005.

musical beauty resided in purely musical form, in the harmonious interplay of musical sounds, rather than in evocation of images, ideas or feelings.[18] The second edition of his book, prepared when Hanslick was working towards tenure, put an even greater emphasis on the idea that the study of music should take after the natural sciences. After Hanslick received tenure, however, he abandoned the Herbartian views that initially spurred his academic career and moved towards a more historicist approach.[19]

Guido Adler, Hanslick's immediate successor at the University of Vienna in 1898 — and already known for his foundational essay, 'The Scope, Method, and Aim of Musicology' ('Umfang, Methode und Ziel der Musikwissenschaft') — went on to found the Musikwissenschaftliches Institut — an achievement that crowned the decades-long quest for institutionalization of musicology in Austria. His vision of musicology as a science was based on the evolutionary theories of Ernst Haeckel.[20] Hugo Riemann, who exerted immense influence on musicology in general and Russian musicology in particular, founded his theory of harmonic dualism on acoustic grounds, i.e. on an explicitly natural scientific basis.

The rhetoric that accompanied the establishment of the first Russian musicological departments shows that Russian scholars and institutions were not so different from Austrian and German ones. The 'scientific basis' of social reform was a rhetorical staple for the new Soviet government. Although 'positivism' became a pejorative term in Soviet parlance, mainly because it was used as such in Lenin's *Materialism and Empiriocriticism* (*Materializm i empiriocrititsizm*, 1909),[21] its derivative construct 'positive knowledge', meaning 'rigorous' or 'empirical' knowledge, was still in use. For instance, a Narkompros decree on artistic education from 1925 read: 'All academic research must be done in the environment of scientific-positive knowledge and must be based on Marxism.'[22] In the autumn of 1921, three new institutions for humanities research were established: the

[18] Eduard Hanslick, *On the Musically Beautiful: A Contribution Towards the Revision of the Aesthetics of Music*, trans. Geoffrey Payzant, Indianapolis, IN, 1986.

[19] Kevin Karnes, *Music, Criticism, and the Challenge of History: Shaping Modern Musical Thought in Late Nineteenth-Century Vienna*, Oxford and New York, 2008, pp. 29–37.

[20] For a detailed analysis of Haeckel's influence on Adler see Benjamin Breuer, 'The Birth of Musicology from the Spirit of Evolution: Ernst Haeckel's Entwicklungslehre as Central Component of Guido Adler's Methodology for Musicology', unpublished PhD dissertation, University of Pittsburgh, 2011.

[21] Vladimir Lenin, *Materializm i empiriocrititsizm: Kriticheskie zametki ob odnoi reaktsionnoi filosofii*, Moscow, 1909.

[22] Tsentral'nyi gosudarstvennyi arkhiv literatury i iskusstva Sankt Peterburga (hereafter, TsGALI), f. 82, op. 3, d. 7, l. 29.

Russian Institute of Art History in Petrograd (Rossiiskii institut istorii iskusstv, RIII) was reorganized from a pre-revolutionary institution of higher education into a research centre in September,[23] the State Academy of Artistic Sciences (Gosudarstvennaia akademiia khudozhestvennykh nauk, GAKhN) was founded in Moscow in October[24] and the State Institute of Music Science (Gosudarstvennyi institut muzykal′noi nauki, GIMN) opened its doors in Moscow in November.[25] All three existed for a decade until they were either shut down or merged with other research institutions around 1930.

When the Institute of Art History was on the verge of reorganization into a research institute, the musicologist Boris Asaf′ev made ample use of positivist rhetoric, explaining why it was necessary to have a musicological research department.[26] Not unlike Adler's 'Scope, Method, and Aim of Musicology', his 'Explanatory memorandum' legitimized the need for music scholarship and spelled out the principles on which the new discipline of musicology was to be founded.[27] First and foremost, Asaf′ev argued, the new Soviet musicology had to differ from the approach to the history and theory of music that was offered at the Conservatory. For decades, music history and theory had indeed been valued at the conservatories only insofar as they helped create a well-rounded composer or performer. Confined to this subservient position, music scholarship along the conservatory model had not been helpful in fostering musicology's self-awareness as an academic discipline.[28] Asaf′ev thought that, on the contrary, music studies should be an independent and rigorous branch of scholarship, and musicologists rightful members of the scientific community.[29]

Likewise, when the Scientific-Artistic Commission of Narkompros was about to be reorganized into the State Academy of Artistic Sciences,

---

[23] TsGALI, f. 82, op. 1, d. 103, l. 18.

[24] Iuliia Iakimenko, 'Iz istorii "chistok apparata": Akademiia khudozhestvennykh nauk v 1929–1932, *The New Historical Bulletin*, 12, 2005 <http://www.nivestnik.ru/2005_1/11.shtml> [accessed 30 January 2017] (para. 4 of 36).

[25] Mikhail Ivanov-Boretskii, *Piat′ let nauchnoi raboty Gosudarstvennogo Instituta muzykal′noi nauki [GIMN′a]*, Moscow, 1926, p. 4.

[26] Some would call Boris Asaf′ev one of the 'founding fathers' of Russian musicology, not least because of his efforts in the early institutionalization of the discipline.

[27] Guido Adler and Erica Mugglestone, 'Guido Adler's "The Scope, Method, and Aim of Musicology" (1885): An English Translation with an Historico-Analytical Commentary', *Yearbook for Traditional Music*, 13, 1981, pp. 1–21.

[28] For details, see Olga Panteleeva, 'St Petersburg Conservatory and the Beginnings of Russian Musicology', in Marina Frolova-Walker (ed.), *Rimskii-Korsakov and His World*, Princeton, NJ, 2018, pp. 223–47.

[29] TsGALI, f. 82, op. 3, d. 1, l. 12v.

its Council invited the physicist Nikolai Uspenskii to talk about the uses of science in the study of art. Uspenskii portrayed art and science not as opposites but rather as two different forms of knowledge, brought closer together by the momentous revolutionary shift. He used this similarity to argue that it was necessary to study art by methods borrowed from physics, acoustics, optics, mathematics, mechanics and experimental psychology.[30] As in Europe, in Russia the institutional position of the humanities clearly depended on the ability of scholars to locate their discipline firmly within 'scientific-positive knowledge'. In the following sections I discuss the reasons why science accrued such prestige in nineteenth-century Russia and show how this prestige affected writing on music.

Scientific progress as social progress
Political reforms and scientific revolution in 1860s Russia went hand in hand, as Alexander II's decrees undid some of the strict limitations imposed on the educational system by his predecessor Nicholas I. That political progress was spurred by its scientific counterpart was an idea which gained a foothold in Russian society during that decade, when the growing movement against an autocratic system of government was inspired by scientific progress. During that 'golden age' of Russian science, Nihilist and Populist philosophers promoted an appreciation of science among the broader reading public and beyond the academic community. Nihilists such as Dobroliubov, Chernyshevskii and Pisarev were convinced that science was the best remedy for the social ills that plagued the country. The famous physiologist Ivan Pavlov reminisced that 'under the influence of the great minds of the 1860s, particularly that of Pisarev, our intellectual interests were directed toward natural science, and many of us decided to study the natural sciences at universities'.[31] The scientific mind-set flourished in literature as well. Bazarov in Turgenev's *Fathers and Sons* (*Ottsy i deti*, 1862) was a medical student, and rumour had it that Kirsanov in Chernyshevskii's *What Is to Be Done?* (*Chto delat'*, 1863) was modelled after the physiologist Sechenov.[32] In the 1880s a new generation stepped to the fore that had been brought up in the climate dominated by such adepts of science as Pisarev. As a result of their efforts, the scientific mindset had spread into much broader circles of the educated class. People who were not natural scientists by vocation carried these convictions to their areas

[30] Rossiiskii gosudarstvennyi arkhiv literatury i iskusstva (hereafter, RGALI), f. 94, op. 1, d. 4, ll. 7–8v.
[31] Alexander Vucinich, *Science in Russian Culture*, 2 vols, Stanford, CA, 1963–70, 2, p. 19.
[32] Ibid., p. 126.

of intellectual activity. Ultimately, it was this generational identification with scientific philosophy that brought about the positivist turn in the Russian humanities. In the study of music this turn coincided with the 1886 establishing of the first chair in music history and aesthetics at the St Petersburg Conservatory, held by Liverii Sakketti (Liberio Sacchetti).

The Russian reception of positivism
Another way in which science acquired its elevated status was through Russian echoes of positivism — a philosophical current whose main goal was to endow science with ultimate prestige. As much as positivism changed since its formulation in the mid-nineteenth century, the different versions had one belief in common: that science was capable of uncovering laws that underlie the universe and therefore could be applied to both the natural world and human society. As Michael Singer has pointed out, this expectation was the primary basis for the prestige of natural sciences, and has survived well into the present day.[33] Most famously formulated in August Comte's *Cours de philosophie positive* (1830–42) and developed in the mid-nineteenth century by his followers John Stuart Mill and Émile Littré, positivist precepts and their various mutations came to permeate late nineteenth-century European thought predominantly without reference to either their early roots or even to the term itself. They are known today as nineteenth-century positivism.

Positivism first made an appearance in Russian culture as early as the 1840s, only a few years after Comte's treatise was finished. Private correspondence and diaries by Belinskii and Chernyshevskii show that both were familiar with Comte's philosophy already in the late 1840s.[34] However, positivist ideas achieved prominence in Russia only at the end of the 1860s, when the Russian sciences began to flourish. The most detailed explications of Comte's philosophy appeared in writings of Vladimir Lesevich, published by the influential monthly, *Otechestvennye zapiski*.[35] However, the writer who advocated most ardently for positivism in the public domain was Pisarev. In his gargantuan article, 'Historical Ideas of Auguste Comte' ('Istoricheskie idei Ogiusta Konta', 1865–66), published over four issues of the journal *Russkoe slovo*, he praised Comte's goal to 'create positive politics, to discover in the life of human societies immutable

---

[33] Michael Singer, *The Legacy of Positivism*, Basingstoke, New York, 2005, p. 90.
[34] Thomas Nemeth, 'Comtean positivism in Russia', in *The Early Solov'ev and His Quest for Metaphysics*, New York, 2013, pp. 229–38.
[35] Vladimir Lesevich, 'Filosofiia istorii na nauchnoi pochve', *Otechestvennye zapiski*, 182, 1869, 1, pp. 163–96; Vladimir Lesevich, 'Pozitivizm posle Konta', *Otechestvennye zapiski*, 183, 1869, 4, pp. 361–98.

natural laws, and to develop scientifically the kind of social order that would reconcile all reasonable demands in a higher unity'.[36] By society's natural laws Pisarev meant Comte's law of three stages: the idea that both human societies and scientific disciplines pass three stages of development — theological, metaphysical and positive. Sociological positivism in particular found fertile ground in the Russian intellectual climate through the work of the famous sociologist Maksim Kovalevskii.[37] One of the most trenchant dissenting voices belonged to the religious philosopher Vladimir Solov'ev, whose attacks on positivism were proof of a presence in Russian thought that was impossible to ignore.[38]

Positivist precepts were disseminated not only via publications that explicitly referred to Comte but through more elusive channels as well. Many writers adopted aspects of positivist thinking while refusing to acknowledge it as such. For instance, its repercussions can be found in the writings of such authors as Herbert Spencer and Hippolyte Taine, whose influence on Russian thought was profound. The label 'positivism' changed drastically over the years, and its subsequent meanings had little to do with Comte's views. The concept became notoriously ambiguous. Therefore, rather than referring to a specific school of philosophy, I use the term 'positivism' in a broad sense, as an umbrella concept for several core ideas that underlay much of the thinking on music in the period from the 1880s to the 1920s.

Discourse on music in the popular press
The most important of these core ideas was that music scholarship should concern itself with the search for universal laws that govern both the historical development of music (and of art and society in general) and music's inner workings. This general idea often gave rise to the following sub-ideas: first, that theoretically determined laws should have predictive and prescriptive power over the practice of music; and second, that this search should be carried out with the help of the methods and rigour of the natural sciences, to whose status the humanities should aspire. Those who advocated a scientific study of music rejected the established Romantic notion of music as an ineffable form of art. For them, music could and should be understood rationally.

---

[36] Dmitrii Pisarev, 'Istoricheskie idei Ogiusta Konta', in *Istoricheskie eskizy: Izbrannye stat'i*, Moscow, 1989, pp. 340–504 (pp. 340–41).
[37] Andrzej Walicki, *A History of Russian Thought from the Enlightenment to Marxism*, Stanford, CA, 1979, p. 362.
[38] Nemeth, 'Comtean positivism in Russia', p. 236.

From the late seventeenth century onwards the Russian *nauka* has had a broad meaning which was comparable to that of the German *Wissenschaft*, insofar as both words encompassed notions of science and scholarship. For late nineteenth-century and early twentieth-century Russian sources, 'science' is a more exact equivalent of *nauka* even when the sources deal with music or art studies. After all, this was what most of the authors meant by studying music in accordance with the positivist spirit: studying it scientifically, by discovering its laws and applying methods from the natural sciences.

To see how these ideas fuelled writing on music, let us take a look at how three different writers engaged with Eduard Hanslick's *On the Musically Beautiful* during the last decade of the nineteenth century. By 1885, when a full translation was published by Mikhail Ivanov in 1885,[39] Hanslick's name already was being referred to not only in specialized discussions of music aesthetics but also in fields as removed from music as law. The translation elicited a flurry of responses. For the most part, they were dripping with vitriol because by the turn of the century the value Hanslick placed on the autonomy of music was already seen as utterly unscientific. Hanslick's famous metaphor comparing music to a moving arabesque as the most precise expression of a musical form that was beautiful in and of itself seemed to draw the greatest ire from Russian critics of all stripes. In the following section I will consider how three critics attacked the idea of music's autonomy not on nationalist grounds, but because it contradicted what they saw as the scientific approach to the study of music. Coming from various social and intellectual backgrounds, all three argued that a truly scientific study of art would understand it as an integral part of the material and social world.

i. The marriage of science and revolution
Appeals for a holistic study of art echoed through Sergei Kazanskii's article, 'One of the Reactionary Doctrines in the Field of Aesthetics (On Hanslick)' ('Odna iz reaktsionnykh doktrin v oblasti estetiki [O Ganslike]', 1890), published in the short-lived, but seminal journal, *Artist*.[40] Kazanskii had a colourful biography. In addition to being a music critic, he belonged to the Moscow branch of the terrorist organization *Narodnaia volia* (*The People's Will*, or *The People's Freedom*) — responsible for assassinating Alexander II

---

[39] Eduard Ganslik, *O prekrasnom v muzyke: dopolnenie k issledovaniiu estetiki muzykal'nogo iskusstva*, trans. Mikhail Ivanov, Moscow, 1885.
[40] Sergei Kazanskii, 'Odna iz reaktsionnykh doktrin v oblasti estetiki (O Ganslike)', *Artist*, 6, 1890, pp. 39–44, and 7, 1890, pp. 19–31.

in 1881.[41] He was exiled to Western Siberia for helping publish the group's newspaper in illegal print shops, just before Lenin went into his Siberian exile in 1897–1900. The article in question seems to have been written in exile.[42] Evoking the Comtean definition of 'positive' — that which is real rather than chimerical, useful rather than futile[43] — Kazanskii pointed out that Hanslick still dwelt in the metaphysical age, thinking it was 'possible to know the absolute, to comprehend the true essence of things'.[44] What was possible to know was not the essence but the relationship between things. Kazanskii believed, as many did at the turn of the twentieth century, that the universe was bound together by invisible forces that connected all phenomena. 'So, in our scientist's opinion', Kazanskii wrote, 'there are things that can be comprehended in and of themselves [...]. If Dr Hanslick does not recognize the contemporary doctrines of unity of matter,[45] conservation of energy, and so on, then he should at least acknowledge the unity that is brought to the external world by the spirit studying it'.[46] In a twist that brought a core idealist precept firmly into the realm of the scientific, Kazanskii concluded that Hanslick's idea of beauty as autonomous (and therefore divorced from human perception) was unscientific. Kazanskii also couched his opposition to Hanslick in terms of class. According to him, Hanslick was expressing views of the most powerful class in Europe, the bourgeoisie, which understood music as an innocuous and meaningless plaything for the privileged, ignoring music's capability of effecting a positive social change and thus entrenching social inequality.

ii. Genetic connections
Like his Bayreuth namesake, the Russian zoologist and psychologist Vladimir Aleksandrovich Vagner (1849–1934) did not think highly of Hanslick's theory. Vagner was the first scientist in Russia to apply evolutionary theory to psychology, focusing on the evolution of instincts within the framework of Haeckel's biogenetic law. He was married to the

---

[41] Grigorii Bernandt and Izrail´ Iampol´skii, *Kto pisal o muzyke: bio-bibliograficheskiii slovar´ muzykal´nykh kritikov i lits, pisavshikh o muzyke v dorevolyutsionnoi Rossii i SSSR*, 4 vols, Moscow, 1971–89, 2, p. 9.

[42] His reviews stopped in 1888, and resumed in 1896 but in Tiflis, where he was allowed to settle after his Siberian exile. Between 1888 and 1896 Kazanskii only produced four large theoretical essays for *Artist*. *Kto pisal o muzyke*, 2, pp. 9–10.

[43] Quoted in Singer, *Legacy of Positivism*, pp. 10 and 13.

[44] Kazanskii, 'Odna iz reaktsionnykh doktrin', p. 43.

[45] He likely meant the law of conservation of matter.

[46] Kazanskii, 'Odna iz reaktsionnykh doktrin', p. 44.

pianist Maria Apollonovna Krishtofovich, a pupil of Nikolai Rubinshtein, and their Moscow house on Malaia Tsaritsynskaia street, typically for its time, became a juncture of the musical and scientific worlds.[47]

A professional scientist, Vagner was well aware of Comte and other positivist writers.[48] His review of Hanslick was published in the reputed journal, *Voprosy filosofii i psikhologii*, which operated on the crossroads of philosophy and the natural sciences.[49] Appropriately, Vagner's argument relied on a mixture of humanities and scientific knowledge, and did not make distinctions between the two. For instance, he quoted at length from Hippolyte Taine's *Philosophy of Art*, the Russian translation of which enjoyed wide popularity and multiple reprints.[50] Taine stipulated that a work of art was thoroughly conditioned by its social context. Meticulous descriptions of landscape and climate, and of social and political conditions abounded in this study, which aimed to explain national spirit in art. Such details, Taine claimed, could help a historian not only understand the laws that shape artistic creation, but also formulate an aesthetic criterion: the best art was that which captured the national character most comprehensively. According to Vagner it was precisely the lack of such catholicity that made Hanslick's approach unscientific.

Advocating a holistic study of music, Vagner referred to his own actual scientific expertise as well. As a geneticist, Vagner wrote, he could only support Hanslick's intention of importing methods of natural history to the study of aesthetic issues. But insisting on the autonomy of music, Hanslick forgot about 'the fundamental principles of natural sciences […] about the genetic connection of all phenomena, and thus about the necessity of studying them by proceeding from the simplest to the more complex'.[51] A *Brokgauz i Efron* entry on Hanslick authored by Sergei Bulich — a linguist, ethnographer and the first dean of the first music department at the Institute of Art History — praised Vagner's 'well-aimed objections' to Hanslick's theory and added that Neustroev and Sacchetti supported

---

[47] Boris Lukin, 'Pervyi redaktor "Prirody" V. A. Vagner', *Priroda*, 48, 1987, pp. 48–58 (p. 50).

[48] His magnum opus, *Biologicheskie osnovaniia sravnitel'noi psikhologii*, opened with three chapters on, respectively, theological, metaphysical and scientific world-views in comparative psychology. Vladimir Vagner, *Biologicheskie osnovaniia sravnitel'noi psikhologii*, Moscow, 2005.

[49] Vladimir Vagner, 'O prekrasnom v muzyke', *Voprosy filosofii i psikhologii*, 29, 1895, pp. 478–502.

[50] Ibid., pp. 492 and 496.

[51] Ibid., pp. 478–79.

Vagner's position.⁵² Evidently, a scientist's opinion on an aesthetic issue carried much weight in musical circles at the turn of the century.

iii. Psychology as a branch of physiology
Aleksandr Neustroev's book, *Music and Feeling* (*Muzyka i chuvstvo*, 1890) engaged with Hanslick primarily from a psychological perspective.⁵³ Having studied law at the University and piano and compositional theory at the Conservatory, Neustroev was an assistant to the chief custodian of The Hermitage museum in St Petersburg, Andrei Ivanovich Somov — the father of the painter Konstantin Somov. One of the founders of *Mir iskusstva*, Konstantin was friends with the Neustroev family and often stayed at their dacha in Martyshkino.⁵⁴

Neustroev's approach drew on one of the central scientific trends of the time: studying a causal relationship between physiology and psychology and thus promoting a materialistic understanding of the human psyche. The questions he asked were: 'Is it possible to narrow down the seeming diversity of music's influence to some general law; is it possible to get to the root of the question of how music can affect us if it is purified of all incidental admixtures imparted by associations; in other words, what is its physiological and psychological effect on man?'⁵⁵

Borrowing classifications of feelings from Adolf Horwicz's *Psychological Analyses on a Physiological Basis: An Attempt at a New Foundation of Psychology* (1872),⁵⁶ Neustroev laid out his own ranking of feelings aroused by music. These could be of two kinds: 'formal feelings' and 'sympathetic feelings'.⁵⁷ By the latter Neustroev meant empathy. The former, however, were vague and unformed, and thus did not lend themselves to specific descriptions. These feelings, such as tension and relief, could be aroused musically by employing such devices as dissonances, suspensions and syncopations on the one hand, and resolution and faster tempi on the other. If nudged in the right direction by the properties of the musical material, these vague primary feelings, such as longing, were able to

---

⁵² Sergei Bulich, 'Muzyka', in *Entsiklopedicheskii slovar' Brokgauza i Efrona*, ed. I. Ie. Andreevskii, St Petersburg, 86 vols, 1890–1907, 20, pp. 127–45.

⁵³ Aleksandr Neustroev, *Muzyka i chuvstvo: materialy dlia psikhologicheskogo osnovaniia estetiki muzyki*, St Petersburg, 1890.

⁵⁴ Alexandre Benois, *Memoirs*, London, 1960.

⁵⁵ Neustroev, *Muzyka i chuvstvo*, p. 2.

⁵⁶ Adolf Horwicz, *Psychologische Analysen auf physiologischer Grundlage. Ein Versuch zur Neubegründung der Seelenlehre*, 2 vols, Halle, 1872.

⁵⁷ *Elementargefühle, formale Gefühle* or *vage Gefühle* in German terminology.

develop into specialized feelings, such as grieving for a lost friend.[58] In the mid-nineteenth century it was precisely Hanslick's disavowal of the subjective feelings aroused by music that elevated his theory from mere music criticism into the status of scholarship. By the end of the century, as the purview of science widened in the popular imagination, it became commonplace to think of subjectivity itself as the material for objective scientific inquiry.

A political prisoner rotting in Siberia, a privileged member of artistic circles and a famous natural scientist all argued against the idea of music's autonomy and exceptionalism and claimed that it could not be studied in isolation from both society and nature. Like Kazanskii, Neustroev and Vagner, many writers who contributed to this discourse at the turn of the century did not specialize in music, but their writings appeared in widely read and influential journals and therefore lent these people a powerful voice. Crucial to the arguments of all three critics, the connection between music and 'life' (understood generally to be the social and material world) remained central to writings of Soviet musicologists three decades later.

Networks: Professional and personal

But through what kind of channels did positivist ideas travel from late imperial to Soviet Russia? These precepts could hardly be found in the writings of the famous nineteenth-century music critics who are conventionally considered the ancestors of Russian musicology. In his article, 'Music, Musical Science and Musical Pedagogy', Aleksandr Serov expounded a utilitarian view of musical science as an explanation of the works of genius. For him, the idea that theory was to hold any prescriptive power over practice was laughable. Although some of his organicist terminology would resurface decades later in the writings of Soviet theorists, the ethos of his advocacy of music scholarship was fundamentally different: for him, a composer, it was a means to an end.[59] German Larosh echoed Serov in rejecting a prescriptive view of music scholarship in an article entitled 'The Historical Study of Music'.[60] Conceding that the study of music should not be held to any utilitarian standards more than any other branch of 'pure' science, he nevertheless established a definite hierarchy between music history as a part of general history, and music

---

[58] Neustroev, *Muzyka i chuvstvo*, pp. 67–68.
[59] Aleksandr Serov, 'Muzyka, muzykal′naia nauka, muzykal′naia pedagogika', *Epokha*, 6, 1864, pp. 100–24, and 12, 1864, pp. 1–18.
[60] German Larosh, 'Istoricheskoe izuchenie muzyki', *Russkii vestnik*, 70, 1867, 8, pp. 690–706.

history as a part of specialized musical knowledge, on a par with harmony and counterpoint. For us musicians, he claimed, the latter was more important. For him, the current dominance of natural sciences in the study of music (i.e. Helmholtz's acoustics) represented merely a stage in the development of music historiography and by no means its goal. Finally, he was unequivocally against studying art in natural-scientific terms, believing that these terms could explain only the material of art but not its meaning. Neither did Vladimir Stasov, who repeatedly ranted against the 'scholastic' Westernized education at the conservatories, consider music scholarship to have an independent professional identity.

The idea that music scholarship was a branch of science able to discover the laws of music was so established in the late nineteenth century that we find it in writings of authors as diverse as Kazanskii, Neustroev and Vagner — authors who have received virtually no attention in the historiography of Russian music criticism. At the same time, in the work of such towering figures of nineteenth-century thought on music as Serov, Stasov and Larosh, this postulate, which became a fixture in the output of early Soviet musicologists, is barely to be found. The personal and professional paths through which positivist precepts travelled to the first generation of Soviet musicologists often included unlikely characters. Let us now trace one such path.

A well-known lawyer, philosopher and sociologist, Vladimir Taneev (1840–1921) valued Comte's work highly, regarding him as the founder of scientific philosophy. Adopting Comte's law of three stages, Taneev wrote that positivism was 'a movement that superseded the fictitious ideas of theology and metaphysics in science, practice and art'.[61] Fifteen years older than his brother Sergei Taneev (1856–1915), Vladimir was a significant influence on the future composer. When the young Sergei lived in Paris he wrote to his family, 'It was somewhat strange to meet people, whose names I knew only from Volodia's books. [...] [W]hen people said "Taine" I used to think of a book; it never occurred to me that someone could say, "Here is Taine" and show me not a book, but a person'.[62] Having grown up in a household where Hippolyte Taine's works were known simply as 'Taine', Sergei Taneev was acquainted with scientific philosophy and its application in the humanities — a theme that occupied him throughout his life. Many years later he wrote in his diary: '[R]ead many articles from

---

[61] Quoted in Petr Alekseev, *Filosofy Rossii XIX–XX stoletii*, 4th edn, Moscow, 2002, p. 786.

[62] Quoted in Grigorii Bernandt, *S. I. Taneev*, Moscow, 1983, p. 36.

the philosophical dictionary and from Meyer to extract proof of a close relationship between philosophy and natural sciences'.[63] Most tellingly, as the epigraph to his life's work — *Convertible Counterpoint in the Strict Style* (*Podvizhnoi kontrapunkt strogogo pis'ma*), in which he codified the relationship between voices in counterpoint in mathematical formulas — he took Leonardo da Vinci's phrase, 'No human investigation can be called true science without passing through mathematical tests'.[64]

A life-long professor at the Moscow Conservatory and a co-founder of the Moscow People's Conservatory, Sergei Taneev was a mentor to several generations of Moscow musicians. Nadezhda Briusova (1881–1951), who would later become a prominent musicologist at the State Academy of Artistic Sciences and one of its staunchest Marxists, considered Taneev to be one of the crucial influences on her musicological career.[65] In 1900–07 Briusova underwent extensive theoretical training in Taneev's class that included counterpoint, canon and fugue, as well as musical forms.[66] Two years after graduation she would go on to author a programmatic brochure on the 'science of music'. In Taneev's class, Briusova met Boleslav Iavorskii (1877–1942), her future colleague at the Academy, whose theory of symmetric modes would later exert vast influence on the development of Soviet music theory.

Iavorskii studied with Taneev in 1899–1903 and thus overlapped with Bruisova by three years. The poet Andrei Belyi, recalling the names of people who frequented the Symbolist gathering 'Free Aesthetics', described Briusova and Iavorskii as colleagues. More importantly, he emphatically portrayed them as members of the scientific camp, to which Belyi was averse:

> A couple of acerbic, dry theorists of music, thoroughly: N. Ia. Briusova and the ironically reserved and taciturn Iavorskii. Agile as a lizard, the talkative sister of the poet [...] suggested — scientifically: why don't we retune our tunings into out-of-tunings? Why don't we have our rows within tone rows? [...] The silent Iavorskii [...] exceeded even Briusova in his intellect, but uninspired was this skull [...]. For years Briusova carried

[63] Entry of 11 October 1901 in Sergei Taneev, *Dnevniki*, ed. Liudmila Korabel′nikova, 3 vols, Moscow, 1981–85, 2, p. 273.

[64] In Taneev's book the phrase is given in Italian: 'Nissuna humana ivestigatione si po dimandare vera scientia, s'essa non passa per le mattematiche dimmonstratione.'

[65] Natal′ia Minor, 'Problemy massovogo muzykal′nogo vospitaniia v pedagogicheskom nasledii N. Ia. Briusovoi', unpublished PhD dissertation, Moscow State Pedagogical University, 1998, p. 19.

[66] Bernandt, *Taneev*, pp. 270–72.

a 'whole-tone' scale in her pocket, so she could take it out, like a tape measure, to measure in centimetres — Bach, Beethoven, following her brother's principles — 'To measure and to quantify!'[67]

Other than her conservatory studies, Nadezhda Briusova never attended a university but was home-schooled by her brother, the poet Valerii Briusov (1873–1924). Eight years older than his sister, Valerii was a defining influence on her.[68] In a memoir, Briusov described the intellectual climate of their household: '[T]he 1860s were coming; "rays of light" started penetrating the "realm of darkness" of the Moscow merchantry. [...] My father hit the books [...] reading Marx and Buckle, Darwin and Moleschott, all those works whose titles were on everyone's lips. [...] I learned about Darwin's ideas and principles of materialism before I learned multiplication.'[69] Despite belonging to the Symbolist movement, Valerii Briusov had a longstanding connection to positivism, albeit a tangled one.

In 1909 Briusov published an article in a major periodical, *Russkaia mysl'*, in which he elaborated on the concept of 'scientific poetry' — one of the quirky Russian repercussions of positivism.[70] For Briusov, the intellectual activity behind scientific and artistic pursuits was essentially the same, but the method was different. As opposed to analytical methods, poetry was destined to bring together all the advances of science, which specialized branches of science were unable to synthesize. The poet's creative intuition was thus the best tool for divining the connections 'between the elements of world and life', which had not yet been discovered scientifically.[71] Harnessing the idea of the interconnectedness of phenomena in the physical world, one of the core ideas of the scientific, as well as mystical, world-views, Briusov sought to bridge the divide between the two. At the very end of his life, Briusov still applied the epithet 'positivist' to himself without a second thought.[72]

---

[67] Andrei Belyi, *Mezhdu dvukh revolyutsii*, Leningrad, 1934, pp. 238–39.

[68] Quoted in Minor, 'Problemy massovogo muzykal'nogo vospitaniia', p. 21.

[69] Valerii Briusov, *Dnevniki. Avtobiograficheskaia proza. Pis'ma*, ed. Evgeniia Ivanova, Moscow, 2002, p. 164.

[70] The article was titled, 'The Literary Life of France. Scientific Poetry', and was essentially a review and summary of René Ghil's *De la poésie scientifique*, published in Paris earlier that year. Valerii Briusov, 'Literaturnaia zhizn' Frantsii, II. Nauchnaia poeziia', *Russkaia mysl'*, 6, 1909, pp. 155–67.

[71] Ibid., p. 162.

[72] In his speech at a celebration in honour of his fiftieth birthday, held on 16 December 1923 at the State Academy for Artistic Sciences, he recalled his fierce polemics with Viacheslav Ivanov, 'who brutally reproached me for this realism in symbolism, this positivism in idealism'. Valerii Briusov, 'Otvetnaia rech'', in *Valeriiu Briusovu: sbornik*

As much as through printed media, positivist precepts were disseminated by word of mouth, travelling through familial and professional networks. Rarely based on a thorough knowledge of the writings of Comte and his followers, these precepts interbred with such unlikely bedfellows as Symbolism and mysticism, further obscuring their uncertain pedigree. This tightly bound cluster of familial, friendly and collegial relationships is illustrative of how ideas circulated in the artistic circles of the Russian *fin de siècle*, in which most people knew each other and in which the ideological was closely interwoven with the personal.

Briusova and Iavorskii

In November 1909, at the famous Symbolist 'Society for Free Aesthetics' (Obshchestvo svobodnoi estetiki), Nadezhda Briusova gave a talk entitled 'The science of music, its historical development, and its present state' ('Nauka o muzyke, ee istoricheskie puti i sovremennoe sostoianie').[73] Briusova's essay was a prime example of the positivist precepts that underpinned early Russian attempts to create a coherent methodology for studying music:

> Scientific inquiry should yield exact knowledge of the laws that govern the sounding temporal life of [the musical] world. The method of the science of music is the same as the method of all natural sciences that examine the physical structure of any world. It involves experimenting on individual living creatures, which provides the opportunity to comprehend the general laws of life of the world that we study — since any living part of the world, in abiding by its laws, is tantamount to the whole world.[74]

Positioning music within the natural world was a leap Briusova had to make to carry out her positivist agenda. Briusova understood music as something that had a life of its own, had a knowable essence and, most importantly, constituted a reality external to the human mind. This claim slotted into the venerable tradition of organicism started by Jean-Jacques Rousseau and most famously exemplified in Herbert Spencer's essay, 'The

posviashchennyi 50-letiiu so dnia rozhdeniia poeta, ed. Petr Kogan, Moscow, 1924, p. 55.

[73] Subsequently published in the influential Symbolist art journal, *Vesy*, and later as a separate book: Nadezhda Briusova, 'Nauka o muzyke, ee istoricheskie puti i sovremennoe sostoianie. Doklad, prochitannyi v Obshcheste svobodnoi estetiki 11 noiabria 1909 g.', *Vesy*, 11–12, 1909, pp. 185–211; Nadezhda Briusova, *Nauka o muzyke, ee istoricheskie puti i sovremennoe sostoianie*, Moscow, 1910.

[74] Ibid., p. 1.

Social Organism', first published in 1860.[75] Such organicist metaphors were firmly established in Russian writing on music as well. For instance, Serov likened 'musical organisms' to the well-organized system of human muscles and skeleton.[76] Briusova, however, went so far as to identify methods of natural sciences — and by extension, methods of the science of music — as primarily 'experiments on living creatures'.

Next, she argued that the most important element of music was its temporal aspect — musical form unfolding in time. This temporal aspect was defined by tension and resolution, which, in turn, was made possible by the hierarchy of more and less stable tones of the mode: 'The laws of motion, instability and tension are the only laws that govern life of the sonic-temporal matter.'[77] Movement was thus always teleological, aiming to resolve into stability. She condemned equal temperament, in which the 'natural relationships' of tones were distorted and mechanized.[78] Oppositions between the living and the dead, and between the natural and the mechanistic, were central to Briusova's rhetoric. For her, true science was defined by its interest in 'life'. Adopting a ubiquitous trope of the time, Briusova maintained that old 'scholastic' science could never keep pace with the actual development of composition and was only able to codify styles *ex post facto*, once they had become mechanistic, and the composers had already moved on to a different style.[79] The new science, however, purported to study music in real life and discover its actual laws.

Briusova also wrote extensively on the predictive and prescriptive power of science. The idea that once the laws of social life were discovered, people would be able to predict the future and shape it as desired, harkened back to Comte. Indeed, it was the *raison d'être* of Comte's whole programme. For him, positive science was a means towards a political reorganization of society. Briusova was convinced that the new science of music would possess the prescriptive power of a scientific modal system, and would replace the contemporary *ad hoc* approach to composing music.[80]

Briusova's ideas bore a striking resemblance to the work of Boleslav Iavorskii, whose 'theory of modal rhythm' laid the foundation for Soviet

---

[75] The Russian translation was published in a collection of Spencer's essays in 1899–1900: Gerbert Spenser, *Opyty nauchnye, politicheskie i filosofskie*, ed. N. A. Rubakin, 3 vols, St Petersburg, 1899–1900.

[76] Serov, 'Muzyka, muzykal′naia nauka', p. 117.

[77] Briusova, *Nauka o muzyke*, p. 36.

[78] Ibid., p. 22.

[79] The model that Briusova extrapolated to all music theory had its roots in the rules for composition codified in the seventeenth-century *stile antico*.

[80] Bruisova, *Nauka o muzyke*, pp. 44–45.

and post-Soviet music theory. To be exact, her writings explained the shared conceptual foundations that underpinned the work of both scholars. A large part of Iavorskii's lasting legacy in Soviet and post-Soviet musicology was his theory of modes. Mode, for Iavorskii, was any system of hierarchically organized stable and unstable tones. This system produced tension and resolution, which in turn shaped musical time. His theory of modal rhythm (*ladovyi ritm*), hinged on the symmetry of the tritone within the octave. He considered the tritone to be the most unstable interval, governing all other intervals. According to this theory, the whole twelve-tone pitch space was comprised of 'tritone systems' — nodes that included a tritone and both its inward and outward resolutions. Different combinations of these nodes would result in stable modes (such as major and minor) and unstable ones, in which even stable tones possessed unresolved tension. Iavorskii pictured his theory as a spiral system of musical space, organized into tritone systems positioned within the circle of fifths. Such was the general law that applied to all kinds of music. Naturalizing this law, Iavorskii wrote that folk music, blissfully ignorant of the artifice of European music theory, conformed to this law better than professional music.

Like Briusova's 'Science of music', the opening sentences of Iavorskii's *The Structure of Musical Speech* (*Struktura muzykal'noi rechi*, 1908) emphasized the equivalence of music and life: 'Musical speech is not a monument to life that has passed, but a manifestation of life itself, life that is happening at the moment, and therefore unfolding in time.'[81] Binary relationships between life and death, and between organicism and mechanism, abounded in Iavorskii's study as well.[82] Attempting to find a causal relationship between musical form and aspects of human physiology and perception, Iavorskii claimed that 'the largest span of continuous and coherent musical speech corresponds to the longest duration of breath in a living creature, and to the longest basic unit of its continuous attention'.[83]

In his article, 'Text and Music' ('Tekst i muzyka', 1914), he attempted to show that the law of tension and resolution he worked out for music was, in fact, an overarching law that applied to verbal speech as well. Elaborating on the concept of *intonatsiia* — the precursor of Asaf'ev's more well-known theory — Iavorskii wanted to establish the primacy of intonation as a vehicle of meaning.[84] *Intonatsiia* was also the life force that organized

[81] Boleslav Iavorskii, *Stroeniie muzykal'noi rechi: materialy i zametki*, Moscow, 1908, p. 2.
[82] Ibid., p. 4.
[83] Ibid., p. 8.
[84] Boleslav Iavorskii, 'Tekst i muzyka', *Muzyka*, 163, pp. 8–9.

speech into a succession of tensions and resolutions. The ultimate goal of music scholars, for him, was to formulate 'a possibly perfect and complete theory on the structure of musical speech' — a single law that would remain true independently from its particular manifestations, which were inferior to the law itself.[85]

Briusova and Iavorskii belonged to the first generation of scientifically minded music scholars who practised what the previous generation had only preached: discovering the laws of music. Their original theories and their first publications in the late 1900s had a direct bearing on the further development of musicology in the Soviet Union. Both Briusova and Iavorskii went on to be active members of the Music Department of the State Academy of Artistic Sciences in the 1920s, thus carrying the principles they worked out in the last decade before the Revolution through into the decades after it.

'Nauchnost'' and Marxism

In the summer of 1922, some twelve musicology students at the newly reorganized Institute for Art History were celebrating the end of their first academic year in a new capacity as researchers. For that, they had to thank their mentor Boris Asaf'ev. They sent him a thank-you note, handwritten by Aleksei Finagin, one of Asaf'ev's pupils. Finagin and friends praised Asaf'ev for putting an end to the epoch of dilettantes in the study of music. By dilettantes they meant such writers as Odoevskii, Stasov, Serov, Larosh, Sokal'skii and Taneev, since these writers did not rely on any kind of unified methodology. For the first generation of Soviet-raised musicologists, Asaf'ev was a unifying figure who consolidated scattered approaches and created true scholarship:

> In you, Boris Vladimirovich, we, the young scholars, hail the man who categorically broke with dilettantism in the study of music; a scholar who gave us his own, new, revitalizing method [...]; finally, a person who managed to attract the younger generation, and thus laid the foundation for his own 'school'.[86]

The contents of this letter would later reappear in a widely read and cited publication — the five-year report on the activities of the Music Department (1925).[87] Furthermore, the image of the new rigorous discipline

---

[85] Iavorskii, *Stroeniie*, p. 12.
[86] TsGALI, f. 82, op. 1, d. 122, ll. 59v–60.
[87] Aleksei Finagin, 'Obzor deiatel'nosti Razriada istorii muzyki RIII za 5 let ego

of musicology, which replaced the old 'amateur' attempts at studying music, resurfaced in Lunacharskii's article, 'One of the Breakthroughs in the Study of Art', which praised the department's great strides towards building a Marxist musicology.[88]

Indeed, musicologists were acutely aware of their status as pioneers, professionals now working at academic institutions. Therefore, much of their effort was devoted to formulating new methodologies that would yield *nauchnye*, i.e. scientific discoveries of the laws of music. Historians as much as theorists were fond of large-scale concepts borrowed from sociology and the natural sciences. A theory that promised an overarching explanation of historical laws, dialectical materialism offered an attractive framework. After all, according to Engels, dialectics was 'the science of general laws of motion and development of nature, human society and thought'.[89] Lenin, too, explained the appeal of Marxism by 'the fact that it unites a rigorous and most lofty scientism [*nauchnost'*] (being the last word in social science) with revolutionism'.[90]

Marxism and positivism are widely considered to be antagonistic philosophies — Marx himself used to rant against Comte and his 'Scheisspositivismus'.[91] However, the particular interpretations of these philosophies in the minds of Soviet musicologists were not incompatible. First, the conviction that the development and internal workings of societies (and by extension of the arts) are governed by universal, immutable laws explicable through scientific inquiry laid the groundwork for a wide acceptance of Marxist social determinism. Second, the idea that phenomena should be studied in their dynamic development, in motion, and in the context of their mutual relationship to other phenomena, lay at the centre of the Soviet interpretation of Marxist dialectics. A related idea, that artistic phenomena should be studied holistically, since they were 'alive' and bore resemblance to living, moving and changing organisms, paved the way for both Marxist 'dialectical development' and the natural scientific thrust of Soviet musicology in the 1920s. From this, it followed that the study of art should mimic the methodology of the natural sciences whenever possible, and should draw on scientific knowledge in fields

sushchestvovaniia', *De musica*, 1, Leningrad, 1925, pp. 100–16.

[88] Anatolii Lunacharskii, 'Odin iz sdvigov v iskusstvovedenii', *Vestnik kommunisticheskoi akademii*, 1926, 15, pp. 85–107.

[89] Quoted in David Joravsky, *Soviet Marxism and Natural Science, 1917–1932*, New York, 1961, pp. 5–6.

[90] Ibid., p. 3.

[91] Ibid., p. 5.

such as acoustics, physics and physiology for an explanation of musical phenomena. Third, the premise that all art was socially embedded closely paralleled the core Marxist tenet that the social reality is primary and determines the production of ideas. An extension of this premise was the idea that results of scholarship should benefit society directly.

These convergences explain why many Soviet musicologists of the 1920s embraced Marxist ideas willingly and enthusiastically — a fact that has been barely acknowledged in previous research. Throughout the 1920s scholars kept advocating for the academic value of research avenues that predated the rise of Marxism. The compatibility between the old, pre-revolutionary and the new, Marxist research methods was widely acknowledged at the institutes. As late as 1929 Petr Kogan, director of the State Academy of Artistic Sciences, claimed that scholars who were yet to adopt the Marxist theoretical framework nevertheless produced research that could be valuable to Marxists.[92]

In the Institute's internal records, the term 'Marxism' was used interchangeably with the term 'sociological method'. The department within the Institute that was responsible for developing the Marxist study of art was called the 'Sociological Committee'. Indeed, the sociological study of music was thriving. For instance, the Music Department of the Institute of Art History had a special section called the Office for the Study of Music of Daily Life (Kabinet po izucheniiu muzykal'nogo byta). One of its projects was the study of the behaviours of concert and theatre audiences. A progress report for January–March 1928 stated that the department developed observational methods and questionnaires that would measure the audience's reaction to music, applying what they called a 'theory of learned reflexes'.[93] A collection of articles devoted to *muzykal'nyi byt* dealt with eighteenth-century Russian music — early opera as well as domestic music-making — widening the purview of musicology from the canon of masterworks to music as social practice.[94]

In 1924, the musicologist Roman Gruber gave a talk at the Music Department of the Institute of Art History entitled 'Contemporary musicology and dialectical materialism'.[95] In the spirit of positivism, this was an attempt to use what Gruber thought to be a rigorous scientific method for the study of music. Gruber believed that the

---

[92] RGALI, f. 941, op.1, d. 141, ll. 2–21.
[93] TsGALI, f. 82, op. 3, d. 31, ll. 174–77v.
[94] *Muzyka i muzykal'nyi byt staroii Rossii: materialy i issledovaniia*, ed. Boris Asaf'ev, Leningrad, 1928.
[95] TsGALI, f. 82, op. 3, d. 10, ll. 6–6v.

Marxist method was based on four principles: 1) the principle of constant change of all that is; 2) the principle of the universal interconnectedness of phenomena; 3) the principle of discrete, step-wise development in which quantity is transformed into quality; 4) the principle of dialectical (contradictory) development.[96] Indeed, the continuity of these points with pre-revolutionary precepts is striking. The first and second postulates had been in circulation in Russian humanities thought for several decades. As for the basic concept that would later become a bugbear of Soviet ideology — the causal understanding of base and superstructure — Gruber claimed that the classics of Marxism admitted that the relationship between base and superstructure was indirect and that there existed mediating factors between the two (something Gruber called 'society's psyche'). Therefore, it was possible for the superstructure to influence the base. In 'the complex system of interrelations' between base and superstructure Gruber saw a flexible research instrument capable of producing an objective analysis of reality without squeezing it into a procrustean bed of rigid formulas.[97] To prove the 'scientific legitimacy' of musicological pursuits from the viewpoint of dialectical materialism, Gruber claimed that 'Dialectical materialism is similar to certain approaches [...] in contemporary (particularly Russian) musicology that some musicologists developed independently and by way of purely musical considerations'.[98] Developing these ideas, in 1927 Gruber published an article entitled 'On the "Formal Method" in Musicology', in which he argued that the formal method, rooted in the methodology of natural science, provided a solid foundation for the 'sociological method' (a.k.a. Marxism) to build upon.[99]

One of Nadezhda Briusova's early talks at the Academy repeated verbatim passages from her article, 'Nauka o muzyke', while taking the scientistic pathos up a notch — now Briusova used the term 'musical biology' to mean analysis of musical forms.[100] While in the early 1920s her work still dealt with predominantly formal issues such as the function of the bar line,[101] it soon shifted towards the 'sociological' approach. In 1925 she gave a talk entitled 'Music and Revolution' at the joint session of the music theory group and the Commission for the Study of Revolutionary

[96] Ibid.
[97] TsGALI, f. 82, op. 3, d. 10, ll. 6–6v.
[98] TsGALI, f. 82, op. 3, d. 10, l. 6v.
[99] Roman Gruber, 'O "formal'nom metode" v muzykovedenii', *De musica*, 3, 1927, pp. 39–53.
[100] RGALI, f. 941, op. 5, d. 1, ll. 4–5v.
[101] RGALI, f. 941, op. 5, d. 1, ll. 13–13v.

Art.[102] Briusova's understanding of music's nature as the system of tension and resolution, propelling music forward (i.e. Iavorskii's theory of modes) had not changed since 1909. That idea, however, proved to be an ideal vantage point from which to theorize revolutionary music. 'The nature of musical material', Briusova said in her talk, 'which possesses two colours: tension and resolution, makes it the most capable [art] to convey the struggling will, the revolutionary thrust'.[103] It is remarkable how easily the new topical subjects flowed from Briusova's pre-revolutionary rhetoric, steeped in scientistic discourse.

Natural scientific rhetoric
Another direction Soviet musicologists pursued was tethering musicology to the natural sciences. One way to do this was through empirical research. For instance, the acoustics laboratory and instrument-building workshops at the State Institute of Musical Science indeed made use of natural scientific methods. At the Academy, Boleslav Iavorskii collaborated with the psychologist Sof′ia Beliaeva-Ekzempliarskaia on establishing empirical foundations for his theory of modes, doing experimental work on perception.[104] Another avenue was applying a natural scientific vocabulary to musicological studies via metaphor. Most of the theories put forth by the Academy's musicologists used terms evoking biology, math and physics, which aimed to impart a certain gravitas to the study of musical form and aesthetics.

One such product of the Academy's Music Department was Georgii Konius's theory of 'metrotectonism'. In 1928 he presented this method to his colleagues in a talk entitled 'Principles of disassembling the skeletons of musical bodies'.[105] In an attempt to impart a semblance of a natural law to his theory of musical form, Konius claimed that 'A musical organism is characterized by a musical-physiological process of steady pulse, which creates pulse waves or cells, of which a musical organism is born'.[106] The gist of his method was, in fact, quite simple: 'Having found the location of the joints [*tochki sochleneniia skeletal*] we can measure the constitutive parts and determine their relationship to each other, as well as to the

---

[102] RGALI, f. 941, op. 5, d. 18, ll. 9–10v.
[103] RGALI, f. 941, op. 5, d. 18, l. 9.
[104] RGALI, f. 941, op. 5, d. 10, l. 119. See also, Ol′ga Serova, 'Sof′ia Nikolaevna Beliaeva-Ekzempliarskaia — vypusknitsa MVZhK', *Razvitiie lichnosti*, 2, 2012, pp. 40–58; Boleslav Iavorskii and Sof′ia Beliaeva-Ekzempliarskaia, *Struktura melodii*, Moscow, 1929.
[105] RGALI, f. 941, op. 5, d. 36, ll. 27–28.
[106] RGALI, f. 941, op. 5, d. 36, l. 27.

entire work.'[107] Thus his concern was with breaking down the musical form into smaller fragments and finding the ratios between them. Regular musical metre he called 'skeletal structure', relegating various non-metrical fragments of musical syntax to the category of epithelium. This method, Konius stated, allowed him to discover the commonalities between apparently dissimilar musical pieces and therefore the 'musical-biological foundations of the structure of musical organisms'.[108] Leonid Sabaneev's 'biometric method' aimed to find the 'positive characteristics of style' by measuring the frequency with which certain motives appeared in a musical work, thus capturing the originality of a composer's style.[109] Emilii Rozenov's theory of 'rational aesthetics' rested on the biological concept of the self-preservation instinct. According to Rosenov, the survival instinct compels humans to be alert to their surroundings, but also to spend as little energy on this task as possible. When external stimuli exceed the mind's ability to process them, the cognitive faculties shut down, resulting in unpleasant feelings and negative aesthetic judgement. On the other hand, when a work of art offers too little stimuli (for instance, by relying on over-familiar forms), the mind wastes energy by processing the stimuli too quickly. This causes feelings of boredom and impatience, also leading to negative aesthetic judgement. Therefore, in order for the listener to experience aesthetic pleasure, the sum of the stimuli should match the ability of the mind to process them.

When these theories were presented at the Academy's meetings, the audience generally did not question how exactly science related to music in these theories and accepted them as legitimate. Sheila Fitzpatrick has called such thought 'eccentric', and rightly so.[110] However, schooled in unqualified reverence for the natural sciences, musicologists saw the theories not as eccentricities but as bold steps towards scientific progress.

Musicology during the Cultural Revolution
During the general reorganization of Soviet culture known as the Cultural Revolution, the institutes were dissolved and the musicological paradigm of the 1920s came to an end. The term 'Cultural Revolution' was introduced into historiographic vocabulary by Sheila Fitzpatrick in 1978 in her groundbreaking volume, *Cultural Revolution in Russia: 1928–1931*. Fitzpatrick saw

[107] RGALI, f. 941, op. 5, d. 36, l. 27v.
[108] Ibid.
[109] RGALI, f. 941, op. 5, d. 10, ll. 230–230v.
[110] Sheila Fitzpatrick, 'Cultural Revolution as Class War', in *The Cultural Front: Power and Culture in Revolutionary Russia*, Ithaca, NY, 1992, pp. 115–48 (p. 140).

the change as rooted in educational and hiring policies that fostered upward social mobility among the proletariat (*vydvizhentsy*, as she called them). In an effort to create new proletarian elites and simultaneously oust *spetsy* of the old guard, educational opportunities were created that made it possible for working class *vydvizhentsy* to move up to white collar jobs in culture, technology and administration.[111]

The overhaul of the Academy's staff is documented in the minutes of a meeting that took place in June 1930: 'We must consider it desirable to create an institution of researchers of the second category with the goal of attracting young Marxist forces, both with and without Party membership (in the first place from activist workers).'[112] Since the beginning of that year, appointing new employees and denying the requests of current employees to retain their positions became routine practice at the Academy.[113] The career of Nikolai Cheliapov is a good case in point. He was the son of peasants, a graduate of the Law Faculty of the Moscow University and an administrator at a number of Soviet cultural institutions, including the Komakademiia, but most conspicuously he was the editor-in-chief of *Sovetskaia muzyka* (the most important Soviet musicological journal) and the head of the Composers' Union — in other words, a member of the working class whose rise in the Soviet musical world was meteoric. He was appointed Chair of the Music Department at some point after 25 November 1929 and before 13 February 1930, when his name appears in Music Department's archive for the first time.[114] That day marked a change in policy, personnel and rhetoric. The very first time Cheliapov's name was mentioned as the chair of departmental meetings, Georgii Konius was demoted from a full-time (*shtatnyi*) to a part-time (*vneshatnyi*) employee.

These policies successfully drove out anybody who could not adapt, but their effects were not exclusively negative. For instance, the same document that contains the first mention of Cheliapov's name and the decision to demote Konius also mentions that four young researchers (two of them women) had been accepted to the department. One of these youngsters was Viktor Tsukkerman, who went on become an influential music theorist and a creator of 'holistic analysis'. This Marxist-inspired analytical method that attempted to unify content and form became

[111] Ibid., p. 147.
[112] RGALI, f. 941, op. 5, d. 53. l. 119v.
[113] See, for instance, RGALI, f. 941, op. 5, d. 53, ll. 33–33v.
[114] The document was minutes of a meeting of the Music Department's presidium on 13 February 1930. RGALI, f. 941, op. 5, d. 53, ll. 14.

celebrated both in the Soviet Union and, much later, in the West.[115] Born in 1903 in a shtetl (Brailov) in Ukraine, Tsukkerman was able to rise to prominence due to the fact that the most serious obstacles to a successful career — his social class and his Jewishness — were rendered irrelevant by the policy that fostered upward social mobility among disadvantaged populations.

However, the mutation of academic vocabulary into militant Marxist rhetoric was far more damaging to musicological methodologies of the 1920s than a wave of new hires. Since the publication of Fitzpatrick's seminal book, various scholars have offered new frameworks for understanding Cultural Revolution. For instance, Michael David-Fox argues against a historiographic trend that adopted Fitzpatrick's periodization of Cultural Revolution as a clearly bounded period from 1928 to 1931. David-Fox has proposed that thinking about Cultural Revolution as a discrete historical episode is too reductive to be helpful in explaining the process of ideological transformation. Instead, he suggests the Cultural Revolution was not a period but a foundational idea: that a political revolution is only possible when it works in tandem with revolutionizing culture and belief systems. As such, the idea of cultural revolution originated long before the October Revolution. Throughout the 1920s many authors proposed a range of strategies for reshaping the cultural legacy of the late imperial era. Much of the musicological work of the 1920s could be understood as developing such strategies. What distinguished the period of the Great Break ('velikii perelom') is that in 1928 this multiplicity of ideas about what should constitute cultural revolution was subsumed by a simplistic and militant understanding of cultural revolution, as an 'all-out struggle against bourgeois culture and its carriers became the new orthodoxy'.[116]

In the arts, such a militant idea, which had a rich pre-revolutionary history but became increasingly orthodox in the late 1920s, was the idea that art should be inextricably bound to life — anti-autonomy of music taken to the extreme. In scholarship, as well, many an academic career was ended through accusations about research that was 'divorced from life'. Understanding of what constituted 'life', too, became increasingly

---

[115] For further details, see Daniil Zavlunov, 'The "tselostnyi analiz" (holistic analysis) of Zuckerman and Mazel', *Music Theory Online*, 20, 2014, 3 <http://www.mtosmt.org/issues/mto.14.20.3/mto.14.20.3.zavlunov.html> [accessed 28 April 2018], and Ellon D. Carpenter, 'The Theory of Music in Russia and the Soviet Union, ca. 1650–1950', unpublished PhD dissertation, University of Pennsylvania, 1988.

[116] Michael David-Fox, 'What Is Cultural Revolution?', *Russian Review*, 58, 1999, 2, pp. 181–201 (p. 198).

restrictive. The idea itself was present long before 1928, but it was only during the Great Break that it started to be enforced as the only viable way of thinking about art. Contrary to the view of this transition as a set of repressive policies implemented from above, the musicologists themselves had significant agency in this change.[117] Tracing how this idea developed in Boris Asaf'ev's writings and how it affected his relationships with his colleagues at the Institute of Art History will help illustrate this point. In the rest of the article I will discuss several ways in which this shift played out in musicological discourse, and what it meant for Soviet musicology's awareness of itself as an academic discipline.

The trope of 'music and life'

As Elina Viljanen has demonstrated, Asaf'ev's initial desire to formulate an overarching law of musical organization was deeply rooted in the pervasive search for unity that characterized the 'musical metaphysics' of the Russian *fin de siècle*.[118] However, during his stint as the head of musicology at the Institute, Asaf'ev's vocabulary clearly shifted towards thinking about music as an inherently social practice (disparate influences were typical for Asaf'ev, whose thinking was eclectic).

In 1924, Asaf'ev published an essay entitled 'Composers, keep up!' in which he urged his fellow composers to 'try living in the present and attempt to refract it'. By this, he meant decentring sonata form and the symphony as the most prestigious achievements of professional music and embracing musical theatre, folk song and even the sounds of the street. 'Hurry to create music for the sake of the life that has developed around you', Asaf'ev wrote, 'and not for the sake of some "ephemeral dream".'[119] In the same year, responding to a *Glavnauka* circular that asked research institutions how their work 'reflected Lenin's personality and ideas',[120] Asaf'ev spelled out what he took to be the legacy of Lenin (who died earlier that year):

[We must] persistently study the interaction of music and the social environment [*byt*], thus paving the way for an accessible art of music, [and

---

[117] For instance, see Raku, 'Sotsial'noe konstruirovanie "sovetskogo muzykovedeniia"', and Ksenia Kumpan, 'Institut istorii iskusstv na rubezhe 1920–1930 godov', in M. E. Malikova (ed.), *Instituty kul'tury Leningrada na perelome ot 1920-kh k 1930-m godam*, St Petersburg, 2011, pp. 540–637.

[118] Viljanen, 'The Problem of the Modern and Tradition'.

[119] The essay is translated and provided with a commentary in Frolova-Walker and Walker, *Music and Soviet Power*, pp. 124–27.

[120] TsGALI, f. 82, op. 1, d. 152, l. 30.

understand] musical forms not as formal [...] schemes, but as aggregates naturally crystallized in the process of organic development of musical language.[121]

At the same time, in 1924 these ideas were not yet explicitly connected with Marxism for Asaf´ev: in October 1924 he explicitly disavowed dialectical materialism. In the discussion following Gruber's aforementioned talk on musicology and dialectical materialism he claimed that his approach was independent, self-sufficient and not indebted to dialectical materialism.[122]

In late 1927, Asaf´ev accused his colleagues at the musicology department of fleeing from life's pressing issues and hiding in the ivory tower of historicism with its natural-scientific focus. He proposed a complete reshaping of the musicology department that would purge all disciplines which did not contribute to the study of social realities past and present. In a document entitled 'Preliminary work plan of the Music Department', Asaf´ev spelled out the new principles:

> 1. The Department's work should come as close as possible to tackling musical modernity and the problems it poses; 2. The basis of all music-scholarly work should be music in its sound and motion. [...] The Department has no right whatsoever to flee contemporary music and music culture for past's sake; 3. No single area of musicology, researched by the Department's sections, should eschew organic connection with the work of the rest of the Department; 4. Every section of the Department understands music as a social phenomenon. Thus, as intriguing or interesting independent self-sufficient development of disciplines that analyse music as a physical, biological or some other world of phenomena might be, it cannot take place at the Department; 5. [it is necessary] to stop the Department's apparent sprawling into adjacent peripheral disciplines and its ambition to cover areas that belong to specialized research institutions.[123]

Asaf´ev now regarded natural-scientific approaches as incompatible with the Marxist study of music. Supported by the Institute's Board of Directors, he implemented this reform singlehandedly, pushing for a decisive turn from historical and natural-scientific approaches to a sociological method.

---

[121] Asaf´ev's letter to Finagin. Kabinet rukopisei Rossiiskogo Instituta Istorii Iskusstv (hereafter, RIII), f. 68. op. 1, d. 78, ll. 63–63v. Undated, but clearly referring to the circular from Glavnauka.
[122] Ibid.
[123] TsGALI, f. 82, op. 3, d. 31, l. 58.

In a letter to the musicologist Aleksandr Ossovskii, Asaf′ev trumpeted 'battles' for socially relevant music.[124] He compared the Institute's research versatility to a cancerous tumour that grew in its pursuit of 'acoustics for acoustics' sake' and 'historicism for historicism's sake' (which he crossed out and changed to the punchier 'past for past's sake').[125] Asaf′ev's style in these communications shows a predilection for colourful, if crude, metaphors, and a preference for a broad-brush style ('past' instead of 'historicism').

This reform sacrificed the positions of several scholars at the Institute. But more importantly, it drove a wedge between Asaf′ev and the group of scholars led by his former comrade-in-arms, Aleksei Finagin, who was also eventually forced to leave the Institute. Finagin, like many others, could not tolerate the new restrictive intellectual environment and was sure to have conveyed his indignation to Asaf′ev. In letters to Andrei Rimskii-Korsakov (the composer's son), also a prominent figure at the Music Department, Finagin expressed his desire to continue their work outside of the Institute, where they could advance scholarship without 'interventions from B. V. [Asaf′ev], Simeon [Ginzburg] and Glavnauka', and where they could be free from 'demagogical phraseology'.[126] However, as Rimskii-Korsakov pointed out, during the Great Break such plans were utopian at best.[127]

While the continuity in Asaf′ev's coupling of 'music and life' throughout the 1920s is obvious, only in 1927 did he turn this idea against his colleagues. Throughout his career, Asaf′ev proved to be highly adaptable to the ideological climate of the time. Unlike the academic careers of some musicologists working at the Institute, Asaf′ev's career survived the purges and the loss of an institutional platform. Since the demise of the Institute, Asaf′ev's musicological career was based at the conservatories in Moscow and Leningrad, where for two more decades he continued to perform the tortuous ideological balancing act of adjusting to continuously changing policies. Eventually, he earned the highest honour that existed in Soviet academia when he was named a member of the Academy of Sciences of the USSR — an achievement unparalleled in Russian musicology.

It is likely, therefore, that in 1927 Asaf′ev correctly identified the imminent change in rhetoric and decided to implement it pre-emptively at the department for which he was responsible. This was a strategic choice:

---

[124] The letter was intended to persuade Ossovskii to work alongside Asaf′ev in the reorganized Department.
[125] RIII, f. 22, op. 1, d. 27, l. 25.
[126] RIII, f. 8, razdel VII, ll. 4–4v.
[127] RIII, f. 68. op. 1, d. 82, l. 6.

if he were to regain control of the Music Department at the Institute — control which he had temporarily relinquished while working at the Leningrad Conservatory — Asaf'ev would effectively wield ideological control over both music departments in Leningrad and, therefore, over the city's entire musicological infrastructure. Although nearly all musicologists accepted Marxism as a valid research framework, some managed to make it through the ordeal of the Cultural Revolution, while others forfeited their academic careers. Ultimately, who got to stay and who had to leave had less to do with ideological or methodological differences per se, and more with dexterity in navigating social and political change.

The changing meanings of 'science'
In February 1928, upon hearing the director Fedor Shmit's report on the Institute's activities in the preceding year, the Scholarly-Artistic Section of the State Academic Council issued an official resolution. It was decidedly unsympathetic, reprimanding the entire Institute for its lack of a clear-cut ideological orientation:

> The Sociological Committee still functions as a superstructure, and its methods have not yet penetrated all organs of the Institute's organism. Acknowledging the difficulties that switching to the track of sociological method entails (for instance, the absence of a sufficient quantity of Marxist art scholars), one must note that the Institute's work lacks a dominant ideological idea.[128]

The Department of Literature took the heat for 'the dominance of the formal method, [which] contradicts the Marxist study of literature'.[129] The Music Department was criticized for working outside the purview of music scholarship, for a 'chronological understanding' of modernity (i.e. one that did not emphasize ideologically significant recent events), and for its insufficiently sociological methods.

Responding to a smear campaign in the press that portrayed the Academy of Artistic Sciences as anti-Marxist, the State Academic Council created a commission to evaluate the Academy's work in early 1929. This evaluation reflected a new idea of what counted as science:

> [The Academy's] workers [...] are predominantly 1) alien not only to the Marxist, but to the materialist worldview in general, 2) to a

[128] TsGALI, f. 82, op. 3, d. 31, l. 173.
[129] Ibid.

HOW SOVIET MUSICOLOGY BECAME MARXIST 107

considerable extent removed from the challenges that are being posed to the art of our Soviet modernity and 3) some of them are only employed as researchers, while in fact they are dilettantes-art lovers. [...] [T]he Academy's work [...] is characterized by a predominantly [...] formal method of research with strong leanings towards abstract idealism. [...] A wide variety of philosophical conceptions (except Marxism) are present there, from positivism to mysticism; the Department [of General Theory of Art] [...] deems itself to be creating a 'purely-scientific', independent from 'worldviews' (of course from the Marxist one first and foremost), 'philosophy' of art, and for the entire duration of Academy's work it has been [...] a centre of reactionary thought in the field of art studies.[130]

Claiming that some of the employees were not professional scholars but merely 'art-lovers' carried the implication that from that point on, scholars' professional identity hinged on their allegiance to Marxism. Putting 'purely scientific' in sarcastic scare quotes, the report signalled that empirical research without the lens of Marxist theory no longer qualified as science. Both on a smaller scale at the musicology department at the Institute of Art History, and on the level of the entire institutes, the natural-scientific focus in the study of art had become invalid. Since science had been associated with social progressivism for more than half a century, the unscientific was also seen as socially reactionary. The title of Sergei Kazankii's article, 'One of the Reactionary Doctrines in the Field of Aesthetics', foreshadowed the Soviet use of the adjective 'reactionary' as a rhetorical tool of unique potency. It was used pervasively as a stand-in for 'backward', pre-Soviet and therefore anti-Soviet. In the previous quotation 'reactionary' is explicitly equated with non-scientific (signalled by scare quotes and accusations of dilettantism). Infractions against Marxist science were by extensions infractions against the social order.

These revised criteria for the concept of 'science' had swift consequence for policies that affected research institutions. The commission recommended that the Academy appoint a Communist majority in its presidium and among the heads of individual departments 'in order to ensure direct Marxist leadership'.[131] As discussed above, this reorganization was accomplished, leading immediately to a striking change in musicological rhetoric as well as in the range of possible research

---

[130] Arkhiv rossiiskoi akademii nauk (hereafter, RAN), f. 350, op. 1, d. 242, ll. 7–8.
[131] The document that contains the evaluation is undated but it must have been produced before 25 November 1929 because it was officially presented at Narkompros before or on that day. RAN, f. 350, op. 1, d. 242, l. 6.

topics. As if a new discourse fostered outside the walls of the Academy — in Komakademiia perhaps? — was being imported wholesale, a new vocabulary, such as the famous phrase, *zagnivaiushchaia burzhuaziia* (rotting bourgeoisie) started to dominate musicological meetings.[132] After undergoing ideological purges, the Institute of Art History merged with the Academy of Artistic Sciences and several other Moscow institutions to form the State Academy of Art History. This event effectively marked the end of the early Soviet musicological paradigm.[133]

Conclusion

The turn towards Marxism as the sole legitimate theoretical framework cost numerous scholars their careers. The violence with which these changes were enacted was legitimized not only by the official policies of the Cultural Revolution, but also by the historical prestige that some of its precepts had accrued before the October Revolution. To reiterate, these core precepts were: 1. that study of the humanities should be as scientific as possible (although the meaning of 'scientific' eventually shifted away from an emphasis on natural science); 2. that art should be studied as inextricably bound to the material and social world; and 3. that artistic form should be studied in its dialectical development, not as a dead abstraction. All three surface in a passage from Finagin's yearly report on the Music Department's activities from 1925:

> The history of scientific institutions suggests that a scientific organization is solid and strong only as long as it does not lose its organic connection to the relevant demands of reality with which it is contemporaneous — therefore, the Department's Council [renounces] both abstract theorizing, unconnected as it is to life, but which some researchers may not have yet outgrown, and the narrow professionalization of practising musicians. [...]. When it comes to the necessity of the Marxist approach [...] the Department Council believes that the Marxist method is a method of accounting for past experience and the direction of human activity on the basis of the laws of dialectical development. Applying it to the study of art, if it aspires to become a science, is only possible on the condition of adhering to that 'scientific materialism' which lies in studying specific material according to the laws of scientific thought.[134]

---

[132] See, for instance, Arnol'd Al'shvang's talk, 'Posleimpressionisticheskaia stadia razvitiia burzhuaznogo muzykal'nogo stilia', RGALI, f. 941, op. 5, d. 64, ll. 31–35.

[133] Kumpan, 'Institut istorii iskusstv', p. 635.

[134] TsGALI, f. 82, op. 3, d. 1, l. 54.

From the moment of its inception early Soviet musicology had been conditioned by a long pre-revolutionary positivist tradition. The state's emphasis on a scientifically-based social order was in agreement with the positivist understanding of science — and by extension scientifically-oriented humanities — as providing the means to a better way of life. Given their general conceptual similarities, some precepts of positivism (in its generalized and anonymized late nineteenth-century iteration) prepared musicologists to accept Soviet interpretations of Marxism as a promising new method which could be seamlessly connected with existing theoretical frameworks. Many musicologists readily accepted Marxist philosophy because it coincided with the academic ideals on which they had been raised. The ones who did not explicitly advocate Marxism nevertheless had deep respect for the sociological aspect in the study of art. Musicologists were proud to be a part of state institutions and eagerly worked on research tasks passed down from above.

When the research institutes came under attack for being not Marxist enough, the resulting shift did not represent a radically different paradigm supplanting an older one with which it was at odds. It is more likely that the intransigent rhetoric was a means to an end: removing the old guard from key positions in Soviet humanities, in the 'all-out struggle against bourgeois culture and its carriers'.

4

The Birth of the Soviet Romance from the Spirit of Russian Modernism

PHILIP ROSS BULLOCK

To describe an artistic genre is not just to propose an account of its principal formal features, but also to situate it within a particular linguistic or national culture. Equally, it is to invite a historical analysis of its evolution over time. It is for this reason that we talk about the English and Italian sonnet, just as we talk about the romantic elegy, the realist novel, the naturalist drama or the symbolist poem. It is this intersection of spatial and temporal elements — the definition of distinct national canons, as well as major artistic movements (although there is frequently an overlap between these two categories) — that means that the genres of works of art are as susceptible to ideological interpretation as their content. This is especially the case in Russian culture, where radical historical discontinuities — say, for instance, the processes of Europeanization initiated by Peter the Great, the reign of Nicholas I, the reforms of Alexander II, the revolutions of 1905 and 1917, the Stalin era, Khrushchev's 'Thaw' or the collapse of the Soviet Union — have radically shaped the ways in which narratives of artistic evolution have been constructed. At the same time, the fact that Russian society from the eighteenth century onwards has very often imported models of culture from the West has meant that translation, imitation, adaptation and eventually rivalry have become key metaphors when it comes to the discussion of the historical development of the Russian arts.[1]

In the case of music, it is the formation of a supposedly Russian canon that has tended to predominate in criticism, whether in the nineteenth century or in the Soviet period, and which has subsequently formed the basis of recent revisionist criticism seeking to expose the ideological presuppositions of nationalism itself.[2] By contrast, studies of genre per

---

[1] See, for instance, David Gasperetti, *The Rise of the Russian Novel: Carnivalization, Stylization, and Mockery of the West*, DeKalb, IL, 1998.

[2] See, most influentially, Richard Taruskin, *Defining Russia Musically: Historical and Hermeneutic Essays*, Princeton, NJ and Oxford, 1997. See also, Marina Frolova-Walker,

se have figured less prominently (which is not to say that genres have not been studied in terms of their historical situation, whether synchronically or diachronically).[3] Moreover, where they do exist, such studies often serve to reinscribe, rather than challenge conventional historical periodizations of Russian culture, as — with good reason — do important recent accounts of Russian music's intellectual and institutional contexts.[4] This issue is particularly acute when it comes to tracing the development of Russian music from the late nineteenth century through to the first decades of the twentieth, and especially across the seemingly decisive cultural break represented by the October Revolution of 1917. In the case of opera, for instance, the death of Nikolai Rimskii-Korsakov in 1908 seems to mark a terminal point in the evolution of a genre that would be reborn only in the works of Dmitrii Shostakovich some two decades later, firstly in *Nos* (*The Nose*, 1927–28), and then, most importantly, in *Ledi Makbet Mtsenskogo uezda* (*Lady Macbeth of the Mtsensk District*, 1930–32).[5] The emigration of major early twentieth-century composers such as Sergei Rakhmaninov and Aleksandr Glazunov similarly promotes the perception of discontinuity as a key feature of the historical development of the symphony. Although the career of Nikolai Miaskovskii suggests one way in which the symphony did indeed survive in Russian culture from the early twentieth century onwards, and the premiere of his Sixth Symphony in 1924 was a major event in early Soviet musical life, it is instead the premiere of Shostakovich's first essay in the form in 1926 that seems to mark its rebirth in its new, Soviet incarnation. When it comes to chamber music, and in particular the string quartet, the relative paucity of canonical examples from the nineteenth century, and the prominent repositioning of the genre as part of Socialist Realism's emphasis on learning from the classics,[6] means that important

---

Russian Music and Nationalism: From Glinka to Stalin, New Haven, CT and London, 2007, and Rutger Helmers, *Not Russian Enough? Nationalism and Cosmopolitanism in Nineteenth-Century Russian Opera*, Rochester, NY, 2014.

[3] See, for instance, Richard Taruskin, *Opera and Drama in Russia as Preached and Practiced in the 1860s*, Ann Arbor, MI, 1981.

[4] Examples here include Rebecca Mitchell, *Nietzsche's Orphans: Music, Metaphysics, and the Twilight of the Russian Empire*, New Haven, CT and London, 2015, and Amy Nelson, *Music for the Revolution: Musicians and Power in Early Soviet Russia*, University Park, PA, 2004.

[5] For treatments of opera which do reach across the revolutionary divide, see Simon Morrison, *Russian Opera and the Symbolist Movement*, Berkeley, CA and London, 2002, and Tatyana Sirotina, 'Russian Opera (1901–1936): Musical Experiments and Paths of Development', unpublished PhD dissertation, University of Manchester, 2007.

[6] Katerina Clark, 'Shostakovich's Turn to the String Quartet and the Debate about Socialist Realism in Music', *Slavic Review*, 72, 2013, 3, pp. 573–89.

historical continuities (as in the case of Misakovskii's quartets of the early 1930s) are effaced in favour of a narrative that foregrounds moments of rupture.[7]

In the case of art-song, it might appear at first glance that its history is also one decisively split across the revolutionary divide. As a genre associated with both the polite space of the bourgeois salon and Russia's tradition of lyric poetry, it seems an unlikely genre to have flourished in the revolutionary, collective atmosphere of the 1920s, let alone one that might embody continuities with turn-of-the-century modernism. Such indeed is the impression given by Soviet-era criticism, and this article will begin by surveying influential historical introductions to the genre from this period in order to show how they have promoted a clear-cut distinction between song's pre- and post-revolutionary incarnations. It will then go on to argue that such an interpretation overlooks the very substantial continuities that characterized the development of art-song as a genre, whether traced through the careers of individual composers, the reception of modernist poetry in music or the history of the song recital as a form of social practice. In particular, poetry proves to be a productive way of assessing elements of continuity and change in the art-song repertoire, precisely because it establishes a palimpsestic link between the literary culture of one era and the musical culture of another.[8] The perception of significant continuities between Russian art-song of the turn of the twentieth century and developments in the early Soviet period rests, moreover, not just on historical hindsight, but also on the evidence of contemporary documents and criticism. The decisive break in the evolution of Russian art-song in the early decades of the twentieth century came, it will be argued, not in 1917, but during the final years of the 1920s, when Stalin's first Five-Year Plan was accompanied by a 'cultural' revolution that was directed against artistic modernism and such remnants of the culture of the past as had

---

[7] Of the many pressing issues in the historiography of twentieth-century Russian music, a reassessment of the importance of Miaskovskii, both as a creative artist and as a key figure within Soviet music is one of the most urgent. See, in this respect, Patrick Zuk, 'Nikolay Myaskovsky and the Events of 1948', *Music and Letters*, 93, 2012, 1, pp. 61–85, and 'Myaskovsky and the "Regimentation" of Soviet Composition', *Journal of Musicology*, 31 2014, 3, pp. 354–93.

[8] Although beyond the scope of the present article, Russian art-song in the wake of Rakhmaninov is of considerable interest from the point of view of its musical means and offers case studies as varied and inventive as their composers' taste in poetry, as witnessed by, say, the terse, almost expressionistic musical language of Miaskovskii's songs, particularly his settings of Gippius, and the lush expressivity of Aleksandrov's Kuzmin songs.

survived and even flourished in the years immediately after the October Revolution.⁹

*   *   *

Written by the leading Soviet scholar of the genre, Vera Vasina-Grossman, the two most influential monographic treatments of Russian romance in the nineteenth and twentieth centuries respectively entrench a seemingly categorical divide between the classical and Soviet repertoires and deny the profound continuities that existed between them. In *Russkii klassicheskii romans XIX veka* (The Nineteenth-Century Russian Classical Romance, 1956), for instance, Vasina-Grossman traces the evolution of art-song in Russia from the dilettante salon romances of the early nineteenth century to the late works of Chaikovskii and Rimskii-Korsakov, with which, she argues, 'the great period of the development of the Russian classical art-song [*romans*] closes in on itself'.¹⁰ The reason behind such a categorical claim is simple enough: Russian modernism proves to be too great a stumbling-block to an understanding of developments around the turn of the century. For Vasina-Grossman, modernism is indicative of a stylized and over-aestheticized attitude to form, an imitative attitude to Western European influences (she cites Hugo Wolf and Claude Debussy in particular), a failure to draw organically on the roots of folk culture, an unnatural treatment of human speech and a withdrawal by composers into the world of elite cliques.¹¹

Nonetheless, some song composers are recognized by Vasina-Grossman, principally on account of their supposed 'realism': here, she cites Sergei Taneev, Anton Arenskii, Feliks Blumfel'd, Reingol'd Glier, and — most importantly — Sergei Rakhmaninov, whose music had been comprehensively rehabilitated in the Soviet Union by this point, despite his emigration in 1917.¹² In the case of Rakhmaninov's songs, this process was relatively straightforward, given that all of them were written before

---

⁹ On the late 1920s and early 1930s, see Sheila Fitzpatrick (ed.), *Cultural Revolution in Russia, 1928–31*, Bloomington, IN, 1978, and *The Cultural Front: Power and Culture in Revolutionary Russia*, Ithaca, NY and London, 1992. For a study of Russian and early Soviet piano music that traces a similar trajectory, not least because of the prevailing influence of the music of Skriabin on several generations of composers, see Peter Deane Roberts, *Modernism in Russian Piano Music: Skriabin, Prokofiev, and their Russian Contemporaries*, 2 vols, Bloomington, IN, 1993.
¹⁰ V. A. Vasina-Grossman, *Russkii klassicheskii romans XIX veka*, Moscow, 1956, p. 299.
¹¹ Ibid., p. 300.
¹² Ibid., p. 304.

1916 and hence could be reincorporated into an overarching narrative of Russian music that avoided the question of works composed outside the Soviet Union after the October Revolution. For Vasina-Grossman, Rakhmaninov's songs conform to the classical tradition inasmuch as they retain links to folksong, continue to prioritize accessible melody, employ some of the characteristic genres that had developed during the nineteenth century (the elegy, the oriental song and various dance forms) and enjoyed great popularity with a wide range of audiences.[13] The most significant reason for her approval, however, is their seeming resistance to the kind of innovative trends that were otherwise typical of the early twentieth century: 'considering Rakhmaninov's vocal works as a whole, we must admit that they are essentially directed against modernism.'[14] Vasina-Grossman even downplays the experimental qualities of his final set of songs, the *Shest' stikhotvorenii* (Six Poems), op. 38 (1916). Settings texts by leading symbolist poets (Aleksandr Blok, Andrei Belyi, Igor' Severianin, Valerii Briusov, Fedor Sologub and Konstantin Bal'mont) that had been selected for the composer by Marietta Shaginian, and exploring a rather more complex and adventurous musical language than his earlier songs, the cycle is interpreted by Vasina-Grossman as 'both a fascination with modernism, and an internal attempt at overcoming this fascination'.[15]

The ideological contexts that shaped *Russkii klassicheskii romans XIX veka* meant that it was never likely to respond positively to musical or literary modernism; published in 1956, it betrays the evident influence of Stalinist attitudes. By the time Vasina-Grossman came to publish her study of the Soviet art-song tradition, however, attitudes to modernism had changed considerably:

> Fifteen to twenty years ago all varieties of Russian modernism struck us as almost identical, we clearly saw how alien they were, and at times even how dangerous they were in respect of the progressive ideological movements of the age. We saw their retrospectivism, their subjectivism — all the ills of the Russian intelligentsia that were characteristic of the pre-revolutionary era.
>
> But now, as well as this, something else has become clear: that within modernism a battle raged, that its best and most talented representatives

---

[13] Ibid., pp. 305–06.
[14] Ibid., p. 318.
[15] Ibid., p. 336. For an account of the genesis of the cycle, see Richard D. Sylvester, *Rachmaninoff's Complete Songs: A Companion with Texts and Translations*, Bloomington and Indianapolis, IN, 2014, pp. 234–56. See also, Marietta Shaginian, 'Vospominaniia o Sergee Vasil'eviche Rakhmaninove', in *Sobranie sochinenii*, 9 vols, Moscow, 1971–75, 9, pp. 363–436.

clearly sensed the hopelessness [*ushcherbnost'*] of their social and artistic position, something which allowed both Aleksandr Blok and Valerii Briusov to take up such prominent positions within Soviet poetry.[16]

This highly contingent view of modernism shapes Vasina-Grossman's *Mastera sovetskogo romansa* (Masters of the Soviet Romance, 1968, revised edition 1980) profoundly. Avoiding 1917 as a moment of decisive rupture, she argues instead that 'the history of the Soviet art-song begins more or less in the middle of the 1920s. Most of the romances which appeared in the first years after October seem to be a strange anachronism: both their choice of texts and the manner of their musical embodiment are completely the same as before the Revolution'.[17] Faced with the very substantial continuities that characterized the development of art-song in Russia around 1917, she simply ignores the early Soviet repertoire as little more than a historical and ideological anachronism, proposing instead a decisive break somewhere in the mid-1920s, after which a thorough-going Sovietization of the repertoire could take place.

The impact of modernist poetry on a number of early-Soviet song composers, as well as the organic links between aspects of the pre- and post-1917 song repertoire, mean that Vasina-Grossman at least acknowledges the historical significance of a number of works from the early 1920s. Her acceptance proves, however, to be limited and tendentious. Writing of Anatolii Aleksandrov's settings of the poetry of Mikhail Kuzmin, for instance, Vasina-Grossman claims that the composer overlooked the most important developments in Soviet poetry (here, she names Vladimir Maiakovskii and Sergei Esenin, Nikolai Aseev and Dem'ian Bednyi, Eduard Bagritskii and Boris Pasternak, Nikolai Tikhonov and Il'ia Sel'vinskii), suggesting that 'the inertia of the pre-revolutionary era was too strong and revealed itself, of course, in the durability not just of poetic tastes, but also in musical language'.[18] In fact, it was very often a composer's choice of poet that was used to characterize his relationship to modernism. In the case of Nikolai Miaskovskii, for instance, Vasina-Grossman expresses a strong preference for his settings of classical poetry, even whilst cataloguing his considerable investment in modernist poetry and asking, in particular, 'what, in the 1900s, was Miaskovskii searching for in the poems of Zinaida Gippius, a mannered and pretentious, albeit talented

---

[16] V. A. Vasina-Grossman, *Mastera sovetskogo romansa*, Moscow, 1968; 2nd edn 1980, p. 102 (here and subsequently, all references will be to the revised, second edition).
[17] Ibid., p. 11.
[18] Ibid., p. 107.

poetess, and the host of a literary salon that was at the heart of Russian decadence?'.[19] As well as many songs to texts by Gippius, Vasina-Grossman notes Miaskovskii's broader interest in symbolist verse (Bal'mont and Viacheslav Ivanov especially), yet it is his settings of the early nineteenth-century poet Evgenii Baratynskii that draw both her greatest approval and most detailed commentary: 'if we turn to the songs of op. 1 (the cycle *Razmyshleniia* [Meditations] to texts by Evgenii Baratynskii, 1907), then we will sense in them above all a vital continuity with the best and most noble traditions of the Russian romance, traditions which are understood not in the spirit of learning, but of creativity.'[20] The key phrase here is 'vital continuity' (*zhivaia preemstvennost'*). A central task of Soviet criticism, especially after the establishment of Socialist Realism with its emphasis on learning from the classics of nineteenth-century realism, was to distinguish between productive and acceptable forms of continuity with the past, and those aspects of Russian culture whose importance had to be downplayed or denied altogether.[21] In a literal sense, there can be no continuity between Miaskovskii's settings of Baratynskii, whose musical language is described by Vasina-Grossman as 'restrained, simple, classically poised',[22] and the heritage of the nineteenth-century Russian art-song. There can, of course, be a dialogue, but Vasina-Grossman's purpose is not to propose an intertextual reading of Russian music across the generations (unlike, say, the Russian Formalists, whose experiments in literary history explicitly foregrounded the evolution of both genre and tradition through a series of non-consecutive 'knight's moves', generational leaps and intergenerational struggles). Rather, she seeks to institute a clear and coherent narrative of the development of the art-song as a genre that effaces the modernist tradition, or at least relegates it to a marginal place in that narrative.

Few of Vasina-Grossman's claims should surprise, given the context in which they were produced. Nonetheless, they are worth reviewing in some detail because they are indicative of broader trends in Soviet music

---

[19] Ibid., p. 43.
[20] Ibid., p. 35.
[21] See, for instance, Marina Raku, *Muzykal'naia klassika v mifotvorchestve sovetskoi epokhi*, Moscow, 2014, and Pauline Fairclough, *Classics for the Masses: Shaping Soviet Musical Identity Under Lenin and Stalin*, New Haven, CT and London, 2016. A return to the classics was not limited to official culture at this time, even if it was partly dictated by political factors. For a study that explores how a series of writers — Iurii Tynianov, Vladislav Khodasevich and Mikhail Bulgakov — appropriated the legacy of Pushkin in their own writing, see Angela Brintlinger, *Writing a Usable Past: Russian Literary Culture 1917–1937*, Evanston, IL, 2000.
[22] Vasina-Grossman, *Mastera sovetskogo romansa*, p. 37.

historiography. Take, for instance, Galina Soboleva's two short, popular histories written for mass audiences in the 1980s: *Russian romans* (The Russian Art-Song, 1980) and *Russkii sovetskii romans* (The Soviet Russian Art-Song, 1985). Following Vasina-Grossman's lead, she divides song into a classical and a Soviet period and sees the turn of the twentieth century as a period of decline, followed by a renaissance from the mid-1920s onward.[23] This emphasis on two distinct traditions was characteristic of earlier scholarship too. Indeed, in the work of Boris Asaf'ev, the Russian romance tradition appeared to belong entirely to the past. In the chapter devoted to art-song in his *Russkaia muzyka ot nachala XIX stoletiia* (1930, translated into English in 1953 by Alfred J. Swan as *Russian Music from the Beginning of the Nineteenth Century*), Asaf'ev argued that the Revolution demanded a new type of lyricism ('here there is no longer any room for the romance') and suggested that composers risked isolating themselves from new audiences ('as individualistic lyricism moves away from the street and settles, behind thick walls and heavy curtains, into the quiet of lonely contemplation, the rift between artistic creation and the tastes of the majority of listeners, becomes more dangerous').[24] Similarly, the essays included in Asaf'ev's edited collection, *Russkii romans: opyt intonatsionnogo analiza* (The Russian Art-Song: An Attempt at an Intonational Analysis, 1930) dealt entirely with the nineteenth-century repertoire (Glinka, Dargomyzhskii, Balakirev, Borodin, Musorgskii and Rimskii-Korsakov), as did his own introduction ('Vazhneishie etapy razvitiia russkogo romansa' ['The most important phases in the development of the Russian art-song']).[25] Earlier in his career, Asaf'ev had showed greater interest in the modern development of Russian song, publishing — under the pseudonym of Igor' Glebov — a short pamphlet on Taneev, as well as two editions of a bibliography of poems set to music by Russian composers that included many works dating from the immediate pre- and post-revolutionary periods.[26] Nonetheless, it is clear that by the 1930s his attitude had become less inclusive and hence

---

[23] G. Soboleva, *Russkii romans*, Moscow, 1980, and *Russkii sovetskii romans*, Moscow, 1985. See, also, V. Muzakelevskii, *Sovremennaia tema v russkom sovetskom romanse*, Leningrad, 1964, for an attempt to connect the social engagement of the contemporary Soviet romance with the nineteenth-century tradition, bypassing turn-of-the-century modernism almost entirely.

[24] Boris Asaf'ev, *Russian Music from the Beginning of the Nineteenth Century*, trans. Alfred J. Swan, Ann Arbor, MI, 1953, pp. 89–90.

[25] B. V. Asaf'ev (ed.), *Russkii romans: opyt intonatsionnogo analiza*, Moscow and Leningrad, 1930.

[26] Igor' Glebov, *Romansy S. I. Taneeva*, Petrograd, 1916, and *Russkaia poeziia v russkoi muzyki*, Petersburg, 1921; Petrograd, 1922.

more indicative of mainstream Soviet attitudes when it came both to the legacy of turn-of-the-century modernism and its relationship with Soviet culture in the Stalin era.

A similar picture obtains when it comes to the main literary bibliographies of Russian song, explicitly so in the case of G. K. Ivanov's *Russkaia poeziia v otechestvennoi muzyke (do 1917 goda)* (Russian Poetry in Russian Music [up to 1917]), and also in the various *Biblioteka poeta* anthologies of Russian song texts that appeared in 1936, 1950, 1957, 1965 and 1988.[27] Despite changing attitudes to the literary canon over the Soviet period, such publications reinforce a history of Russian song that had implicitly come to its conclusion in the late nineteenth century, and certainly by the time of the October Revolution. To be sure, there have been some subsequent attempts at correcting and complementing the picture, including bibliographies of settings of the poetry of Akhmatova, Tsvetaeva, Mandel´shtam, Pasternak and even Ivanov, as well as revisionist studies of forgotten or neglected composers.[28] Yet the accumulated legacy of Soviet-era criticism continues to make itself felt in concert programmes, recordings and even scholarship, where the main focus remains on the nineteenth-century tradition, with a smaller body of work considering the Soviet period, yet relatively little attention is given to the extensive and organic connections that linked the two. In the West in particular, overwhelming interest in the life and works of Dmitrii Shostakovich has tended to shape assumptions about Soviet cultural politics in a way that continues to exclude alternative narratives and experiences, and although song came to constitute a very profound means of artistic expression in his later years, his career promotes a deceptive account of the genre's evolution, especially in the early Soviet period.

---

[27] G. K. Ivanov (ed.), *Russkaia poeziia v otechestvennoi muzyke (do 1917 goda)*, 2 vols, Moscow, 1966–69. The major anthologies of Russian song texts included in the *Biblioteka poeta* series are I. N. Rozanov (ed.), *Pesni russkikh poetov (XVIII–pervaia polovina XIX veka)*, Leningrad, 1936, *Pesni russkikh poetov*, 2nd edn, Leningrad, 1950, and *Pesni russkikh poetov*, 3rd edn, Leningrad, 1957; and V. E. Gusev (ed.), *Pesni i romansy russkikh poetov*, 2nd edn, Moscow and Leningrad, 1965, and *Pesni russkikh poetov*, 3rd edn, 2 vols, Leningrad, 1988.

[28] Bibliographies of modernist poetry set to music include Boris Rosenfel´d (ed.), *Anna Akhmatova, Marina Tsvetaeva, Osip Mandel´shtam i Boris Pasternak v muzyke: notografiia*, Stanford, CA, 2003; Pavel Nerler and Aleksandr Dunaevskii, 'Notografiia: muzykal´nye sochineniia na stikhi Osipa Mandel´shtama', *Sem´ iskusstv*, 1 (2016), and P. V. Dmitriev (ed.), *Poeziia Viacheslava Ivanova v russkoi muzyke: notograficheskii spravochnik prizhiznennykh publikatsii, 1913–48*, St Petersburg, 2013. Surveys of song in this period include T. Levaia, 'Poeziia simvolizma v romansovoi lirike', in *Russkaia muzyka nachala XX veka v khudozhestvennom kontekste epokhi*, Moscow, 1991, pp. 41–56 and Konstantin Pluzhnikov, *Zabytye stranitsy russkogo romansa*, St Petersburg, 2004.

THE BIRTH OF THE SOVIET ROMANCE

*   *   *

A preliminary step in reconstituting the modernist history of art-song both before and after 1917 must be to reconsider and even reorder the perceived hierarchy of composers' reputations, where both the biographies and lyric output of Rakhmaninov, Prokof'ev and Stravinskii have tended to give a misleading impression of the development of genre. Rakhmaninov wrote his last songs in 1916; emigration, with its attendant loss of attachment to both nation and language, constituted a terminal point in his interest in lyric forms. Prokof'ev's early output included three groups of songs (opp. 9, 23 and 27) and his miniature *scena*, *Gadkii utenok* (The Ugly Duckling, op. 18), all written between 1910 and 1916, as well as two sets of songs (opp. 35 and 36) that date from 1920 and 1921 (the first a set of five wordless vocalises that were later transcribed for violin and piano, the second a series of five settings of Bal'mont, written when composer and poet were neighbours in France). Thereafter, Prokof'ev would not revisit song until after his return to the Soviet Union, when he produced works far closer in aesthetic to Soviet norms (mass songs, folksongs and settings of Pushkin written just before the centenary of the poet's death in 1937).[29] In the case of Stravinskii, song occupied a relatively marginal place in his Russian period, and even before his emigration, his 'rejoicing discovery' of the irregularities of Russian folk prosody meant that he had abandoned the principles of text-setting that had been central to the Russian art-song tradition throughout the nineteenth and early twentieth centuries.[30] If this list is widened to include Nikolai Metner (who was certainly highly regarded by Rakhmaninov at least), then the picture may need to be modified slightly. Before 1917, Metner had set a substantial number of poems by Pushkin, Tiutchev and Fet, as well as a very large corpus of texts by Goethe, Heine and Nietzsche. This pattern continued after he moved to Western Europe in 1921, and suggests that despite Metner's geographical

---

[29] For a survey of these works, see N. Rogozhina, *Romansy i pesni S. S. Prokof'eva*, Moscow, 1971, and Philip Ross Bullock, 'The Songs of Sergei Prokofiev: Texts and Contexts, Imitations and Interrogations', *Three Oranges*, 11, 2006, pp. 17–22. On the Soviet period in particular, see Eugenia E. Joukova, 'The Songs and Song Cycles of Sergei Prokofiev (1930–1950)', unpublished PhD thesis, University of Illinois at Urbana-Champaign, 2007.

[30] Richard Taruskin, 'Stravinsky's "Rejoicing Discovery": In Defense of His Notorious Text-Setting', in Ethan Haimo and Paul Johnson (eds), *Stravinsky Retrospectives*, Lincoln, NE, 1987, pp. 162–99. For a pithy overview of Stravinskii's songs, see Richard Taruskin, 'In Stravinsky's Songs, the True Man, No Ghostwriters', in *Russian Music at Home and Abroad*, Berkeley and Los Angeles, CA and London, 2016, pp. 503–07.

displacement from his homeland, Russian songs could represent a kind of nostalgic affinity with the culture of the past. What links all these composers is, of course, their status as émigrés. In particular, their prominence in the critical literature suggests that, when it comes to song at least, the distinction between Soviet and émigré maps onto a broader set of discontinuities, whether between pre- and post-revolutionary periods, the between the aesthetics of modernism and (eventually) Socialist Realism, and even between word and music itself (at least in the case of Stravinskii). In each case, 1917 functions as a metonymic representation of a creative hiatus within the evolution of song as an artistic genre.

Yet such an account pays excessive attention to composers whose works give a potentially misleading impression of the development of song as a genre. In particular, it effaces substantial continuities in both the composition and performance of song across the revolutionary divide, and which can be traced by examining other composers' contribution to the Russian song tradition and how this was represented in the critical literature of the time. Here, three composers — Mikhail Gnesin (1883–1957), Nikolai Miaskovskii (1881–1950) and Anatolii Aleksandrov (1888–1982) — stand out as being in need of substantial reconsideration, both when it comes to the evolution of early Soviet culture out of elements of turn-of-the-century modernism, and for their particular exploration of the possibilities of art-song. Between them, they represent both the Moscow and the St Petersburg schools of compositions (Aleksandrov trained at the Moscow Conservatoire, Miaskovskii and Gnesin at the St Petersburg, although Miaskovskii also had private lessons with Glier in Moscow). Most crucially, they all illustrate the close relationship between musical and literary modernism in the first decades of the twentieth century.

One of the leading composers of song in the early twentieth century and a key figure in the musical reception of modernist verse was Mikhail Gnesin, whose four book of songs entitled *Iz sovremmennoi poezii* (From Cntemporary Poetry), op. 2 (1907), op. 5 (1908–09) op. 16 (1915) and op. 22 (1915–16) set verses by Vol′kenstein, Bal′mont, Sologub, Blok, Ivanov and Akhmatova. Other major vocal works from this period include *Posviashcheniia* (Dedications), op. 10 (1912–14), to texts by Ivanov, Bal′mont and Sologub, *Rosarium*, op. 15 (1914), to texts by Ivanov, and *Iz Shelli* (From Shelley), op. 18 (1915), based on translations by Bal′mont. Gnesin's engagement with Russian modernism expressed itself not just in his musical responses to symbolist poetry; he also collaborated closely with Vsevolod Meierkhol′d, using musical notation as a means of transcribing the rise, fall and rhythm of theatrical declamation.[31] After 1917, however, Gnesin's interest in modernist verse waned, and he turned instead to a series of settings of Jewish poetry — his *Stranitsy iz 'Pesni pesnei'* (Pages from the 'Song of Songs'), op. 33 (1926), and the *Evreiskie pesni* (Jewish Songs), op. 37 (1927).[32] Gnesin's later works have tended to efface the importance of his contribution to modernist art-song. Nonetheless, a number of these works were republished in the early Soviet period, as attested both by the holdings of libraries in Moscow and St Petersburg, and by lists of scores issued by the music branch of the Soviet state publishing house and advertised on the back pages of editions of his Jewish songs, opp. 33 and 37. Indeed, Gnesin's turn to Jewish music did not put a stop to his interest in literary modernism entirely; in 1927, his setting of Sof´ia Parnok's *Saficheskie strophy* (Sapphics), op. 26, was published in Moscow, part of the rather surprising endurance of Sappho's poetry in early Soviet song.

Gnesin's songs to symbolist texts all date from before 1917, and were an important factor in creating the preconditions for other composers' engagement with modernist poetry well into the 1920s. Similarly, Miaskovskii devoted himself extensively to symbolist poetry before 1917; unlike Gnesin, however, he continued to set modernist texts well into

---

[31] M. F. G., 'Obraztsy ritmicheskoi interpretatsii stikha u russkikh kompozitorov', *Liubov´ k trem apel´sinam*, 1914, 1, pp. 48–51. Brief accounts of Gnesin's lectures on 'musical reading in drama' were published in *Liubov´ k trem apel´sinam*, 1914, 1, p. 60, and 2, 1914, pp. 60–61. See, also, S. Bondi, 'O "muzykal´nom chtenii" M. F. Gnesina', in M. F. Gnesin, *Stat´i, vospominaniia, materialy*, ed. R. V. Glezer, Moscow, 1961, pp. 80–101.

[32] Gnesin was not alone in moving away from literary and musical modernism towards an interest in Jewish national music. See, for instance, Leonid Sabaneev, *Aleksandr Abramovich Krein* (Moscow, 1928), which traces Krein's early interest in leading modernist poets such as Blok, as well as his subsequent interest in Jewish texts. See also, Sabaneev, *Evreiskaia national´naia shkola v muzyke* (Moscow, 1924). An interest in modernist poetry was not necessarily incompatible with a commitment to Jewish cultural politics, and one cannot assume that a turn to Jewish nationalism was a direct corollary of Soviet nationalism. For an overview of Gnesin's career which highlights his pre-revolutionary interest in Zionism — 'another messianic dream' to match his interest in the Revolution — see James Loeffler, *The Most Musical Nation: Jews and Culture in the Late Russian Empire*, New Haven, CT and London, 2010, pp. 202–09. Gnesin also makes a number of appearances in Klára Móricz's study of the activities of the Obshchestvo evreiskoi narodnoi muzyki (Society for Jewish Folk Music), founded in St Petersburg in 1908 and reorganized after 1917 as the Obshchestvo evreiskoi muzyki (Society for Jewish Music). Significantly, part of the work of the society involved creating a 'classical' art-song repertoire out of a song culture that had largely been a folkloric one up to that point, even if doing so was achieved by taking the stock formulae of Russian musical orientalism and applying them to Jewish works. See Klárá Móricz, 'Jewish Nationalism à la Russe: The Society for Jewish Folk Music', in *Jewish Identities: Nationalism, Racism, and Utopianism in Twentieth-Century Music*, Berkeley and Los Angeles, CA and London, 2008, pp. 11–91.

the 1920s. Moreover, many of these works continued to be republished well into the Soviet period and constitute one of the seeming continuities between the pre- and post-1917 contexts, and even into the Stalin period. Tracing the history and evolution of Miaskovskii's songs is not always easy, however, given his habit of revising his earlier works and often republishing them with different titles and different opus numbers. There are settings of Bal'mont — most notably the cycle *Madrigal* (written 1908–09, first published in Vienna in 1925 and in Moscow in 1945), but also the twelve songs of *Iz iunesheskikh let* (From the Days of Youth) that were written between 1903 and 1906, collated in 1945 and partially published only in 1956.[33] Miaskovskii's *Tri nabroski* (*Three Sketches*, eventually numbered as op. 8) are settings of Ivanov that date from 1908 which were first published in Berlin in 1913 and reissued in Moscow in 1945. There are also settings of Baratynskii (*Razmyshleniia* [Meditations], op. 1, written 1907, published 1922, 1926 and 1944), Blok (*Shest' stikhotvorenii* [Six poems], op. 20, written 1921, published 1922), Tiutchev (*Na sklone dnia* [At the Close of Day], op. 21, written 1922, published 1923 and 1944) and Del'vig (*Venok poblekshii* [A Faded Garland], op. 22, written 1925, published 1926).[34]

It is, though, Miaskovskii's twenty-three settings of the poetry of Zinaida Gippius that constitute his most sustained and extensive engagement with modernist poetry and which illustrate the prominent role played by symbolist verse in both pre- and post-revolutionary musical culture (even when Gippius herself had gone into emigration and positioned herself as one of the most virulent critics of Soviet rule). The songs were published in various groups from 1906 onwards:

6 *stikhotvorenii Z. Gippius* (6 Poems of Zinaida Gippius), St Petersburg, 1906

Iz Z. Gippius: Tri p'esy dlia odnogo golosa i f-p. (From Z. Gippius: Three pieces for solo voice and piano), Berlin, Moscow and St Petersburg, 1913

Iz Z. Gippius: Dve p'esy dlia peniia i fortepiano (From Z. Gippius: Two pieces for voice and piano), Moscow and Leipzig (n.y.)

---

[33] The publication of *Madrigal* in Vienna forms of the collaboration between leading Soviet composers of the 1920s and early 1930s and the Viennese published, Universal Edition, which has been studied in detail in Olesia Bobrik, *Venskoe izdatel'stvo 'Universal Edition' i muzykanty iz sovetskoi Rossii: istoriia sotrudnichestva v 1920–30-e gody*, St Petersburg, 2011.

[34] Publication details compiled on the basis of Russian library holdings and on N. Miaskovskii, *Izbrannye proizvedeniia*, ed. R. Glier et al., 12 vols, Moscow, 1953–56, 11: *Vokal'nye proizvedeniia*.

THE BIRTH OF THE SOVIET ROMANCE

Iz Z. Gippius: Vosem' nabroskov dlia peniia i fortepiano (From Z. Gippius: Eight sketches for voice and piano), Moscow, 1917

Iz Z. Gippius: Vosem' nabroskov dlia peniia i fortepiano (From Z. Gippius: Eight sketches for voice and piano), Moscow, 1921

Na grani: Deviat' p'es 'Iz Z. N. Gippius' dlia golosa i fortepiano (po starym eskizam) (On the Border: Nine Pieces 'From Z. N. Gippius' for voice and piano [based on old sketches]), Moscow and Petrograd, 1922

Predchuvstvie: Shest' nabroskov dlia peniia i f-p (Premonition: Six sketches for voice and piano), Vienna and Leipzig, 1927

Iz Z. Gippius: Tri p'esy dlia odnogo golosa s f-p (From Z. Gippius: Three pieces for solo voice and piano), Moscow, 1946

These sets of songs are, though, not discrete cycles; rather, their contents often overlap, as Miaskovskii recast (and sometimes revised) them for various publications (see table 1). In terms of their publication history, Miaskovskii's settings of Gippius extend across more than two decades, between 1906 and 1927, and some of them even made a brief reappearance in the mid-1940s.[35] They form one of the most visible instances of how songs written and in some instances published before 1917 continued to circulate into the 1920s, illustrating the evolution of art-song as a genre across the revolutionary divide. However, the legacy of Miaskovskii's early songs was partially eclipsed, whether by his later settings of Lermontov (1935–36, published 1937), Shchipachev (1940, published 1941) and Burns (1946, published 1947), or his reputation as a leading Soviet symphonist. Nonetheless, it is clear that they retained a sufficiently prominent place in cultural memory to have been adduced as supposed proof of the composer's lifelong decadence by Tikhon Khrennikov at the First Congress of Soviet Composers in 1948.[36]

---

[35] These, along with other works by Miaskovskii, were published by Muzfond, and may possibly reflect a decision by the Composers' Union to use its financial resources to support the composer. The relative autonomy of Muzfond at this time has been adduced as one of the major reasons behind the attacks on Shostakovich, Miaskovskii, Prokof'ev and other leadings composers in 1948, when the Union was brought more decisively under centralized control. See Kirill Tomoff, *Creative Union: The Professional Organization of Soviet Composers, 1939–1953*, Ithaca, NY and London, 2006.

[36] 'Doklad general'nogo sekretaria soiuza sovetskikh kompozitorov T. Khrennikova', in M. Koval' et al. (eds), *Pervyi vsesoiuznyi s'ezd sovetskikh kompozitorov: stenograficheskii otchet*, Moscow, 1948, pp. 26–27, cited in Patrik [i.e. Patrick] Zuk, 'Romansy N. Miaskovskogo na slova Z. Gippius', in N. Deriareva and N. Braginskaia (eds), *Sankt-Peterburgskaia konservatoriia v mirovom muzykal'nom prostranstve: kompozitorskie, ispolnitel'skie, nauchnie shkoly 1862–2012*, St Petersburg, 2013, pp. 218–23 (p. 223). Writing of Miaskovskii's Lermontov settings in 1938, Vasina-Grossman welcomed them as a departure from the heightened declamatory style of the early Gippius songs and a turn

Table 1: Miaskovskii's settings of the poetry of Zinaida Gippius

	1906	1913	n.y.	1917	1921	1922	1927	1946
'P′iavki' ('Leeches')	x					x		
'Nichego' ('There is nothing')	x					x		
'V gostinoi' ('In the drawing room')	x			x	x			
'Serenada' ('Serenade')	x							
'Pauki' ('Spiders')	x					x		
'Nadpis′ na knige' ('An inscription in a book')	x					x		
'Protivorechiia' ('Contradictions')		x						x
'Odnoobrazie' ('Monotony')		x						x
'Krugi' ('Circles')		x						x
'Luna i tuman' ('Moon and fog')			x					
'Krov′' ('Blood')			x					
'Neskorbnomu uchiteliu' ('To a carefree teacher')				x				
'Dar' ('The gift')				x	x		x	
'Bol′' ('Pain')				x	x		x	
'Tak-li' ('Like so?')				x	x		x	
'Zaklinanie' ('Incantation')				x	x		x	
'Vnezapno…' ('Suddenly…')				x	x		x	
'Petukhi' ('Cocks')				x	x		x	
'Strany unyn′ia' ('Lands of melancholy')						x		
'Nadpis′ na konverte' ('Inscription on an envelope')						x		
'Tsvety nochi' ('Night flowers')						x		
'Mgnovenie' ('A moment')						x		
'Pyl′' ('Dust')						x		

Noted in particular for his music for solo piano (including fourteen sonatas and a substantial body of smaller works), as well as for various chamber ensembles (most notably four string quartets), Anatolii Aleksandrov was equally renowned as a composer of songs. The substantial (although still incomplete) four-volume edition of his songs that was published in the early 1970s contains a total of 119 works written between 1912 and 1968.[37] As far as his choice of poetry is concerned, from the 1930s onwards Aleksandrov set a large number of texts by contemporary Soviet poets (Stepan Shchipachev, Samuil Marshak, Sergei Severtsev and Margarita Aliger), as well as exploring aspects of the nineteenth-century classical tradition (Baratynskii, Pushkin, Fet and Tiutchev). His songs also illustrate a sustained interest in foreign poetry in Russian translation. If his three settings of the Georgian romantic poet Nikoloz Baratashvili in versions by Pasternak look like an attempt to appeal to Stalin (whilst also reflecting the fact that many leading poets had taken refuge in translation at this time), then other works are more evidently indicative of his cosmopolitan literary tastes, as well as of the prominence of translation in the Russian literary tradition. There are, for instance, songs to texts by modern French poets such as Remy de Gourmont, Emile Verhaeren and Paul Verlaine, settings of the renaissance poet, Pierre de Ronsard, and an early group of three songs to verses by the Persian poet Hafiz in translations by Fet.

Aleksandrov's Hafiz songs reveal a significant feature about the survival and subsequent development of Russian song across the revolutionary divide. Originally written in 1912, they were first published by Gutheil in 1917, before eventually being reissued in 1926. Similarly, his settings of Gourmont were written in 1915, but still available in a publication dating from 1926 — striking evidence of how the pre-revolutionary repertoire continued to exert an influence on the development of the genre after 1917.[38] It is, though, Aleksandrov's settings of Russian modernist verse that most clearly reveal the vitality of song as an early Soviet genre with organic roots in artistic culture of the late imperial era. Dating from 1915,

---

towards a more relaxed form of vocal style. See V. Grossman, 'Lermontovskie romansy N. Ia. Miaskovskogo', *Sovetskoe iskusstvo*, 2 October 1938, reprinted in N. Ia. Miaskovskii, *Sobranie materialov*, 2nd edn, 2 vols, Moscow, 1964, 1, pp. 140–43.

[37] An. Aleksandrov, *Vokal'nye sochinenii*, 4 vols, Moscow, 1970–73.

[38] The major disruption caused by the interruption of the First World War, the Russian Revolutions of 1917 and then the Civil War is a further factor in the delayed publication of many songs written around this time. Many of the songs of Artur Lur'e, for instance, were published only after the October Revolution, despite belonging more properly to the twilight of imperial Petersburg.

his *Chetyre stikhotvorenii K. Bal'monta i I. Severianina* (Four Poems of Konstantin Bal'mont and Igor' Severianin), op. 5, were republished in Soviet Russia in 1926, despite setting texts by two émigré poets. Only one of them was included in the 1970s edition of his songs, potentially suggesting a certain degree of discomfort on the part of his later editors with the legacy of literary modernism, even in the years of the Brezhnev stagnation. But Aleksandrov's seventeen settings of Mikhail Kuzmin's *Aleksandriiskie pesni* (Alexandrian Songs) were too significant a historical and musical document to be similarly overlooked. Divided into four books and published between 1917 and 1926, they take poems by a leading member of the pre-revolutionary Acmeist school, some of which had already been set to music by the poet himself (he was also a talented amateur composer).[39] The first book of Aleksandrov's settings was published by Gutheil in 1917 as his op. 8. By the time it was reissued in 1926, it had been joined by two further books — Aleksandrov's op. 20 (published in 1923) and his op. 25 (published in 1926). A fourth book appears to have been composed in the late 1920s, although its publication may have been disrupted by the change in the political climate at the time.[40]

Aleksandrov's persistent interest in Kuzmin is significant because although he remained in the Soviet Union after 1917, it is hard to make a case for him as being in any way a revolutionary writer. As Vasina-Grossman admits, 'there can be no comparison between Mikhail Kuzmin and either Aleksandr Blok or Valerii Briusov.' For Vasina-Grossman, his poetry can be tolerated, because 'he shared with them the sense of the hopelessness [*ushcherbnost'*] of modernism, as did, as it happens, many other representatives of his generation'.[41] Moreover, Vasina-Grossman cites Kuzmin's Acmeist manifesto, 'O prekrasnoi iasnosti' ('On beautiful clarity', 1910) as a positive reaction against the abstraction and inwardness of symbolism, and hence — potentially at least — as a kind of realism. Yet this is very much a late-Soviet rationalization of the persistence of pre-revolutionary aesthetics after 1917. As we shall see, contemporary reviews of Aleksandrov's songs frequently singled them out as offering a new form of lyricism that was well attuned to the needs of the age.

---

[39] For a study of Kuzmin's settings of his own poetry, see Philip Ross Bullock, '"An Era of Eros": Hellenic Lyricism in the Early Twentieth-Century Russian Art-Song', in Katerina Levidou, Katy Romanou and George Vlastov (eds), *Musical Receptions of Greek Antiquity: From the Romantic Era to Modernism*, Newcastle upon Tyne, 2016, pp. 260–95.

[40] Only the first three books of Aleksandrov's settings are included in the 1970s edition of his vocal works, although Vasina-Grossman gives details of the fourth book in *Mastera sovetskogo romansa*, p. 107.

[41] Ibid., p. 102.

THE BIRTH OF THE SOVIET ROMANCE

*   *   *

The careers of Gnesin, Misakovskii and Aleksandrov all illustrate how settings of a wide range of poetry — Soviet, modernist, classical and foreign works in translation — survived and even flourished well into the Soviet period. Yet the mere fact of publication gives little indication of significance, which should be traced instead through contemporary reviews of both publications and performance. These give a good indication of the importance of song not just as a hybrid musical and literary genre, but also as a form of social practice embedded in early Soviet culture. Writing in 1926 about the first years of Soviet musical life, Leonid Sabaneev emphasized the continuity of the romance tradition with both composers and performers, as well as highlighting the particular set of social and institutional factors that had facilitated that continuity:

> But the fact that the work of Russian composers has continued to enrich the treasure-trove of the song genre with new achievements, as well as the fact that in general, the art of vocal performance, because it is the most intimate form of musical performance, has been simultaneously the easiest one to organize, and the one most able to cope with the wide range of issues raised by the import of foreign musical novelties — all of this has gone to supporting the vitality of the art of vocal performance at a significant level and has nurtured in the public a taste for chamber song that was only partially expressed beforehand.[42]

In particular, Sabaneev noted that although many of the leading vocalists of the pre-revolutionary period had gone into emigration, a new generation of singers (such as Nazar' Raiskii, Zoia Lodii, Vera Dukhovskaia and F. Petrova) had done so much to promote this seemingly unpropitious repertoire:

> Thanks to these performers, contemporary foreign and Russian musical works continue to be heard from concert platforms, and chamber concerts are even becoming more a popular form of performance than other serious concerts, even if they are still only designed for a relatively limited circle of musical consumers.[43]

---

[42] L. L. Sabaneev, *Muzyka posle Oktiabria*, Moscow, 1926, p. 93.
[43] Ibid., p. 94.

In terms of the composers who had devoted themselves to song, then Aleksandrov was undoubtedly the most visible figure at the time. Viktor Beliaev, writing in 1927, praised his settings of Kuzmin's *Aleksandriiskie pesni*, both for their successful fusion of the best traditions of the past, and for their development of a new kind of vocal lyricism that would be more appropriate for the present day:

> In his *Aleksandriiskie pesni* [...] Aleksandrov has presented a range of models of a completely individual vocal style, which is as distinct from the declamatory style of Dargomyzhskii, Musorgskii and their followers, as it is from the melodious style of Chaikovskii and his imitators. [...] In his songs, Aleksandrov almost completely avoids the salon style which was so characteristic of Chaikovskii and other Russian song composers and strives to create a style of art-song that is the expression of an 'objective' lyricism and the direct opposite of the subjective lyricism of the salon romance.[44]

Beliaev had long been a supporter of Aleksandrov, praising his settings of Kuzmin in print throughout the 1920s. In the first edition of *Sovremennaia muzyka* (Contemporary Music), for instance, he discussed the relationship between the first and second set of songs:

> Aleksandrov's *Aleksandriiskie pesni*, now complemented by four new romances, is capable of producing a deep and powerful impression. Whoever has heard them performed by the composer in an intimate setting will know how many subtle shades they contain and how profoundly they can stir the listener. This new set is more mature than the first, but is replete with that same smell of freshness and directness of creativity. In it, the composer, whilst remaining true to the style of the earlier set, deepens and underscores the stylistic link by means of allusions to the music of the first set, thereby fusing the two groups of romances, separated from each other by a large gap in time, into a single whole.[45]

Here, Beliaev posits an organic connection between the pre- and post-revolutionary songs, seeing the creative promise of the former fully realized in the latter. He returned to the question of Aleksandrov's place in early Soviet musical aesthetics a few years later:

---

[44] V. Beliaev, *Anatolii Nikolaevich Aleksandrov*, Moscow, 1927, pp. 13–14.

[45] V. Beliaev, review of Anatolii Aleksandrov, *Aleksandriiskie pesni. Tetrad' 2aia*, Petrograd, 1923, *Sovremennaia muzyka*, 1924, 1, pp. 26–27.

Aleksandrov is not a 'modernist', if one can use at all a word which often signifies a total spiritual poverty and contemporary artistic vacuity, masked by a 'contemporary' and 'fashionable' exterior. He is by his very nature a traditionalist, combining in his artistic make-up his talents as a musical performer with an independence of musical thought. As a traditionalist, Aleksandrov is more inclined to develop, deepen and refine the existing achievements of Russian music, than to make new discoveries.[46]

For Beliaev, Aleksandrov's principal accomplishment is to bridge the artistic culture of the past with the demands of a new age. His works embody a spirit of creative continuity, and such continuity is perceived as a necessary feature of early Soviet musical culture.

Such views were common enough in *Sovremennaia muzyka*, the journal of the Assotsiatsiia sovremmennoi muzyki (often shortened to ASM, Association for Contemporary Music). Despite its name, the association did not espouse a radically avant-garde attitude to the culture of the past. Rather, it aligned itself with what it saw as the best of the heritage of the pre-revolutionary period, as well as with developments in modern Western Europe music. As well as reviewing works by its members, it also included reviews of its own concerts. On 12 November 1924, for instance, Aleksandrov and his wife gave a recital of songs by Karol Szymanowski (including extracts from his settings of Rabindranath Tagore, Hafiz and the *Songs of an Infatuated Muezzin*, to words by Jarosław Iwaszkiewicz).[47] Then, on 29 April 1928, two of Aleksandrov's own *Aleksandriiskie pesni* were heard with orchestral accompaniment at a concert held in the Great Hall of the Moscow Conservatoire.[48] An earlier modernist periodical, *K novym beregam* (Towards New Shores), very much a precursor to *Sovremennaia muzyka*, also featured regular reviews of concerts featuring the work of contemporary Russian song composers. On 28 February 1923, Nazarii Raiskii and Aleksandr Gol'denweizer performed a selection of Metner's romances at a concert in Moscow.[49] (Gol'denweizer's involvement is striking, given his close association with pre-revolutionary song culture; in early 1907, for instance, he had played the piano in the premiere of

---

[46] Viktor Beliaev, 'Anatolii Aleksandrov', *Sovremennaia muzyka*, 1926, 12, pp. 47–51 (p. 48).
[47] *Sovremennaia muzyka*, 1924, 4, p. 126.
[48] *Sovremennaia muzyka*, 1928, 28, p. 105.
[49] 'Khronika, kontserty', *K novym beregam*, 1923, 1, pp. 46–50. See too Beliaev's laudatory review of new editions of Metner's op. 36 settings of Pushkin (1915) and op. 37 settings of Tiutchev and Fet (1918–20), as well as Sabaneev's short article on the composer in the following edition. *K novym beregam*, 1923, 1, p. 60, and L. Sabaneev, 'Metner', *K novym beregam*, 1923, 2, pp. 21–25. See too V. V. Iakovlev, *Nikolai Karlovich Metner*, Moscow, 1927.

Rakhmaninov's *15 romansov* [15 Songs], op. 26, in Moscow.) In the spring of 1923, the soprano Siranush Kubatskaia gave a concert of Aleksandrov's songs at the Beethoven Hall of Moscow's Bol'shoi Theatre, including the first two volumes of the *Aleksandriiskie pesni*, which were praised by the reviewer as 'not only the most significant of Aleksandrov's own compositions in particular, but also in the modern Russian art-song literature'.[50] Publications of new vocal works by Georgii Katuar, Aleksandr Krein and Samuil Feinberg were warmly welcomed, as were Prokof'ev's settings of Anna Akhmatova ('so limpidly luminous and exhaustive in the fullness of their expressivity that they leave behind an indelible impression').[51]

Yet what of the proletarian musical associations, which are often seen as the antipode of the early Soviet modernists? To be sure, the works of song composers association with the ASM were briefly the target of hostile criticism in the early 1930s, when the cultural revolution was at its height and the proletarians felt emboldened to unleash a virulent attacked on modernists, formalists and those artists whom Leon Trotskii had earlier called 'fellow travellers'. Writing in *Proletarskii muzykant* (Proletarian Musician) in early 1931, for instance, Boris Shteinpress criticized the decadence and aestheticism of a number of leading song composers, especially Aleksandrov.[52] Gnesin too found himself condemned both for his early association with so-called Russian decadence, and then for his 'reactionary Jewish nationalism'.[53] Although he refused to renounce his earlier works, claiming that 'one simply cannot remove the history of the twentieth century from Russian history, that's completely impossible',[54] his emphasis on the continuity of the Russian song tradition found itself in direct opposition to the proletarians' call for a new form of revolutionary culture that rejected the legacy of modernism and looked back to the examples of Beethoven and Musorgskii instead. In fact, the proletarians

---

[50] A. V., 'Khronika, kontserty', *K novym beregam*, 1923, 2, pp. 56–62. In *Music of the Soviet Era: 1917–1991* (2nd edn, Abingdon and New York, 2016), Levon Hakobian gives the date of this recital as 24 March 1923. Elsewhere, he notes other performance of the various volumes of *Iz 'Aleksandriiskikh pesen'* on 28 April 1925 and 5 October 1929.

[51] A. Versilov, review of Sergei Prokof'ev, op 9, op. 18, op. 27, *K novym beregam*, 1923, 3, p. 52.

[52] B. Shteinpress, 'Protiv burzhuaznykh tendentsii v muzyke', *Proletarskii muzykant*, 1931, 2, 20, pp. 28–29.

[53] D. Zhitomirskii, '"Povest' o ryzhem Motele" Mikh. Gnesina', *Proletarskii muzykant*, 1931, 10, 28, pp. 27–31 (p. 31).

[54] B. D., '"Ia slozhnyi chelovek". M. F. Gnesin o sebe i okruzhaiushchei deistvitel'nosti', *Proletarskii muzykant*, 1931, 8, 26, pp. 22–30 (p. 22).

seem largely to have dismissed, rather than attacked, art-song as a bourgeois genre, focusing primarily on jazz, Gypsy music and popular culture as the most dangerous impediments to the development of proletarian culture. Art-song was simply too rarefied, and hence too limited in its potential impact on society, to be the object of sustained ideological criticism.[55]

Paradoxically, however, proletarian organizations could also prove to be surprisingly welcoming of aspects of the art-song tradition, at least in the second half of the 1920s, when the ideological atmosphere was less extreme and when the distinction between the modernists and the proletarians was less clear cut.[56] As well as calling for the development of a new genre, the Soviet 'mass song',[57] critics also emphasized the importance of the legacy of the past, whether in the form of the Russian nineteenth-century tradition (Glinka, Dargomyzhskii and Musorgskii in particular), or the *Lieder* of Beethoven and Schubert (the centenary of whose death was widely marked in the Soviet Union in 1928).[58] In the second half of the 1920s, even the contemporary Soviet repertoire found itself discussed more generously, and reviews of performances published in *Muzyka i revoliutsiia* (Music and Revolution), the organ of the Obedinenie revoliutsionnykh kompozitorov i muzykal'nykh deiatelei (Association of Revolutionary Composers and Music Workers), reveal some striking continuities with the pre-Soviet period. In the spring of 1926, Mariia Olenina-Dal'geim, who had not only contributed to the rediscovery of Musorgskii in the early twentieth century, but also done much to promote the song recital as an institution, returned to Moscow for the first time in more than ten years to give three recitals.[59] Like many recitals at the time, these were broad and anthological in scope: the second (on 21 April) consisted of a selection of

---

[55] For studies of changing Soviet attitudes to popular culture, see in particular Richard Stites, *Russian Popular Culture: Entertainment and Society since 1900*, Cambridge, 1992, and David MacFadyen, *Songs for Fat People: Affect, Emotion, and Celebrity in the Russian Popular Song, 1900–1950*, Montreal and Ithaca, NY 2002. Fairclough likewise notes the widespread hostility among the proletarian musical groups towards popular culture, rather than classical art music (*Classics for the Masses*, pp. 50–57).

[56] For a documentary study of early Soviet musical politics that gives a good impression of such blurred boundaries and shifting allegiances, see Marina Frolova-Walker and Jonathan Walker, *Music and Soviet Power, 1917–1932*, Woodbridge and Rochester, NY, 2012.

[57] L. Shul'yn, 'Massovaia pesnia', *Muzyka i revoliutsiia*, 1926, 2, pp. 18–20, and D. Rovinskii, 'O massovykh pesniakh', *Muzyka i revoliutsiia*, 1926, 2, p. 33.

[58] See, for instance, M. Ivanov-Boretskii's review of Beethoven's settings of Scottish folksongs in *Proletarskii muzykant*, 1931, 5, 23, pp. 47–48, or the list of cheap and accessible editions of songs that was published in *Za proletarskaia muzyka*, 1930, 1, p. 30. See also, M. Bruk, 'Shubert i cgo pesni', *Za proletarskuiu muzyku*, 1931, 16, 26, pp. 6–12.

[59] Alexander Tumanov, *The Life and Artistry of Maria Olenina d'Alheim*, trans. Christopher Barnes, Edmonton, AL, 2000.

folksongs that was followed by romances by Musorgskii, whilst the third (on 8 May) juxtaposed French songs from the medieval period to Gabriel Fauré with Russian songs and Schumann's *Frauenliebe und -Leben*.[60] Later that month, Vera Dukhovskaia sang works by Chaikovskii, Dargomyzhskii and Glinka, as well as more recent songs by Stravinskii and Gnesin, bringing the contemporary scene into dialogue with the nineteenth century.[61] November 1926 saw recitals by Natal'ia Vesnina (16 October) and Ol'ga Bogoslavskaia (26 October) which included Metner's recent settings of Fet, Tiutchev and Pushkin, and a survey of songs by women composers from the early nineteenth century up to the present day (Iuliia L'vova, Liubov' Shekhter, Valentina Ramm and Iuliia Veisberg).[62] That December, Kubatskaia offered a historical overview of Russian song that included not only the dilettante romances of the early nineteenth century and works by Chaikovskii and the *moguchaia kuchka* ('Mighty Handful'), but also romances by Rakhmaninov, Stravinskii, Prokof'ev, Miaskovskii, Krein and Aleksandrov.[63] Song recitals were a prominent feature of Soviet musical life throughout the rest of the 1920s, often combining Russian and foreign repertoires, and making little distinction between pre- and post-revolutionary composers.[64]

If proletarian journals could respond warmly to Soviet Russia's lively culture, then they also carried thoughtful reviews of the contemporary art-song repertoire. In 1926, Anatolii Drozdov reviewed the third volume of Aleksandrov's *Aleksandriiskie pesni* in terms that were as appreciative of their poetry as they were of their music:

> M. Kuzmin's *Aleksandriiskie pesni* are one of the rare highpoints in the art of poetry. The poet has taken not the grandly heroic era of classicism, but the late era of its decadence (its waning) and has revealed its very essence, translating every nuance of this interesting way of life. And if the *Aleksandriiskie pesni* are fascinating in and of themselves, then they

[60] Vs. Liutsh, 'Kamernye kontserty vokalistov', *Muzyka i revoliutsiia*, 1926, 5, p. 31.
[61] Ibid.
[62] Ibid.,, 11, pp. 31–32.
[63] Ibid., 12, p. 31.
[64] See, for instance, Georgeii Poliakovskii, 'Avtorskii kontsert S. N. Vasilenko', *Muzyka i revoliutsiia*, 1927, 2, p. 31, and regular reviews by Vs. Liutsh: 'Kontsery vokalistov', *Muzyka i revoliutsiia*, 1927, 2, p. 33; 'Kontserty vokalistov', 1927, 3, p. 35; 'Kontserty vokalistov', 1927, 4, p. 32; 'Kontserty vokalistov', 1927, 5–6, p. 45; 'Kontserty vokalistov', 1927, 10, pp. 27–28; 'Kontserty vokalistov', 1927, 12, pp. 30–31; 'Kontserty vokalistov', 1928, 2, p. 33; 'Kontserty vokalistov', 1928, 3, pp. 38–39; 'Kontserty vokalistov' and 'Vecher frantsuskoi pesni', 1928, 5–6, pp. 48–49; 'Itogi vokal'nykh kontsertov', 1928, 2, pp. 34–35, and 'Obzor vokal'nykh kontsertov', 1929, 3, pp. 37–38.

are doubly interesting as themes for musical composition; the musical element is embedded in the verse form itself of the *Aleksandriiskie pesni*, and their content calls for musical setting, with its many references to dancing, flutes, tambourines, the sound of the sea, etc. But the challenges of embodying them in music are equally great, and are to be found in the complexity of their rhythmical construction, and — most of all — in the subtlety of the stylistic problem that the stylized theme of the work forces upon the composer. It seems that the main task of the composer in setting the *Aleksandriiskie pesni* to music should be the preservation of the harmony between musically retrospective means (the evocation of antiquity) and the means available to a contemporary composer. It is precisely this sense of harmony that we can discern in the volume of songs by An. Aleksandrov under review here.[65]

A review of a concert performance of all three groups that took place on 26 February 1927 made similar claims and referred to Aleksandrov's 'radiant, objective and somewhat abstract lyricism' as being 'absolutely alien to modish mannerism, affectedness or shrill innovation'. Yet the critic sounded a note of caution too. Observing that Aleksandrov's musical language had its roots in 'Metner [...], Debussy and middle-period Skriabin', he suggested that they were 'very far removed from our contemporary life' and that 'one wishes for something greater, something more modern from such a master of vocal style as Aleksandrov'.[66] If this review suggests that after a decade of continuity and evolution, critics were beginning to seek new things from the art-song repertoire, then there seemed little risk, for the time being at least, that composers would be criticized, whether for their choice of poets, or their musical language. Writing in late 1928, the same critic who had called for Aleksandrov to explore new themes, praised Miaskovskii's recent settings of Del′vig: '*Venok poblekshii* [A Faded Garland] should be considered one of the most successful vocal cycles of Miaskovskii and one of the most interesting works of our art-song literature.' Indeed, Miaskovskii's songs, for all their complexity, were 'probably no less rich and significant than his work in the field of the large musical forms — the symphony and the sonata'.[67]

---

[65] A. Drozdov, review of An. Aleksandrov, *Iz 'Aleksandriiskikh pesen' M. Kuzmina. Tetr. III, 1926*, *Muzyka i revoliutsiia*, 1926, 6, pp. 39–40 (p. 39).

[66] Vs. Liutsh, 'Avtorskii vecher An. Aleksandrova', *Muzyka i revoliutsiia*, 1927, 3, p. 34.

[67] Vs. Liutsh, review of N. Miaskovskii, op. 22, *Venok poblekshii*, *Muzyka i revoliutsiia*, 1928, 10, pp. 45–46 (p. 45).

* * *

As this article has sought to demonstrate, the Russian art-song tradition did not come to an end at some point before the October Revolution, only to be reborn in its new Soviet guise, whether in the mid-1920s or as part of the implementation of Socialist Realism from the mid-1930s. There were, in fact, organic connections between the various phases of Russian song that came before 1917 — whether the early nineteenth-century dilettante tradition, the 'golden age' of the second half of the nineteenth century or, most importantly, the vital interaction between music and poetry that characterized the turn of the twentieth century — and its development in the early Soviet period. If these continuities have been largely effaced in the most prominent and influential instances of the secondary literature, then they are clearly there to be seen in the periodical literature of the time. Soviet criticism was not alone in overlooking this body of material; Western scholars keen to characterize the early Soviet period in terms of its avant-gardism have equally sought to cast 1917 as a moment of decisive rupture, even if for very different reasons.[68] Reconstituting the organic links between Russian modernism of the late imperial era and the musical culture of the early Soviet period helps to illuminate not only broad continuities between the two, but more crucially, establishes the preconditions for a re-evaluation of the art-song tradition in particular. Viewed in this new light, works such as Dmitrii Shostakovich's *Shest' romansov na slova iaponskikh poetov* (Six Romances to Texts by Japanese Poets), op. 21, may take on new relevance. Composed between 1928 and 1932, they are often read in the context of his work on his opera, *Ledi Makbet mtsenskogo uezda*, as well as against the background of his relationship with his first wife, Nina Vazar'. A reading of their literary sources might suggest parallels with Stravinskii's *Tri iaponskikh stikhotvorenii* (Three Japanese Lyrics, 1912–13), as both sets of songs were based on a volume of Japanese poetry in Russian translation that was published in St Petersburg

---

[68] See, for instance, Larry Sitsky, *Music of the Repressed Russian Avant-Garde, 1900-1929*, Westport, CT and London, 1994. Similarly, Detlew Gojowy's emphasis on avant-gardism leads him to misread the profound influence of the Russian Silver Age on the work of Artur Lur'e. See *Arthur Lourié und der russische Futurismus*, Laaber, 1993, as well as his *Neue sowjetische Musik der 20er Jahre*, Laaber, 1980. For an influential attempt at distinguishing between modernism and a more politically engaged avant-garde, see Peter Bürger, *Theory of the Avant-Garde*, trans. Michael Shaw, Minneapolis, MN, 1984.

in 1912.[69] Yet a reading of Shostakovich's songs in terms of their place in the early Soviet song tradition potentially exposes links not to other works by the composer, still less to other settings of related texts, but to the kind of compositions by figures such as Aleksandrov, Gnesin and Miaskovskii that have been considered here, as well as other song composers whose work has yet to be considered in any detail. The legacy of turn-of-the-century modernism for early Soviet culture has been extensively explored in the case of literature, yet a similar process has yet to be undertaken when it comes to art-song, and remains an urgent priority for contemporary scholarship, as well as an alluring field for adventurous performers.

[69] G. Kopytova, 'Poeticheskie istochniki vokal'nogo tsikla D. D. Shostakovicha (Shest' romansov na slova iaponskikh poetov', in O. Digonskaia and L. Kovnatskaia (eds), *Dmitrii Shostakovich: Issledovaniia i materialy. Vypusk 3*, Moscow, 2011, pp. 176–205.

5

In Search of Russia:
Sergei Rakhmaninov and the Politics of Musical Memory after 1917

REBECCA MITCHELL

In August 2015, Russian Culture Minister Vladimir Medinskii demanded that the body of composer Sergei Rakhmaninov be exhumed from its final resting place in Valhalla, New York and reinterred in Russia. Though Medinskii's blustering demand ultimately met with little interest from Russian politicians and open dismissal from the composer's descendants,[1] his claim that this 'greatest of Russian geniuses' had been 'recently portrayed in the West in an utterly wrong way' was a contemporary reframing of a longer history of Soviet attempts to reclaim a 'correct' interpretation of the composer's legacy.[2] Already in the immediate aftermath of the Great Patriotic War, K. Kuznetsov had observed in the leading music journal, *Sovetskaia muzyka*, that Rakhmaninov's dying wish 'was to be buried at the end of the war in Moscow's Novodevichii Monastery cemetery' where Chekhov, Skriabin and 'a whole series of people, whom he [Rakhmaninov] particularly loved and valued' were also laid to rest.[3]

Numerous scholars have examined the current Russian state's nation-building project to redefine its relationship to its own imperial past

---

[1] James Barron, 'Family Balks at Talk by Russia to Move Rachmaninoff's Remains', *New York Times*, 6 September 2015 <https://www.nytimes.com/2015/09/07/nyregion/family-balks-at-talk-by-russia-to-move-rachmaninoffs-remains.html> [accessed 14 July 2018].

[2] Iuliia Generozova, 'Medinskii vystupaet za vozvrashchenie prakha Rakhmaninova iz SSHA v Rossiiu', *Kul'tura*, August 15, 2015 <http://tass.ru/kultura/2188793> [accessed 29 January 2017]. This was not Medinskii's first fascination with the fate of bodily relics: in Russian State Duma discussions in 2008, it was Medinskii who suggested that the time had come to remove Lenin's corpse from the mausoleum and bury it. See Alexei Yurchak, 'Bodies of Lenin: The Hidden Science of Communist Sovereignty', *Representations*, 129, 2015, 1, pp. 116–57.

[3] K. Kuznetsov, 'Tvorcheskaia zhizn' S. V. Rakhmaninova', *Sovetskaia muzyka*, 4, 1945, pp. 25–51 (p. 42). For a reiteration of this claim in a later period, see Nikolai Bazhanov, *Rakhmaninov*, Moscow, 1983, p. 324.

and the first wave of émigrés who fled the October Revolution of 1917.[4] Given the émigré community's obsession with preserving 'Russian' memory and culture after the upheavals of 1917, the desire to reintegrate émigré experience into the narrative of Russian national culture is not surprising. But it heightens the importance of finally granting critical attention to how the émigré community itself actually sought to redefine 'Russianness' within a transformed socio-political context after 1917, and how this effort interacted with renewed post-war interest in 'Russianness' in the Soviet Union.[5] This article uses Rakhmaninov as a lens in order to explore shifting conceptions of 'Russianness' in the years after 1917, as the musician was gradually transformed into a site of memory that articulated an idealized definition of 'Russianness'. This construction evolved through the development and interaction of émigré and Soviet public and private discourses that framed Rakhmaninov's music and life in nostalgic terms after the upheavals of 1917, culminating after the composer's 1943 death in a definition of Russianness stripped of (most) political and historical baggage and celebrating an eternalized, purified image of Russian culture. Despite continued variations in Soviet and émigré memory cultures after 1943, they ultimately existed within a single continuum whose shared overarching understanding of 'Russianness' retains currency today.

By defining Rakhmaninov as a site of memory, this article builds upon Pierre Nora's conception of *lieu de mémoire*, which he defined as 'any significant entity, whether material or non-material in nature, which by dint of human will or the work of time has become a symbolic element of the memorial heritage of any community'.[6] As Richard Taruskin, Marina Frolova-Walker and others have shown, aurality, music and musicians have served as key symbols in the construction of Russian national identity.[7]

---

[4] Galina Rylkova, *The Archaeology of Anxiety: The Russian Silver Age and Its Legacy*, Pittsburgh, PA, 2008; Svetlana Boym, *The Future of Nostalgia*, New York, 2001; Greta N. Slobin, 'The "Homecoming" of the First Wave Diaspora and Its Cultural Legacy', *Slavic Review*, 60, 2001, 3, pp. 513–29; eadem, *Russians Abroad: Literary and Cultural Politics of Diaspora (1919–1939)*, Brighton, MA, 2013.

[5] On the emphasis on maintaining Russian cultural life and institutions in emigration, see Marc Raeff, *Russia Abroad: A Cultural History of the Russian Emigration, 1919–1939*, Oxford, 1990.

[6] Pierre Nora (ed.), *Realms of Memory: The Construction of the French Past*, 3 vols, New York, 1996–98, 1, p. xvii. See also, Nora, 'Between Memory and History: Les Lieux de Mémoire', *Representations*, 26, 1989, pp. 7–24. Nora acknowledged that his understanding of the concept expanded from physical to conceptual over the course of his research. See *Realms of Memory*, 1, pp. xv–xxiv.

[7] Marina Frolova-Walker, *Russian Music and Nationalism: From Glinka to Stalin*, New Haven, CT, 2008; Richard Taruskin, *Defining Russia Musically*, Princeton, NJ, 2001; idem,

Though far from the only figure associated with Russian culture and identity after 1917, Rakhmaninov arose as a central figure in the quest both by Russian émigrés and citizens of the new Soviet state to define 'Russianness' in relation to their own past and future. In interpreting Rakhmaninov's music and actions from their divergent contexts, both émigré and Soviet admirers participated in the transformation of Rakhmaninov into a site of memory, a nostalgic symbol of 'true Russian' identity that existed in an idealized past, eternally distinct from the desacralized present.

As a cultural-intellectual historian, I am interested in probing how musical meaning is constructed by audiences, musicians, critics and interpreters. Whereas earlier musicological analyses of Rakhmaninov's music have tended to highlight the question of the composer's stylistic 'traditionalism' versus 'modernism', this article applies reception history to explore the multiple meanings audiences ascribed to both musical compositions and the composer himself.[8] As Neil Gregor has argued, audiences do not simply internalize meanings inscribed into an artistic work by an author or by professional commentary. Rather, the construction of meaning of a given composition or artistic work consists of the creative intersection between the work, authorial intent, and individual and collective response.[9]

In order to access questions of reception and the links between Rakhmaninov and emerging memory culture after 1917, this article examines private and public discourse surrounding the composer. While émigré and Soviet periodicals provide insight into public framings of the composer, the private realm of reception is accessed through the considerable Russian-language correspondence received by Rakhmaninov and preserved at the Library of Congress.[10] Although letter writers self-

---

Russian Music at Home and Abroad, Berkeley, CA, 2016.

[8] For a summary of the modernist vs. traditionalist polemic with reference to Rachmaninoff, see for instance Robin S. Gehl, 'Reassessing a Legacy: Rachmaninoff in America, 1918–43', unpublished PhD dissertation, University of Cincinnati, 2008, pp. 3–7; Richard Taruskin, *Music in the Early Twentieth Century: Oxford History of Western Music*, Oxford, 2006, pp. 550–60. On Rakhmaninov's life and career, see Sergei Bertensson and Jay Leyda, *Sergei Rachmaninoff: A Lifetime in Music*, New York, 1956.

[9] Neil Gregor, 'Music, Memory, Emotion: Richard Strauss and the Legacies of War', *Music and Letters*, 96, 2015, 1, pp. 55–76. For similar cultural-historical approaches to music, see Jane Fulcher (ed.), *The Oxford Handbook of the New Cultural History of Music*, Oxford, 2011; Celia Applegate, 'Introduction: Music among the Historians', *German History*, 30, 2012, pp. 329–49.

[10] The source base for the émigré press includes an examination of *Rul'* (Berlin), *Poslednie novosti* (Paris), *Rossiia i slavianstvo* (Paris), *Vozrozhdenie* (Paris) and *Novoe russkoe slovo* (New York). Soviet periodicals include *Sovetskaia muzyka*, *Literatura i*

selected to correspond with the composer, and Rakhmaninov chose to preserve these particular letters, such epistolary sources nonetheless provide a valuable means to measure how both Soviet and émigré listeners internalized, adapted or rejected conceptions of 'Russianness' employed in public discourse.[11]

As émigré and Soviet memory cultures relating to Rakhmaninov diverged, two distinct but mutually informed images of the composer arose. After a brief discussion of nostalgia as a historical phenomenon, this article looks at how Rachmaninov was framed as the quintessential nostalgic émigré through his publicly reported words and actions.[12] I then explore how Rakhmaninov's image was celebrated by émigrés both in personal letters and in the periodical press, becoming increasingly spiritualized and connected with conceptions of the 'Russian soul' that predated 1917, even as they sought to respond to the challenges of diaspora life. In contrast, in the early Soviet context, interpretations of Rakhmaninov split into two distinct realms. While private letters to the composer similarly celebrated his embodiment of the lost values of old Russia, public discourse questioned the composer's relevance to the new revolutionary state. This bifurcation of collective memory in the Soviet context broke down after 1941, when,

---

iskusstva and *Ogonek*, as well as numerous biographies and studies of the composer published after 1945. Archival sources are drawn primarily from the Library of Congress Rachmaninoff Archive, Washington, DC (hereafter LCRA). The Library of Congress Rachmaninoff Archive contains hundreds of letters in multiple languages; this article is based on examination of approximately 85 Russian-language letter writers as well as occasional letters from Russian émigrés written in English. While some correspondence consists of a single letter, others include several letters to Rakhmaninov. Not all of these can be considered 'fan' letters in a traditional sense. While some of these letters are from Rakhmaninov's former acquaintances, others are from individuals with no prior connection to the composer; still others are from representatives of various Russian émigré or Soviet organizations. Regardless of their former relationship (if any), these letters consistently demonstrate a tendency to frame the composer in terms of his 'Russianness'. For a complete inventory of correspondence to Rakhmaninov, see <http://findingaids.loc.gov/exist_collections/service/music/eadxmlmusic/eadpdfmusic/2015/mu015003.pdf> [accessed 10 July 2018].

[11] On the challenges as well as the potential benefits of fan mail as a source base, see Barbara Ryan and Charles Johanningsmeier, 'Fans and the Objects of their Devotion', *Reception: Texts, Readers, Audiences, History*, 5, 2013, 1, pp. 3–8; Linda M. Grasso, '"You are no stranger to me": Georgia O'Keeffe's Fan Mail', *Reception: Texts, Readers, Audiences, History*, 5, 2013, 1, pp. 24–40. For an example of fan mail analysis in the Russian context, see Anna Fishzon, *Fandom, Authenticity and Opera: Mad Acts and Letter Scenes in Fin-de-Siècle Russia*, Basingstoke and New York, 2013; eadem, 'Confessions of a *Psikhopatka*: Opera Fandom and the Melodramatic Sensibility in Fin-de-Siècle Russia', *Russian Review*, 71, 2012, 1, pp. 100–21.

[12] While Rakhmaninov was not the only cultural figure of the emigration publicly framed in such terms, the consistency of this framing makes him a useful case study.

as the final section shows, both Soviet and émigré interpretations of Rakhmaninov merged into a shared consensus in which the composer was treated unquestionably as an embodiment of 'Russianness'. Despite this confluence, later Soviet interpretations offered a historically and physically bounded memory space of the composer, even while his status amongst émigrés became increasingly disconnected from physical memory.

Nostalgia, memory and Rakhmaninov
In December 1928, the newly-founded Paris periodical *Rossiia i slavianstvo* opened its first issue with a fiery declaration of their mission: together with the political aim of 'freeing Russia' from Communism, they would reunify the 'spiritual culture' of Russia Abroad; by preserving Russia's cultural inheritance, they would overcome political differences dividing the émigré community. Accompanying this statement of intent was a photograph of composer Sergei Rakhmaninov, highlighted as the quintessential symbol of Russian cultural unity.[13] The paper's first issue coincided with Rakhmaninov's first post-revolutionary public concert in Paris. An accompanying commentary called on Russians in Paris to organize a 'Rakhmaninov week' dedicated to the celebration of his distinctly 'national' music.[14]

This fascination with Rakhmaninov as a national unifying figure able to overcome the petty political disputes of the emigration was echoed in later articles as well as other émigré press reports.[15] For Rakhmaninov's 1929 return to Paris, *Rossiia i slavianstvo* ran a lengthy article by Lollii L'vov musing on his meaning for Russian émigrés. 'What does the undying praise and unrivaled success of Rakhmaninov mean for Russia in her current inhuman torments?' he mused. Like the music of Orpheus, he concluded, Rakhmaninov's music had transformative power: in this case, the ability to 'affirm the essence of genuine Russia [...] with his victory he affirms belief in Russia and assures us that Russia is not only that formless chaos, which insane human hands created there [in Soviet Russia]'.[16] Why did such accounts of Rakhmaninov's national unifying power become

[13] 'Nashe politicheskoe litso i nashi zadachi', *Rossiia i slavianstvo* (hereafter, *RIS*) 1, 1 December 1928, p. 1.
[14] Vladimir Pol', 'K kontsertu S. V. Rakhmaninova', *RIS*, 1, 1 December 1928, p. 3. The historical precedent cited was the 'Skriabin Week' held in Russia in 1909.
[15] Il'ia Britan, 'Genii', *Rul'* (no date), LCRA 57/13; Ia. Mul'man, 'Velikii chelovek', *Rul'*, 1109, 29 July 1924, p. 4; B. Shletser, 'Muzykal'nye zametki: Kontsert S. V. Rakhmaninova', *Poslednie novosti*, 4014, 19 March 1932, p. 4; V. Pol', 'Kontsert S. V. Rakhmaninova', *Vozrozhdenie*, 2479, 25 March 1934, p. 3.
[16] Lollii L'vov, 'Rakhmaninov', *RIS*, 52, 23 November 1929, p. 3.

so common in the Russian émigré press of the late 1920s? Here one must consider continuities from pre-revolutionary discourse about Russian music and the historical context which shaped Rakhmaninov reception after 1917.

Perhaps the quintessential emotion associated with the Russian emigration after 1917 was nostalgia: a longing for an idealized, lost world, eternally desired yet out of reach. Svetlana Boym drew attention to the modern emotion of nostalgia as 'a longing for that shrinking "space of experience" that no longer fits the new horizon of expectations'.[17] Evoked as a means of coping with the revolutionary upheavals of modernity, nostalgia involves both a reification of an imagined past, often far removed from reality, and the acknowledgement of the impossibility of return.[18] Amongst Russian émigrés, this obsession with the past was not just the domain of cultural elites — it was a quintessentially modern experience triggered by the trauma of rapid revolutionary events shared by a large swathe of those who survived them. As émigrés set themselves the task of preserving Russian culture and traditions in exile, this widespread sense of temporal displacement acknowledged, in an emotional sense, that the world they commemorated had already ceased to exist (and perhaps had never existed at all). By focusing on this lost 'space of experience' in the aftermath of the 1917 Revolution, nostalgic reflection on 'old Russia' dwelt 'beyond the present space of experience, somewhere in the twilight of the past or on the island of utopia where time has happily stopped, as on an antique clock'.[19] Hence, as Klára Móricz argues, composers like Artur Lur'e (Arthur Lourié) came to embrace a temporal conception 'in which the past predominated' in emigration.[20]

Émigré nostalgia was deeply inflected by concepts and categories developed in imperial Russia. As Katerina Clark has argued with regard to 1920s Petersburg/Leningrad, cultural frames of reference, even in revolutionary periods, are inherited from earlier eras.[21] In the final years of the Russian empire, Rakhmaninov was one of several composers

---

[17] Boym, *Nostalgia*, p. 11.

[18] Peter Fritzsche, 'Specters of History: On Nostalgia, Exile, and Modernity', *American Historical Review*, 105, 2001, 5, pp. 1587–618; Alon Confino, 'Collective Memory and Cultural History: Problems of Method', *American Historical Review*, 105, 1997, 5, pp. 1386–403.

[19] Boym, *Nostalgia*, p. 13.

[20] Klára Móricz and Simon Morrison (eds), *Funeral Games in Honor of Arthur Vincent Lourié*, Oxford, 2014, p. 18.

[21] Katerina Clark, *Petersburg: Crucible of Cultural Revolution*, Cambridge, MA, 1995, p. ix.

interpreted by admirers through the lens of a 'search for Orpheus': the desire for a contemporary Russian composer whose music could overcome the disunifying trends of modernity and reunite Russian culture.[22] In emigration, the glorification of Rakhmaninov as an Orphic figure was inscribed with new meaning: rather than a potential transformer of Russia's future, he became the quintessential example of Russia's inexorably lost past.

Of all the artists, musicians and composers of the emigration, Rakhmaninov was most consistently associated with nostalgia for a lost Russia and served as a reference point for those seeking to make sense of their own traumatic experiences — an evolution made possible through interaction of his own public self-fashioning and the larger reception of his artistry. As Vladimir Satin concluded in a 1930 letter to the composer after Rakhmaninov's recent performance of his Third Piano Concerto, his music allowed listeners to live in the 'good past' ('khoroshee proshloe') and not think about the 'bad future' ('plokhoe budushchee').[23]

Rakhmaninov's public fashioning into an eternalized site of memory arose in part through the numerous interviews and reminiscences attributed to the composer after 1917. In a 1919 English-language interview with *The Etude* magazine, Rakhmaninov emphasized that 'with the exception of a few modernists, all Russian composers deeply absorbed the spirit of Russian folk song'.[24] Emphasizing the central role of melody in Russian music, he claimed that modernist Russian composers were mistaken in abandoning folk music, as only *national* music could provide the basis for truly universal music. Praising Rakhmaninov for 'uncover[ing] the most interesting pages of Russian culture of the recent past', a 1930 interview account in *Rossiia i slavianstvo* emphasized the composer's fascination with Russian Orthodox chant.[25] In his 1933 book, *Rachmaninoff Remembers*, Oskar Riesemann highlighted the composer's deep longing for his lost homeland and his inherently Russian nature, which he framed in racial terms, claiming 'Rachmaninoff is above all Russian — and a Russian who unites within himself all the fundamental characteristics of a people who possess a tremendous wealth of spiritual life', an account that

[22] Rebecca Mitchell, *Nietzsche's Orphans: Music, Metaphysics and the Twilight of the Russian Empire*, New Haven, CT, 2015, pp. 43–49 and 137–64.

[23] Vladimir Satin to S. V. Rakhmaninov, 13 March 1930, LCRA 47/41. Vladimir Satin was Rakhmaninov's brother-in-law.

[24] S. V. Rachmaninoff, 'The Connection of Music and Folk Music', *The Etude*, October 1919, p. 615.

[25] Lollii L'vov, 'U S. V. Rakhmaninova', *RIS*, 74, 26 April 1930, p. 2. See also, L. L'vov, 'Rannie gody Rakhmaninova', *Poslednie novosti*, 5118, 29 March 1935, p. 3.

attracted favourable interest from the literary émigré journal *Sovremennye zapiski*.[26] By 1941, Rakhmaninov offered an even more organic definition of music linking his creativity specifically to his national heritage: 'I am a Russian composer, and the land of my birth has inevitably influenced my temperament and outlook. My music is the product of my temperament, and so it is Russian music.'[27]

Rakhmaninov reiterated that nostalgic longing permeated his art on numerous occasions. In a 1934 English-language interview, Rakhmaninov explicitly connected his lack of compositional inspiration to his exile from his homeland.[28] In a series of interviews recorded by his sister-in-law Sof´ia Satina (unpublished during his lifetime), Rakhmaninov avoided discussing 'present-day Russia' in favour of reminiscing about 'old Russia'.[29] The trauma of war and revolution seldom appeared in these recollections, which instead focused upon defining aspects of eternal 'Russianness', such as the unique 'attraction to the land' that he argued every Russian experienced.[30] The reminiscences were similarly coloured with loving images of church bells and the unifying embrace of Orthodox ceremonies in which 'all cares, all sorrows are forgotten. The old and young, the poor and the rich, the happy and the miserable — all are united in the same brotherly feeling of new hope and joy'.[31] Social unrest, political repression and conflict were minimized in these accounts; the only genuinely negative event in 'old Russia' was Rakhmaninov's final trip to his estate Ivanovka in summer 1917, when he was confronted by a crowd of angry peasants led by a 'Bolshevik agitator'. This rare glimpse of conflict was immediately followed by the observation that he soon thereafter felt the need to leave Ivanovka and ultimately Russia.[32]

---

[26] Oskar von Riesemann, *Rachmaninoff's Recollections Told to Oskar von Riesemann*, New York, 1934, pp. 209–10; M. Aldanov, 'Kritika i bibliografiia', *Sovremennye zapiski*, 56, 1934, pp. 435–36. Rakhmaninov did not approve of Riesemann's biography. See, for instance, Z. Apetian (ed.), *S. Rakhmaninov: Literaturnoe nasledie*, 3 vols, Moscow, 1978–80, 2, pp. 561–63; 3, p. 77. Nevertheless, it was an influential document that helped to shape popular conceptions of the composer.

[27] David Ewan to Sergei Rakhmaninov, 26 February 1941, LCRA 43/57.

[28] Sergei Rachmaninoff, 'The Composer as Interpreter (interview with Norman Cameron)', *The Monthly Musical Record*, 64, November 1934, p. 201. This interview is the source of one of the most popularly quoted comments in later Soviet accounts.

[29] Rachmaninoff, 'Preface', in 'Recollections of a Vanished World', LCRA 50/2. First published (in excerpt) in Sof´ia Satina, 'Iz avtobiografii S. Rakhmaninova', *Novoe russkoe slovo*, 24 June 1973, p. 4.

[30] Ibid.

[31] Rakhmaninov, 'Easter Night in Moscow', in 'Recollections of a Vanished World', LCRA 50/2.

[32] Rakhmaninov, 'Ivanovka', in 'Recollections of a Vanished World', LCRA 50/2. On the

Rakhmaninov's own lifestyle choices were similarly framed as capturing an eternalized image of 'old Russia' in his daily life. According to Alfred Swan, 'Russian spirit and habits were all-powerful in him, and, as soon as the strain of the long concert season was over and he settled down for a while, his way of life became Russian'.[33] As numerous sources attested, Rakhmaninov sought to embody traditional Russian country life in emigration, from his 'Russian' nightshirt, to mushroom gathering, the breakfast food served, and the maid Pasha, who had, it was claimed, accompanied the family from Russia.[34] Such accounts aided in the public fashioning of Rakhmaninov into an embodiment of the lost world of pre-revolutionary Russia.

When Rakhmaninov, through his involvement with a number of charities, sent assistance to impoverished émigrés and both institutions and individuals in the Soviet Union, this generosity was associated with the composer's 'Russian' character.[35] In most of this charitable work he sought to avoid explicitly political organizations, preferring to uphold his status as a cultural rather than political figure.[36] His charitable work did not go unnoticed; Rakhmaninov was regularly celebrated in both the periodical press and in private correspondence for his generosity in supporting fellow Russians in need, both in exile and in the Soviet Union.[37] As interpreted by N. N. Baratov in 1929, Rakhmaninov's return to Paris after years

---

history of these *vospominaniia*, see Apetian (ed.), *Rakhmaninov: Literaturnoe nasledie*, 1, pp. 487–88. This incident is also hinted at in Riesemann, *Rachmaninoff's Recollections*, pp. 184–85.

[33] Katherine Swan and A. J. Swan, 'Rachmaninoff: Personal Reminiscences – Part I', *Musical Quarterly*, 30, 1944, 1, pp. 1–19 (p. 3).

[34] Sof'ia Satina claimed that Rakhmaninov employed almost exclusively Russian servants. See Sof'ia Satina, 'S. V. Rakhmaninov: k 25-letiiu so dnia konchiny', *Novyi zhurnal*, 91, 1968, pp. 115–28 (p. 127). See also Swan, 'Rachmaninoff: Personal Reminiscences', pp. 5–6.

[35] The Library of Congress Rachmaninoff Archive is full of letters thanking the composer for charitable donations. See, for instance, Dr J. M. Goldstein to S. V. Rakhmaninov, LCRA 44/15; Aleksandr Glazunov to S. V. Rakhmaninov, LCRA 44/10; I. Gessen to S. V. Rakhmaninov, LCRA 44/8; Seth Gano to S. V. Rakhmaninov, LCRA 44/4. Of particular value in this regard is Rakhmaninov's correspondence with his secretary Evgenii Somov. See LCRA 41/17-28, 47/61-61.

[36] For a letter of complaint about this, see Boris Brazol to S. V. Rakhmaninov, LCRA 47/35.

[37] M. M. Fedorov, 'Otkrytoe pis'mo S. V. Rakhmaninovu', *RIS*, 3, 15 December 1928, p. 6; Mitropolit Evlogii, Graf P. Ignat'ev and Mikhail Fedorov, 'Sergeiu Vasil'evichu Rakhmaninovu: otkrytoe pis'mo', *RIS*, 107, 13 December 1930, p. 1; Mikhail Fedorov, 'K kontsertu Rakhmaninova', *RIS*, 172, 12 March 1932, p. 1; Lollii L'vov, 'Na kontserte S. V. Rakhmaninova', *RIS*, 173, 19 March 1932, p. 1; Ia. Mul'man, 'Velikii chelovek', *Rul'*, 1109, 29 July 1924, p. 4; 'Shedryi dar' S. V. Rakhmaninova', *Vozrozhdenie*, 4074, 17 April 1937, p. 6.

abroad filled the audience equally with two feelings: artistic pleasure and national pride, the latter awakened by the composer's embodiment of a true generous Russian character.[38] By 1933, M. M. Fedorov called on all Russian émigrés to support Rakhmaninov by attending his benefit concerts in Paris, framing such an activity as both a pleasure and the 'duty' (*dolg*) of a 'Russian person'.[39] While his general avoidance of politics made Rakhmaninov less usable in the political in-fighting of émigrés, it tied him to an idealized and flexible image of cultural Russianness that could be moulded and reinterpreted to suit individual needs.

In contrast to pre-revolutionary critiques that 'melancholic' mood (*toska*) in his music exemplified the sickness of Russian culture, after 1917 Rakhmaninov's perceived melancholic compositional style and traditional compositional approach reinforced his position as a potential site of memory.[40] As Andrew Demshuk has observed in his study of the reception of *Heimat* bells by Silesian expellees, 'as the travails of modernity — nationalism, total war, ethnic cleansing, and more — remade the world, they also remade its soundscape; sounds now interpreted as *archaic* conjured memories of an idealized past world'.[41] In relation to Rakhmaninov, such an observation helps us to move beyond debates about his 'traditionalism' versus 'modernism' and consider instead how his musical style helped to forge the composer into an effective site of memory for many contemporaries. At a time when modernist composers sought to shock or challenge audience expectations, Rakhmaninov's lyricism and perceived romanticism appealed to listeners for whom the soundscape of modernity had awakened nostalgia for an imagined simpler world of the past. Popular accounts of the composer regularly stressed his upbringing in the countryside near Novgorod, his love of Orthodox church bells, sacred chant and the Russian countryside, all of which, it was argued, found aural expression in his compositional works.[42]

---

[38] N. N. Baratov, 'S. V. Rakhmaninov i Soiuz invalidov', *RIS*, 8, 19 January 1929, p. 5.

[39] Mikhail Fedorov, 'K kontsertu S. V. Rakhmaninova', *RIS*, 220, 1 May 1933, p. 3.

[40] Mitchell, *Nietzsche's Orphans*, pp. 137–64.

[41] Andrew Demshuk, 'The Voice of the Lost German East: Heimat Bells as Memory Soundscapes', in A. Demshuk and T. Weger (eds), *Cultural Landscapes*, Munich, 2015, pp. 209–28 (p. 213).

[42] Lollii L'vov, 'Rannie gody Rakhmaninova (k ego segodniashnemu kontsertu)', *Poslednie novosti*, 5118, 29 March 1935, p. 3; M-V, 'S. V. Rakhmaninov', *Novaia zaria*, 21 March 1929, pp. 3–4. Paris-based Russian émigré music critic Boris Shletser (Schloezer) was attacked by fellow Russian émigrés for his alleged hostility to the Russian national music tradition (including Rakhmaninov) and undue embrace of modernist compositional style. See 'Protesty protiv stat´i B. Shletsera o Glazunove: otkrytoe pis´mo N. K. Averino', *Novoe russkoe slovo*, 5851, 2 February 1929, p. 3.

The rise of the recording industry helped to fashion Rakhmaninov into a site of memory at once both material and non-spatial. While music had once been intimately tied to live performance and physical presence in a specific location (whether concert hall, church, or home), Rakhmaninov's extensive recording activity helped to create a sense of commonality that transcended national borders. For admirers who could not attend live concerts, recordings took the place of lived experience, and helped to forge a shared sense of 'Russianness' through the act of listening. Thus, in a 1928 letter from Harbin, Ivan Gumeniuk wrote to the composer that 'we collect all your records [of] Russian music' and that his oldest son Boris, played piano, loved music, and 'listens to your records (Victor) every day'.[43] Similarly, N. Dauge wrote from Riga in 1931 that he and his family would 'constantly listen' to Rakhmaninov's recordings.[44] An internationally renowned concert pianist and composer who regularly crossed national borders, Rakhmaninov's performing career made him a household name, particularly as his recordings gained greater popularity and distribution.

While his own lifestyle choices and interpretations helped shape public discourse, it was nevertheless the broader community that ultimately defined Rakhmaninov's significance as a site of memory. Both Rakhmaninov's melancholic music and his personal life came to serve as a valuable symbol of an eternalized old Russia. While Chopin was cited in the early Russian émigré press as a fellow sufferer whose music was particularly comprehensible to émigrés, it was in the figure of Sergei Rakhmaninov that they found the clearest expression of a distinctively *Russian* émigré artist.[45]

Rakhmaninov and émigré memory

In 1922, émigré poet Konstantin Bal′mont mused wistfully in a letter to Rakhmaninov from Paris that 'when I write to you, in spirit I am in Moscow, in an overfilled hall, and your unerring fingers enchantingly scatter a diamond rain of crystal harmonies'.[46] In 1945 A. F. Greiner went so far as to associate the death of Rakhmaninov with a reenactment of physical exile: 'childhood, youth, Russia, Moscow and Rakhmaninov live

---

[43] Ivan Gumeniuk to S. Rakhmaninov, 23 December 1928, LCRA 44/29.

[44] N. Dauge to S. Rakhmaninov, 5 December 1931, LCRA 43/45. See also, Ivan Sikorskii to S. Rakhmaninov, 10 June 1940, LCRA 47/53.

[45] See, for instance, 'Concert Review', *Teatr i iskusstva*, 2, 1928, p. 2; Mariia Moravskaia, 'Razrushitel′naia muzyka', *Novoe russkoe slovo*, 2863, 27 November 1920, p. 5.

[46] Konstantin Bal′mont to S. Rakhmaninov in Apetian (ed.), *S. Rachmaninov: Literaturnoe nasledie*, 3, pp. 399–400.

together inseparable in my heart', he recalled, but 'with the departure of Sergei Vasil'evich, Moscow and Russia have again departed as well'.[47] Letters to the composer from émigrés in Harbin, Berlin, Paris and New York and countless articles in the Russian émigré press repeated the refrain that Rakhmaninov and 'old Russia' — the Russia of memory — were intimately linked. Thus, Mariia Gagarina, reflecting on Rakhmaninov's death in 1943, mourned that 'Sergei Vasil'evich embodied in himself and in his music everything that is most elevated, the very best features, the entire soul of Russia and it seems to me that, with his death, we are deprived here in exile [*na chuzhbine*] of a piece of our dear, beloved homeland'.[48]

But what precisely was this genuine 'Russianness' that Rakhmaninov and his music were believed to preserve? And, equally important, what did this understanding of 'Russianness' exclude? On one hand, some attributes émigré correspondents celebrated in Rakhmaninov recalled pre-revolutionary notions of the 'Russian soul': emotional, spiritual, universal and at eternal odds with Western, rational culture.[49] On the other hand, émigré constructions of 'Russianness' took place within a context of trauma and loss, as well as their need to define their place both within numerous diasporic contexts and their attitude toward emergent Soviet culture.[50] After all, émigrés preferred to ignore the uncomfortable fact that their eternalized 'Russian soul' had failed to prevent the victory of the Bolshevik Revolution and its secular materialist world-view.[51] Nor was there space in this image for commemorating the actual multi-ethnic and multi-confessional nature of imperial Russia, or engaging with the conflicted social relations and political disputes that had marked the final years of the empire (and that continued to influence the political activities of the émigré community). This underlines the point that a site of memory is a construct. Selection and omission are inherent characteristics of the endeavour.

---

[47] A. F. Greiner, untitled reminiscences, in M. Dobuzhinskii (ed.), *Pamiati Rakhmaninova*, New York, 1946, pp. 41–42.

[48] Mariia Gagarina to Natal'ia Rakhmaninova, 31 March 1943, LCRA 44/26.

[49] A particularly famous iteration of the 'Russian idea' was offered by Fedor Dostoevskii in his speech on Pushkin. See Feodor M. Dostoevsky, 'Pushkin: A Sketch', in Mark Raeff (ed.), *Russian Intellectual History: An Anthology*, Atlantic Highlands, NJ, 1978, pp. 288–300. On the universal (and hence Russian) nature of Rakhmaninov's talent, see for instance Vladimir Pol', 'Kontsert S. V. Rakhmaninova', *Vozrozhdenie*, 2004, 27 November 1930, p. 4.

[50] This claim argues against a tendency to de-historicize conceptions of 'Russianness' and highlights the constructed (and contextual) way through which identity is defined.

[51] For an example of a philosophical attempt to come to terms with this loss, see Nikolai Berdiaev, *Sud'ba Rossii*, Moscow, 2000.

The idealization of Rakhmaninov as an embodiment of 'old Russia' served two practical goals: he was seen as a preserver of genuine Russian culture in exile (*na chuzhbine*), and his music allowed audiences to transcend the struggle of everyday existence and find renewed purpose in life.[52] Both of these accomplishments were cast within a nationalist framing in which 'Russianness' represented an ahistorical image of Orthodox spirituality, a pure Russian landscape (devoid of social conflict) and a vaguely defined humanism. Connections drawn between Rakhmaninov and his patron saint, Sergius of Radonezh, had particular significance for the assertion of the ultimate triumph of a sacred rather than secular vision of Russianness. Thus, the Russian émigré community in Paris declared, '[Rakhmaninov] carries the name of our saint, Sergius of Radonezh, of whom it was prophetically said that "the Russian land will fall when the candles by his relics are extinguished." The prophecy came true — they were extinguished. But not forever', and closed with the wish 'to hear once more in Moscow Rakhmaninov's *All Night Vigil* in the presence of the author'.[53] Here Rakhmaninov was framed as a stand-in for the founder of the famed Holy Trinity Monastery near Moscow, whose relics (and their exposure by the Bolsheviks) had served as a major propaganda target in the early Soviet state.[54] Just as this early anti-religious act had failed to have the intended effect of undermining popular belief in the saint, belief in Russia (as embodied in Rakhmaninov), it was asserted, continued to thrive. Nor was this linking of Rakhmaninov to St Sergius limited to official expressions. In a personal letter to the composer, E. Romanchuk told him how, after her mother's death, she had lost the ability to pray. This tragic loss of belief was overcome, however, when, passing by a church she placed a candle before St Sergius of Radonezh and prayed for Rakhmaninov, in praise that God had sent him.[55] Rakhmaninov, she concluded, had given her the ability to believe again.

Indeed, Rakhmaninov's music was regularly celebrated by admirers for helping them endure suffering and preserving their hope for a better future. Thus, as Duchess Elena Altenburg wrote from Copenhagen in 1921, 'Let your strength be preserved until that bright day, when it will again be possible to work for Russia, recovering from communism, to

---

[52] For reports that emphasize the Russian émigré community's 'pride' in Rakhmaninov's 'Russianness', see also, Iulian Poplavskii, 'Muzyka: Vecher prizrakov i kontrastov', *Teatr i iskusstvo*, 2, 1928, pp. 4–5; idem, 'Sergei Rakhmaninov', *Teatr i iskusstvo*, 19, 1929, pp. 15–16.

[53] 'Rakhmaninovu — Russkaia koloniia v Parizhe', *RIS*, 219, 1 April 1933.

[54] Scott Kenworthy, *The Heart of Russia: Trinity-Sergius, Monasticism, and Society after 1825*, Oxford, 2010, pp. 312–26.

[55] E. Romanchuk to S. Rakhmaninov, 3 March 1929, LCRA 47/37.

praise national [*rodnogo*] art. I fervently wish to live to this epoch [...]. But until this one must endure and deal with *toska* for the motherland'.⁵⁶ By preserving 'true' Russian culture, it was claimed, Rakhmaninov fulfilled a broader cultural mission: preparing the émigré community for return to their homeland once the Bolshevik Revolution should end. Writing from Belgrade in 1929, Colonel Evgenii Garaburda imbued Rakhmaninov's significance with specific political content. 'As a Russian', he wrote, 'I know you of course, our national pride, a genius composer whose works give humanity the highest spiritual pleasure, a brilliant representative of Russian art', and a man who did not forget his fellow countrymen in their hour of need. Rakhmaninov, he concluded emphatically, gave Russians the strength to believe in the 'great national task' of the Russian emigration: to preserve unfettered love for Mother Russia and seek to free her from the yoke of Bolshevik repression.⁵⁷

Rakhmaninov's unique appeal to the 'Russian soul' was regularly singled out as a reason why his compositions were not fully accessible to American or European audiences. In a review for the Paris-based paper *Poslednie novosti*, L. S. argued that Rakhmaninov's 'genuineness' and overabundance of 'Russian soul' (*russkaia dusha*) made it difficult for Western Europeans to understand him.⁵⁸ Riesemann similarly stressed that both the musician's compositional silence after 1917 and the relative lack of interest in his compositions amongst European audiences was due to his enforced residence outside his homeland, concluding that 'owing to the national element present in almost all music, it is best understood by the people of the composer's own race'.⁵⁹ Such assertions served to maintain a sense of distinction from the various host communities in which émigrés found themselves, reinforcing the call often cited in the émigré press to maintain Russia's cultural distinctness.

Perhaps inspired in part by a pre-revolutionary theme of Rakhmaninov as a unifying Orphic figure, Russian émigrés upheld the composer as a symbol that could unite Russians in exile and in their troubled homeland into a single community of 'genuine' Russia. Asserting that Russia would continue to exist so long as Rakhmaninov lived, in 1931 Lollii L'vov turned

---

⁵⁶ Duchess Elena Altenburg to S. Rakhmaninov, 6 November 1921, LCRA 40/3.

⁵⁷ Evgenii Garaburda to S. Rakhmaninov, 4 January 1929, LCRA 44/26. For similar claims, see M. Veinbaum to S. Rakhmaninov, 21 December 1932, Gosudarstvennyi tsentral′nyi muzei muzykal′noi kul′tury (hereafter, GTsMMK), f. 18, no. 1428.

⁵⁸ L. S., 'S. V. Rakhmaninov (k segodniashnemu kontsertu)', *Poslednie novosti*, 4011, 16 March 1932, p. 3.

⁵⁹ Riesemann, *Rachmaninoff's Recollections*, pp. 247–48. See also V. Pol′, 'Kontsert Rakhmaninova', *Vozrozhdenie*, 3588, 31 March 1925, p. 4.

on its head a lambast of the composer's music published in the Soviet paper, *Vecherniaia Moskva*. Audiences who attended a recent concert of Rakhmaninov's *The Bells* at the Moscow Conservatory were not the outlived dregs of society, as the Soviet periodical had suggested; rather, they proved that 'genuine' Russia continued to exist and Rakhmaninov's music gave them strength to maintain their belief in it, despite the yoke of Bolshevik repression.[60] On the composer's sixtieth birthday in 1933, the Russian colony in Paris emphasized that he was the 'expresser of Russian national genius and sympathizer of all Russians', whether in the 'lands of Golgotha' (i.e., Russia suffering under Bolshevik oppression) or in the 'bitter land of exile'.[61] For the Russian Émigré Society in Prague, Rakhmaninov was 'not just a great artist, but an outstanding Russian person, who deeply loves his suffering motherland and passionately responds to the needs of Russian people, both languishing under the Bolshevik yoke, and spread out around the world'.[62] In this context, the transformative power of Rakhmaninov's music merged with an image of reclaiming a single, unified Russian culture that would ultimately be reunited with its homeland.

As hopes faded that an immediate political upheaval would remove the Bolsheviks from power, discourse gave way to a temporally vague image of Russia's future that focused explicitly on the spiritual side of Russian identity rather than material concerns like physical return.[63] True Russianness, admirers increasingly claimed, was to be found in the *spiritual* preservation of old Russia. Such a shift away from political to predominantly cultural concerns within the émigré community more broadly was acknowledged by writer Vladislav Khodasevich in 1933,[64] but individual émigrés already doubted the practicality of return by the late 1920s, particularly as Stalin's 'Revolution from Above' transformed Soviet

---

[60] Lollii L'vov, 'Rakhmaninov', *RIS*, 172, 12 March 1932, pp. 1–2. See also Riesemann, *Rachmaninoff's Recollections*, pp. 200–03.

[61] 'Rakhmaninovu — Russkaia koloniia v Parizhe', *RIS*, 1 April 1933.

[62] GTsMMK, f. 18, no. 1953, l. 8. For other addresses to the composer that similarly stressed his role as a unifier of Russian culture, see for instance 'Rech' N. I. Astrova', LCRA 57/15; Soiuz russkikh pisatelei i zhurnalistov v Iugoslavii to S. Rakhmaninov, 22 April [1933], LCRA 41/34.

[63] The gradual abandonment of the idea of return similarly led to shifts within the émigré community and government policy to Russian émigrés. For instance, the government of Czechoslovakia, which had initially supported educational efforts for Russian émigrés in Prague reformulated their policy towards the émigrés as they sought better relations with the USSR. See Catherine Andreyev and Ivan Savicky, *Russia Abroad: Prague and the Russian Diaspora, 1918–1938*, New Haven, CT, 2004.

[64] Slobin, 'The "Homecoming" of the First Wave Diaspora and Its Cultural Legacy', p. 513.

society and culture.⁶⁵ In his 1928 letter to Rakhmaninov from Harbin, Gumeniuk closed, not with an assertion of the inevitability of return, but with the rhetorical question whether his children would ever 'see him [Rakhmaninov] in their homeland [*rodina*]', a hope he no longer held for himself or his wife.⁶⁶ Writing for *Rossiia i slavianstvo* in 1930, L'vov was ever more pessimistic, concluding that 'we no longer have Moscow, and Russia burns with a frightful fire'.⁶⁷

Indeed, the brutality of Stalin's Revolution from Above, and the remaking of the physical landscape of their former homeland (mourned in *Rossiia i slavianstvo* by a series of photographs of Orthodox churches destroyed by the Bolsheviks), led L'vov to argue in 1933 that genuine Russianness now *only* dwelt in exile, embodied in Rakhmaninov. The composer's 1917 departure had marked the downfall of the true, inherently musical values of 'Russianness' in Russia; this 'first sign of the departure of music from Russia', had doomed the country 'only to an inhuman cruel physical battle for existence'.⁶⁸ A 1938 performance at the Music Academy in Philadelphia likewise inspired an émigré family to write to Rakhmaninov to empathize with what they interpreted as the composer's musical expression of his longing for his lost homeland. 'We fully recognize and honestly sympathize with you over the lost past, [over the loss of] our motherland', for like all Russians they too suffered 'hours of bitter torment'. Rather than ending with a call for return home, they simply wondered: 'When and how will [our exile] end! God only knows.'⁶⁹ They closed with a classic trope of nineteenth-century Russian identity: their suffering served the purpose of bringing them closer to God.

In this context, the act of listening to Rakhmaninov's music served as a force uniting the exiles into a shared community. Gathering in Riga in 1931 to celebrate the one-year anniversary of their attendance at a Rakhmaninov concert, a group of émigrés mourned that they were unable to attend his concerts in London or Paris that year, but reassured him by letter that

---

⁶⁵ In November 1927, Stalin announced the goals of rapid industrialization and collectivization of agriculture, and in 1928 initiated the First Five-Year Plan, which ushered in a period of revolutionary transformation of economic, social and cultural life. Émigrés who had been hopeful that the previous economic policy of NEP had foreshadowed a slackening of revolutionary fervour and the possibility of some sort of rapprochement with the regime were particularly disheartened.

⁶⁶ I. G. Gumeniuk to S. Rakhmaninov, 23 December 1928, LCRA 44/29.

⁶⁷ Lollii L'vov, 'Rakhmaninov', *RIS*, 104, 22 November 1930, p. 3. See also Lollii L'vov, 'Rakhmaninov', *RIS*, 172, 12 March 1932, pp. 1–2.

⁶⁸ Lollii L'vov, 'Rakhmaninov: ko dniu ego shestidesiatiletiia', *RIS*, 219, 1 April 1933.

⁶⁹ Dobrynin family to S. Rakhmaninov, 22 October 1938, LCRA 43/47.

they maintained their connection with him and with all exiled Russians by 'constantly listening' to his records.[70] For émigrés N. Gersdorf and his wife, a performance of Rakhmaninov's second concerto heard on the radio spoke directly to their 'Russian soul'.[71] For such individuals, 'Russianness' increasingly referred, not to a physical location, but to a perceived community linked by the ineffable bonds of culture. Rakhmaninov's beloved musical harmonies connected the scattered émigré communities into a single Russian cultural milieu. The question of return, if raised at all, was increasingly a question about a distant future, not an immediate desire. This spiritual concept of 'Russianness' was decoupled from physical space, and floated in a timeless realm, the temporality of the emigration itself.

Indeed, Rakhmaninov's explicitly apolitical nature allowed émigrés with dramatically different politics and backgrounds to inscribe their own interpretation of 'Russianness' onto the composer, and even to offer explicit compositional suggestions. In his 1929 letter to Rakhmaninov from Tel Aviv, Russian-Jewish émigré David Shor reflected that contemporary problems could only be solved by reawakening the spiritual qualities of Russianness embodied by Rakhmaninov. 'Humanity needs moral foundations and rules of life, founded upon love and justice', he argued, 'and Providence has chosen tiny Palestine and the people of Israel for this'. Only in Palestine could the 'falseness of European civilization' be overcome and a higher spiritual path be found for humanity. It was in Rakhmaninov, the embodiment of a *Russian* composer, that humanity's moral foundations in the modern age would be revived.[72] Fearing that the distractions of world fame had blocked Rakhmaninov's creative mission, Shor begged the composer to move to Palestine in order to regain the spiritual balance and harmony necessary to allow his compositional gift, silenced in exile, to find expression.

It is unlikely that Evgenii Karlovich Brant, an incurable antisemite who blamed the Jewish people for the Bolshevik Revolution, authored a study of Jewish 'ritual murder' and later collaborated with the Nazi

---

[70] N. Dauge to S. Rakhmaninov, 5 December 1931, LCRA 43/45.

[71] N. Gersdorf to S. Rakhmaninov, 31 August 1940, LCRA 44/26.

[72] David Shor to S. Rakhmaninov, 1929, LCRA 47/52. In his response, Rakhmaninov thanked Shor for his desire to bring him 'harmony', but noted that 'judging from the rare newspaper reports that reach us, there is no "harmony" in Palestine. The entire world now is a troubled sea', and concluded that the only 'harmony and peace' possible was spiritual, which could be achieved in New York as well as in Palestine. See Rakhmaninov to Shor, 13 October 1932, LCRA 41/12.

regime, would have approved of Shor's suggestion that Rakhmaninov relocate to Palestine.[73] Nevertheless, his own 1938 letter to Rakhmaninov from Copenhagen touched on similar themes of the spiritual value of Russianness and included a detailed proposal of the exact symphony that Rakhmaninov should complete, which was to be titled 'The Victory of Good over Evil'. After opening 'with a beautiful, languid, but not deep melody', wrote Brant, 'whose spiritual shallowness would embody the deception of Lucifer', this melody would gradually be transformed into a 'sensual, passionate [melody]' that would ultimately 'overflow into base instinct' (the latter symbolized by the use of 'base rhythms' borrowed from jazz music). After reaching the very edge of the 'abyss', 'the melody must then gradually transform into a clear and elevated [melody]. God's light penetrates the darkness, first in fits and starts, but gradually more and more, and, despite the opposing dark forces struggling to muffle the heavenly melody, in the end it is victorious', wrote Brant. 'In my opinion', he concluded, 'you are, of contemporary composers, the only one with the strength to write the symphony'. Eager to explain his interpretation of world history (and the place of Rakhmaninov's music therein), he continued, 'our world is now at a crossroads — it came to the edge of the abyss, but one already senses that, with God's Providence, the world will renounce evil [zlo] and again follow the path of goodness [dobro], in order to finally unite with God'.[74] Regardless of political tendencies, these admirers all were united in a shared image of a cultural 'Russianness' in which truth and higher spirituality was preserved through the composer's music.

In all these examples, Rakhmaninov was framed as an Orphic figure, whose music preserved an inherent 'Russianness' (though the specific content of that 'Russianness' varied depending on the listener). Devoid of clearly defined political content (apart from a generally anti-Bolshevik slant), increasingly detached from physical space, and selective in its iteration, Rakhmaninov and his music came to preserve the image of Russianness as émigrés wanted to define it: transcendent, human, spiritual, eternal and without conflict. As Rakhmaninov's music was transportable outside of the original physical space in which it had been composed, and

[73] Manfred Shrubi and Oleg Korostelev, *Psevdonimy russkogo zarubezh'ia: materialy i issledovaniia*, Moscow, 2016; Evgenii Brant, *Ritual'noe ubiistvo u evreev*, Belgrade, 1926.

[74] Evgenii Karlovich Brant to S. Rakhmaninov (7 November 1938). LCRA 42/66. For another example of a programmatic musical interpretation suggested to Rakhmaninov, see S[ergei] Gusev-Orenburgskii to Sergei Rakhmaninov, undated [after 1924], LCRA 44/25.

was open to interpretation across a range of political views, it became a particularly productive site of memory for the émigré community.

Early Soviet responses to Rakhmaninov: Collective memory divided
'Dear Sergei Vasil′evich', wrote Olga Knipper-Chekhova, actress and widow of Anton Chekhov, on 1 January 1918, 'you abandoned Russia, but for some reason I wanted to write you a few words'. Resentment struggled with longing in her epistle, and she ultimately penned a simple New Year's greeting, ending with the wish that life would soon become easier, and that Rakhmaninov 'would again return to Russia'.[75] Mariia Chartorizhskaia echoed this sentiment in her 1921 letter to the composer, greeting him on his Name Day and desiring 'that you will return to Russia as soon as possible'. However, this initial joyful wish was soon followed with the confession that 'I am convinced that you cannot even imagine how we live', nor 'what the memory of our sunny former life and even more our memories of you and your music mean to us'.[76] Such letters suggest that for Rakhmaninov's admirers and friends who remained behind in Soviet Russia, he was as important a symbol of collective memory as he was for the émigré community.

In contrast to the relatively unified collective memory that took shape around Rakhmaninov in emigration, the early Soviet years witnessed a bifurcation of collective memory between public and private realms. As the Bolshevik regime sought to forge the 'new Soviet man' and transform the mental as well as the physical world around them, music emerged as a cultural front in the struggle between the new revolutionary mentality and the outlived bourgeois culture of the tsarist era. Within this context, musical and artistic preferences were politicized, even while the Soviet state did not create a unified image of what constituted genuine proletarian culture until the 1930s.[77] Two distinct spaces of collective memory emerged in relation to Rakhmaninov: the 'public' discourse of musical specialists and government officials, who struggled amongst themselves to define the future of music in the revolutionary state; and the 'private' discourse of those who interpreted their views of the composer in categories and language decoupled from the revolutionary discussions circulating

---

[75] Olga Knipper-Chekhova to S. Rakhmaninov, 1 January 1918, LCRA 43/30.
[76] Mariia Chartorizhskaia to S. Rakhmaninov, 25 September/8 October 1921, LCRA 43/3.
[77] Amy Nelson, *Music for the Revolution: Musicians and Power in Early Soviet Russia*, University Park, PA, 2004, p. 20.

around them.[78] Private celebration of Rakhmaninov as an embodiment of the humane values of old Russia struggled with a public discourse that generally sought to decouple Rakhmaninov-the-man (a bourgeois White émigré and class enemy) from his popular music.

Of course, much as Rakhmaninov's Soviet admirers continued to cling to an image of music as embodying a higher reality, they resembled their émigré compatriots in that this space had temporally shifted after 1917 to a space of memory and nostalgia rather than a breathlessly awaited future. The nostalgic language expressed in letters to the composer and in private diary reflections resembles the concept of 'internal emigration' that became popular amongst dissidents of the later Soviet period. In his study of collective memory in the Soviet Union, James Wertsch traces the concept of 'internal emigration' back to at least 1946 and defines it as 'a process whereby individuals created an inner existence that stood apart from their public life'.[79] In the 1920s, I would argue that memory and nostalgia played a key role in the *preservation* of an inner existence separate from public life. Rakhmaninov was valuable as a symbol of this past world in part *because* of his absence from contemporary Soviet Russia; as an absent figure whose music still evoked memories of a vanished world, he served as an eternalized representative of the world that was lost. As a benevolent (yet distant) figure who provided material support, he was seen to embody the values of old Russia. This is not to suggest that all those who enjoyed listening to Rakhmaninov's music in the 1920s and 1930s opposed the regime. Nevertheless, those individuals who chose to write to the composer after his emigration seem to have inhabited a commensurate space and temporality as the émigrés. The space of internal emigration was a space of idealized memory of old Russia that embodied values that were perceived to have been lost under the new regime.[80]

---

[78] I use 'public discourse' to refer discussions that sought to integrate revolutionary concepts and categories into judgements of music, regardless of how individual participants viewed the music of Rakhmaninov. In contrast, 'private discourse' refers to the shrinking private space in which individuals responded to musical experiences in ways that did not fall within these revolutionary categories or concepts. In the examples discussed here, they generally did not have overtly dissident intent, though they might be interpreted as dissenting or suspicious on account of their discrepancy with 'public discourse'.

[79] James V. Wertsch, *Voices of Collective Remembering*, Cambridge and New York, 2002, p. 140.

[80] In contrast to émigré letters to Rakhmaninov, letters from Soviet citizens in the 1920s–30s tend to come from individuals who were either acquainted with the composer before 1917, or were recipients of aid sent by Rakhmaninov to the Soviet Union.

For his Soviet admirers, Rakhmaninov offered both physical and spiritual nurture. The composer sent extensive material aid to individuals and institutions, receiving numerous letters from his former compatriots in response.[81] Filled with confusion, bewilderment or even betrayal at his departure, letters also regularly evoked a nostalgic image of Rakhmaninov as a living memorial to a lost time, an old Russia now irreversibly lost. While émigrés still had Rakhmaninov in their midst, his admirers left behind suffered a particularly sharp disjuncture between 'old Russia' (of memory, embodied in their distant icon) and 'new Russia' (of current reality that, unlike émigrés, they experienced all around them). When thanking the composer for money or, increasingly, material aid he had sent, they upheld him as the only remaining symbol of genuine 'humanness' in the current age, a remnant of the 'true' Russia swept away by the Revolution. For N. Aleksapol'skii, writing in 1922, the 'best thing' about Rakhmaninov's gift was that it had moral value at a time when human life had become worth little in Moscow.[82] The poet T. Shchepina-Kupernik struggled to unite her earlier memories of the pleasure she had once received from Rakhmaninov's concerts with the physical pleasure now provided by 'daily bread' purchased through his beneficence.[83]

At the same time that Rakhmaninov offered some of his Soviet admirers physical nourishment, he was commonly interpreted by his correspondents as embodying a more spiritual, humane past that had existed in the lost world of old Russia, and that continued to be expressed in performances of his music. In a 1925 letter, Mariia Chartorizhskaia described a concert in which a Rakhmaninov suite was played as an encore. 'Sergei Vasil'evich, do not think that I exaggerate. I cannot describe to you what took place in the theatre… suddenly it was as though the entire theatre as a single person breathed with great joy, then a single sound was voiced: "aaakh — rakh-ma-ni-nov!"' He was as precious to Russians as ever, she insisted, despite his departure abroad.[84] After a performance of Rakhmaninov's *All-Night Vigil* in February 1926, pianist Aleksandr Gol'denveizer likewise reflected in his diary that he heard in it a life-changing spiritual power, which was

---

[81] Many of these letters are preserved in the LCRA. See also, A. F. Gedike, 'Pamiatnye vstrechi', in Z. V. Apetian (ed.), *Vospominaniia o Rakhmaninove*, 2 vols, Moscow, 1957, pp. 35–49 (p. 49).

[82] N. Aleksapol'skii to S. Rakhmaninov, 19 June 1922, LCRA 42/32.

[83] T. Shchepina-Kupernik to S. Rakhmaninov, 14 June, 1922, LCRA 48/16. See also Mikhail Ivanovich Satin to E. I. [Somov], 4 September 1933, LCRA 47/40. Mikhail Satin, a distant cousin of Rakhmaninov's wife, was arrested and sent to the Gulag.

[84] Maria Chartorizhskaia to S. Rakhmaninov, 20 April 1925, LCRA 43/3.

'especially precious in our dark days when coarseness, cruelty and the mockery of everything spiritual have triumphed'.[85] Religious significance was particularly poignant in a 1929 letter from N. Gardenin of Voronezh, who regretted that she could do nothing for Rakhmaninov's kindness to her family except pray in church; as a religious person, she assured him that she would do this.[86]

For Rakhmaninov's former Moscow Conservatory acquaintance Vladimir Vil'shau, the spiritual essence of 'Russianness' represented by Rakhmaninov was exclusionary, embodying a past Russia in which 'non-Russians' were absent. Responding to the same 1926 performance of Rakhmaninov's *All-Night Vigil* as Gol'denveizer, Vil'shau described in a letter how he was 'buried in memories' to the point that he could 'scarcely hold myself together' (despite the fact that this was the first time he had heard the composition). The audience, which was so struck by the music that they 'made not a single sound, not a cough, not a sneeze' and held their applause until the intermission, were explicitly highlighted by Vil'shau as *Russian*. 'Non-[ethnic] Russians [*inorodtsy*] were almost entirely absent', he noted.[87] Thus excluding non-ethnic Russians from his imagined lost Russia, he concluded, 'only now [i.e., after the Revolutions of 1917] do I understand how many of them [non-ethnic Russians] there are. If it continues further like this, then very soon all of Moscow will speak jargon'.[88]

While seldom explicitly political in content, implicit critique of the existing regime combined with an imagined return to an idealized Russian spirit. In 1921, fellow musician Mikhail Slonov wrote to complain of Rakhmaninov's departure and to suggest that his current task should be to write a symphony 'dedicated to the Motherland'.[89] He then detailed the precise content of the envisioned symphony. After an introduction offering

---

[85] Aleksandr Gol'denveizer, *Dnevnik: Tetradi vtoraia-shestaia (1905–1929)*, Moscow, 1997, p. 56. Gol'denveizer continued to have dreams in which Rakhmaninov returned to Moscow through the 1920s. See Gol'denveizer, *Dnevnik: tetrad vtoraia-shestaia*, pp. 251, 281 and 287.

[86] N. Gardenin to S. Rakhmaninov, 31 December 1929, LCRA 44/7. Gardenin was a distant cousin of Rakhmaninov's wife, Natal'ia.

[87] Vladimir Vil'shau to Rakhmaninov, 29 March 1926, in *Russkoe pravoslavnoe tserkovnoe penie v XX veke: Sovetskii period; Kniga 1 — 1920–1930e gody*, Moscow, 2015, pp. 489–90. A censored version of the letter (without reference to 'foreigners') appeared in Apetian (ed.), *Rakhmaninov: Literaturnoe nasledie*, 2, p. 465. For a similarly adulatory account of a 1922 performance of the *All-Night Vigil*, performed in a church in Kazan', see A. F. Samoilov to Rakhmaninov, 10 December 1922, in ibid., p. 490.

[88] Ibid., pp. 490–91.

[89] Mikhail Slonov to S. Rakhmaninov, 1921, LCRA 47/56.

the 'peaceful theme of Orthodox chant', the 'Time of Troubles' would be depicted with 'excerpts of themes of a Jewish and Kazakh character' that would be 'overcome with the strains of a "Slava" chorus [based on the folk song, "Slava na nebe sol′ntsu vysokomu"] that would accompany the crowning of Mikhail Fedorovich [Romanov]'.[90] An Andante with music of a 'German character' would follow to depict the 'influence of Germans on Russia', and then a third movement showcasing the War of 1812 (complete with the *Marseillaise* to symbolize Napoleon's march on Russia). But it was in the fourth movement that Slonov expressed his own commentary on Russia's fate. After an opening dominated by a 'gloomy, Japanese theme', broken off by the 'vigorous saintly theme of the workers', the 'Jewish theme' would return from the Time of Troubles, leading into a section of 'orgy and destruction' depicting the war and revolution. This would ultimately be overcome by the return of the opening Orthodox chant, this time accompanied with a counterpoint melody derived from the 'Slava' chorus. While not explicitly political (the letter is framed entirely in terms of musical themes and movements), the political implications are not difficult to extrapolate. In Slonov's view, (Jewish) Bolsheviks had ushered in the current era of death and destruction, which would be overcome through a return to Orthodoxy and Russian nationalism, and Rakhmaninov was uniquely qualified to compose the musical expression of this future. Such glorifications of Rakhmaninov's 'Russianness' thus co-existed with xenophobia connecting the Bolshevik Revolution to the influence of 'non-Russians'.

It is not surprising that, in contrast with such private nostalgia, early Soviet public discourse disparaged the composer as a relic of 'outlived' bourgeois society; his traditional compositional style and status as an émigré made it difficult to admit him into a temporally forward-looking discourse focused on historical progress. Though not banned, his music drew the critique of musicians who allied themselves to the new regime's revolutionary platform.[91] Music critic Leonid Sabaneev off-handedly dismissed Rakhmaninov as a representative 'not even [of] the yesterday of

---

[90] The reference Slonov gives is to the Slava chorus in Rimskii-Korsakov's *The Tsar's Bride*, which employs the same Russian folk song used in compositions by Musorgskii and Beethoven. The text cited seems to have been inspired by Rimskii-Korsakov.

[91] On the fate of the performance of Rakhmaninov's music, see Pauline Fairclough, *Classics for the Masses: Shaping Soviet Musical Identity under Lenin and Stalin*, New Haven, CT, 2016, pp. 89–90 and 85–91; Nelson, *Music for the Revolution*, p. 73; Marina Frolova-Walker and Jonathan Walker, *Music and Soviet Power, 1917–1932*, Woodbridge and Rochester, NY, 2012, pp. 287–88.

art', but of 'some day last week'.⁹² The 1926 performance of the composer's *All-Night Vigil*, celebrated by Gol'denveizer and Vil'shau privately, was roundly condemned by the proletarian music organization RAPM, which questioned both the historical value of the work and why any sacred music was being performed by the state capella. By 1928 the work had been removed from the repertoire.⁹³ Such attacks intensified in the early 1930s, perhaps sparked in part by Rakhmaninov's condemnation of the Soviet government in a 1931 letter to the *New York Times*.⁹⁴ In a 1931 article for *Vecherniaia Moskva*, a performance of *The Bells* was framed as a surreptitious Orthodox liturgy, performed under the very auspices of Soviet society, and attended by 'a very strange public' consisting of 'old men in long frocks', 'old women in old-fashioned scarves', and an assortment of 'long stockings' and 'lorgnettes' — all physical symbols of outlived, bourgeois culture out of place in the worker's state.⁹⁵

While Rakhmaninov's music gradually returned to performance after RAPM was disbanded in 1932, he continued to be lampooned as an outdated White émigré. Thus, in their 1937 satirical work, *Odnoetazhnaia Amerika*, Soviet satirists Il'f and Petrov caricatured him as cynically performing the role of the tragic émigré for foolish audiences:

> Rakhmaninov, as we were told by a composer-acquaintance, sits in the green room [*artisticheskaia komnata*] and tells jokes before going out on stage. When the bell rings, Rakhmaninov rises from his seat and, assuming the great sorrow of a Russian exile on his face, goes onstage.⁹⁶

---

⁹² L. Sabaneev, 'The Revolutionary Years in Music', *Kul'tura i zhizn'*, 1, 1 February 1922, pp. 51–55, translated in Frolova-Walker and Walker, *Music and Soviet Power*, pp. 75–80 (p. 78).
⁹³ 'The Double-Faced Janus', *Muzyka i Oktiabr'*, 1926, 2, p. 21, translated in Frolova-Walker and Walker, *Music and Soviet Power*, pp. 170–72. See also, Nelson, *Music for the Revolution*, p. 152.
⁹⁴ A. Veprik, *Muzyka i revoliutsiia*, 1929, 2; E. Kann, *Rabis*, 9, 1932. The letter, written in response to Rabindranath Tagore's recent visit to the USSR was signed by Rakhmaninov, Ivan Ostromislenskii and Count Il'ia Tolstoi. It appeared in the 15 January 1931 edition of the *New York Times*. See LCRA 50/3.
⁹⁵ D. G., 'Kolokola zvoniat (ob odnom kontserte v Konservatorii), *Vecherniaia Moskva*, 57, 9 March 1931. The entire article was republished with commentary in El, '"Kolokola" S. V. Rakhmaninova v Moskve', *RIS*, 121, 21 March 1931, p. 3. For descriptions of similar attacks in the Soviet press at this time, see Riesemann, *Rachmaninoff's Recollections*, pp. 200–03.
⁹⁶ Il'f and Petrov, *Odnoetazhnaia Amerika*, Moscow, 1937, p. 148.

In this and other critiques of the time, Rakhmaninov was framed as a symbol of the outlived and backward culture of old Russia, preserved in the emigration.

As the political situation darkened in the Soviet Union, Rakhmaninov's connections with those left behind grew increasingly scant; by 1935, the composer's secretary, Evgenii Somov, informed Rakhmaninov that Stalin's terror had directly affected a number of Rakhmaninov's former pensioners.[97] In response to Rakhmaninov's concern in 1935 that he spent too much of his personal fortune sending aid to others, Somov chided him by directly referencing his meaning for the Soviet Russian population. When recent arrivals from Soviet Russia were asked which Russian émigrés enjoyed the greatest popularity in the USSR, Somov claimed, they invariably answered 'Rakhmaninov of course!' This was not, he concluded, because of the composer's music, which they had not been able to hear for many years, but because of how Rakhmaninov's image had taken shape in exile. 'Your Russianness, your implacability, the absence in all your actions of any sort of compromise, and your large responsive heart', wrote Somov, 'all this, in addition to what your music gives to each of them, is what raises you higher than all others now living in the eyes of your people [*narod*]'.[98] In Somov's view, Rakhmaninov-the-man was, if anything, more important than his music in embodying the true Russianness of the past to those unfortunate Russians still dwelling in the Soviet Union. In this way, the political tensions between Soviet and émigré conceptions of the 1917 Revolution found explicit voice in the conflicting memory culture surrounding Rakhmaninov.

Nostalgia and nationalism: The convergence of memory

In 1945, mourning Rakhmaninov's recent death, Soviet musician Aleksandr Gedike wrote from Moscow to the composer's widow, 'I passionately loved Rakhmaninov both as a person and as a great musician, and he remained in my memory just the same as he was on that evening that I passed in your house with such pleasure'.[99] Gol'denveizer similarly expressed his own unfulfilled 'hope to once more meet in this life with Sergei Vasil'evich, to embrace him and to tell him how dear he is to me and how I love his miraculous music'. Lapsing into his own idealized vision of old Russia, Gol'denveizer mused, 'I often see him in my dreams, arriving in Moscow

---

[97] Evgenii Somov to S. Rakhmaninov, 19 April 1935, LCRA 47/61.
[98] Somov to Rakhmaninov, 26 April 1935, LCRA 47/61.
[99] Aleksandr Gedike to Natal'ia Rakhmaninova, 29 March 1945, LCRA 44/13.

— I see him just as I remember him, still young. His voice sounds so clear to me, as if I hear him in real life'.[100]

At the close of the Great Patriotic War, the reintegration of public and private memories into a single narrative of Rakhmaninov's 'Russianness' was already well underway. Whereas Greta Slobin argues that 'a significant shift occurs in the internal re-evaluation of the émigré legacy begun in the more liberal climate following Stalin's death in 1953', Soviet reassessment of Rakhmaninov's place in Russian culture had already begun ten years earlier amid the patriotic mood of the Great Patriotic War.[101] Interaction and synthesis of émigré and Soviet interpretations of Rakhmaninov yielded shared acceptance of the composer as a site of memory through which 'Russianness' was communicated to a new generation.

Rakhmaninov's outspoken support for the Soviet Union after the invasion by Nazi Germany in 1941 and charity concerts to benefit the Soviet war effort sparked a new official narrative of Rakhmaninov as a 'great patriot', a national hero who was eternally devoted to his homeland. Former acquaintances, now leading members of the Soviet musical establishment, responded with a flood of letters to Rakhmaninov celebrating their shared status as patriotic Russians.[102] The composer's death in 1943 closed off any possible hope of his physical return to Russia, but redoubled his importance as a memory space through which to construct a unified Russian identity. To overcome problematic aspects of his historical views, Rakhmaninov had to be reworked into a tragic national hero, whose 'fatal error' in abandoning his homeland had led to his eternal suffering. This new narrative was already espoused at a memorial meeting on 3 July 1944, at which the idea of opening a Rakhmaninov museum was raised, as well as the plan to collect reminiscences from those who had known him.[103] In his report at the meeting, Gol'denveizer, who in 1926 had celebrated the continued spiritual significance of Rakhmaninov's *All-Night Vigil*, recounted a meeting between the composer and a Moscow musician travelling abroad. Having stumbled across one another in a music store, Rakhmaninov had started to ask about Moscow, but after a few words he 'burst into tears and ran out of the store without saying goodbye'.[104]

---

[100] Aleksandr Gol'denveizer to Natal'ia Rachmaninova, 14 June 1943, LCRA 44/14.
[101] Slobin, 'The "Homecoming" of the First Wave Diaspora and Its Cultural Legacy', p. 519.
[102] Fairclough, *Classics*, p. 187.
[103] A. B. Gol'denveizer, 'Doklady posviashchennye pamiati S. V. Rakhmaninova', GTsMMK, f. 18, no. 2694, ll. 1–2.
[104] Ibid., ll. 16–17.

Gol'denveizer claimed, moreover, that Rakhmaninov had requested 'that his body be taken to Russia' — a physical return to his homeland that had been impossible while he lived.[105]

Inspired in part by materials shared by Rakhmaninov's sister-in-law Sof'ia Satina via VOKS (the All-Union Society for Cultural Ties Abroad, the institution in charge of cultural exchange between the Soviet Union and the West), K. Kuznetsov developed these ideas in his 1945 article for *Sovetskaia muzyka*, which established a standard narrative for later Soviet interpretations.[106] In Kuznetsov's account, Rakhmaninov desired to be buried in Moscow after the war, was indifferent to Orthodox spirituality, fascinated by Russian folk belief, and had mistakenly believed that there would be no place for music in post-1917 Russia — his departure, in short, was entirely caused by professional considerations, which he had, in his final years, realized were mistaken.[107] His lengthy compositional silence was caused in large part by the trauma of departing from his 'beloved motherland, her nature, her day-to-day life [*byt*], her people'.[108] Indeed, even the composer's first large-scale composition finished in emigration, the fourth piano concerto, had, Kuznetsov emphasized, been started in Russia.[109]

The image of Rakhmaninov as a homesick, nostalgic émigré who could never stop thinking of his motherland quickly became a standard

---

[105] Ibid., l. 17. Initial Soviet attempts to reclaim Rakhmaninov's legacy were seen in the publication of a number of pre-1917 letters, reminiscences by acquaintances, and new assessments of his music, including late compositions like the Third Symphony. See Marietta Shaginian (ed.), 'Pis'ma S. V. Rakhmaninova k Re', *Novyi mir*, 4, 1943, pp. 105–13; Georgii Khubov, 'Tret'ia ia simfoniia Rakhmaninova', *Pravda*, 26 July 1943; Igor' Glebov [Boris Asaf'ev], 'Rakhmaninov', *Literatura i iskusstvo*, 14/66, 3 April 1943; Boris Asaf'ev, 'Tret'ia simfoniia Rakhmaninova', *Literatura i iskusstvo*, 25/77, 19 June 1943; K. Kuznetsov, 'Novoe o Rakhmaninove', *Literatura i iskusstvo*, 25 March 1944; Boris Asaf'ev, 'S. V. Rakhmaninov', *Sovetskaia muzyka*, 3, 1953, pp. 55–65.

[106] K. Kuznetsov, 'Tvorcheskaia zhizn' S. V. Rakhmaninova', *Sovetskaia muzyka*, 4, 1945, pp. 25–51. An English-language version of the same article appeared as K. Kouznetsov, 'Sergei Rachmaninoff's Musical Life', *VOKS Bulletin*, 6, 1945, pp. 40–51. On the history of VOKS and its involvement in cultural diplomacy in interwar and post-1945 contexts, see Michael David-Fox, 'From Illusory "Society" to Intellectual "Public": VOKS, International Travel and Party: Intelligentsia Relations in the Interwar Period', *Contemporary European History*, 11, 2002, 1, pp. 7–32; Kiril Tomoff, *Virtuosi Abroad: Soviet Music and Imperial Competition During the Early Cold War, 1945–1958*, Ithaca, NY, 2015, pp. 23–26.

[107] Kuznetsov, 'Tvorcheskaia zhizn' Rakhmaninova', pp. 48–51.

[108] Ibid., p. 48. Kuznetsov does not simply reiterate a simplistic musical interpretation of Rakhmaninov's late works as nostalgic reminiscences of Russia; rather, he emphasizes that the composer was developing a new, mature style.

[109] Ibid., p. 47.

trope in post-war Soviet discussion.[110] If Rakhmaninov had been so passionately devoted to his homeland, however, his Soviet interpreters had to clarify the reason for his departure — a reason, moreover, that could not demonstrate hostility to the Bolshevik regime. Building on these early interpretations, Rakhmaninov's 1917 departure soon came to be labelled a 'fatal error' of judgement that had poisoned his years in emigration. Thus, in a popular biography of the composer in 1946, Igor' Belza claimed that Rakhmaninov's departure abroad 'was connected with the beginning of a deep spiritual crisis'. While the composer had thought that he needed to leave in order to be able to devote himself to his art, this decision was faulty. 'In fact he lost [his ability to serve art], because he loved his homeland too much to be able to easily come to terms with émigré life.'[111] By 1962, another popular biography claimed that Rakhmaninov never intended to be gone for longer than a single winter.[112] This error had a deleterious effect on Rakhmaninov's compositional output, which was repeatedly explained through his loss of creative inspiration when he physically left his homeland.[113] Events and comments contradicting this narrative were often edited out of Soviet sources. The carefully compiled three-volume collection of letters, reminiscences and documents related to the composer published in 1978-80 omitted mention of any Bolshevik 'agitator' in Rakhmaninov's recollections, as well as his discussion of Orthodox spirituality, and the critical letter about the Soviet regime written by the composer in 1931 that had helped spark RAPM's call for a boycott of his music.[114]

Despite the fatal error of leaving his homeland, it was argued, Rakhmaninov had successfully preserved a 'deeply Russian' character.

---

[110] A. Solovtsov, *S. V. Rakhmaninov: lektsiia*, Moscow, 1955, p. 22; O. I. Sokolova, *Sergei Vasil'evich Rakhmaninov*, Moscow, 1983, p. 109; Ossovskii, 'S. V. Rakhmaninov', in *Vospominaniia o Rakhmaninove*, 1, pp. 354-401 (p. 401); 'Stat'i i retsenzii o S. V. Rakhmaninove', GTsMMK f. 18, no. 599.

[111] I. F. Belza, *S. V. Rakhmaninov: populiarnyi ocherk*, Moscow, 1946, p. 11. See also, Apetian (ed.), *S. Rakhmaninov: Literaturnoe nasledie*, 1, pp. 26-29.

[112] N. Bazhanov, *Rakhmaninov*, Moscow, 1962, p. 337. A. Trubnikova argued that the composer had left Russia *before* the October Revolution had taken place. See A. Trubnikova, 'Sergei Rakhmaninov', *Ogonek*, 4, 27 January 1946, pp. 20-21.

[113] Dmitrii Shostakovich, 'Ego tvorchestvo pitali Rodina', *Izvestiia* (31 March 1973), LCRA 88/12.

[114] S. Rakhmaninov, 'Vospominaniia,' in Apetian (ed.), *S. Rakhmaninov: Literaturnoe nasledie*, 1, pp. 51-61. The 'Ivanovka' section of Rakhmaninov's reminiscences had previously been published (also without the section on the Bolshevik agitator) in Sof'ia Satina, 'S. V. Rakhmaninov: k 25-letiiu so dnia konchiny', *Novyi zhurnal*, 91, 1968, pp. 115-28.

While 'Russianness' in the émigré context had been connected with an explicitly spiritualized image of the 'Russian soul', Soviet interpretations focused instead on Rakhmaninov's direct connection to the Russian *narod*. Citing the material provided to VOKS by Sof´ia Satina, Belza argued that Rakhmaninov 'remained a Russian person not only in his background, but in the form of thoughts and feelings. He was deeply interested in the life of the Russian *narod* and the development of its culture'.[115] Similarly, in reminiscences collected from former acquaintances in the 1950s, Rakhmaninov's 'Russianness' was repeatedly emphasized as explicitly connected with his homeland and its residents. 'Serezha loved everything Russian, the Russian people [*narod*], Russian language, Russian nature, Russian art, without limit. He had a wide Russian soul, full of deep and noble feelings.'[116] Indeed, even Rakhmaninov's love of Soviet culture, literature and song (including recordings of the Red Army Chorus) was celebrated.[117] For another former friend, A. V. Ossovskii, it was essential to reject the spiritual aspect of Rakhmaninov's work emphasized by émigrés. 'Rakhmaninov never "was an Orthodox believer" and the *Liturgy* was not written by him because of religious convictions. The national artist-patriot Rakhmaninov sought sources that were ancient Russian, folk, national musical culture and found them in the plentiful treasures of ancient church *obikhod* melodies, preserved in the form of so-called chants.'[118] Above all, Rakhmaninov's patriotic devotion to his homeland was evidenced, it was claimed, by his performance of benefit concerts after the Nazi invasion of the Soviet Union, the proceeds of which were contributed to the Soviet war effort.[119] In this way, Rakhmaninov's post-war Soviet memory evoked nostalgia for an idealized pure space of Russian national identity connected with folk culture that avoided discussion of the political upheavals of the revolutionary age.

The post-war Soviet rediscovery of Rakhmaninov was part of a transnational discussion that involved direct exchange of ideas and interpretations between Soviet and émigré groups. Archival materials and reminiscences of the composer were shared and reprinted by both

---

[115] Belza, *Rakhmaninov: populiarnyi ocherk*, p. 12.
[116] L. D. Rostovtsova, 'Vospominaniia o S. V. Rakhmaninove', in *Vospominaniia o Rakhmaninove*, 1, pp. 242–62 (p. 262). See also *S. Rakhmaninov: Literaturnoe nasledie*, 1, pp. 31–34.
[117] A. Solovtsov, *Rakhmaninov: lektsiia*, p. 23.
[118] A. V. Ossovskii, 'S. V. Rakhmaninov', in *Vospominaniia o Rakhmaninove*, 1, pp. 354–401 (p. 377).
[119] K. Kuznetsov, 'Novoe o Rakhmaninove', *Literatura i iskusstvo* (25 March 1944); GTsMMK f. 18, no. 599, l. 8.

communities, and the Soviet state entered into direct contact with Rakhmaninov's descendants.[120] However, such interaction also laid bare a lasting disjuncture in collective memory between these communities. In the Soviet context, the physicality of Rakhmaninov's link to his homeland was explicitly developed and celebrated. In the Tambov region, local activists united with the larger Soviet musical community to found a Rakhmaninov museum, first in the local proletarian club, but later housed in the physical space of Ivanovka itself, where the restoration of the estate buildings and park began in the 1960s.[121] Indeed, the very physicality of memory was embodied in repeated discussion in the Soviet press of the laying of lilies and earth brought from Russia on Rakhmaninov's grave in New York.[122] In contrast, in his 1946 reminiscences, M. Aldanov noted the renewed interest in Soviet Russia in Rakhmaninov, but concluded 'music is "more apolitical" than other arts, and has less need in an immediate geographic connection with the homeland. Rakhmaninov lived one third of his life abroad, and he continued to work and continued to create. His life was happy — insofar as the life of a great artist can be happy'.[123] Rather than a tragic figure, Rakhmaninov, he insisted, had profited from his emigration, as his world fame dated to his post-revolutionary concertizing activities. Alfred Swan similarly emphasized Rakhmaninov's alienation from Soviet Russia, claiming that the composer lived 'a life tinged with a longing to be in Russia again, *in the Russia of his dreams*. Once (at the station in Vienna)

---

[120] The Soviet publication *Vospominaniia o Rakhmaninove* included texts published in the émigré memorial volume edited by Dobuzhinskii. The émigré paper *Novoe russkoe slovo* published excerpts from the Soviet publication *Vospominaniia o Rakhmaninove* in its 1 April 1973 edition. Sections of Riesemann's memoirs were translated as well. See, for instance, M. S. Nemenova-Lunts (trans.), 'Rakhmaninov o sebe', *Ogonek*, 31 March 1943, p. 12.

[121] N. N. Emel´ianova (ed.), *S. V. Rakhmaninov v Ivanovke: sbornik materialov i dokumentov*, Voronezh, 1971; 'Sergei Rakhmaninov na Tambovshchine: ekskursionnyi putevoditel´', LCRA 88/13; N. Emel´ianova, 'Novyi muzei: po pamiatnym mestam', *Sovetskaia muzyka*, 10, 1968, pp. 158–59.

[122] B. Rozenfel´d and E. Pol´skaia, 'Rakhmaninovskii Aprel´', *Kavkazskaia zdravnitsa*, 59, 24 March 1973, 3; Dmitrii Shostakovich, 'Ego tvorchestvo pitala Rodina'; V. Briantseva, 'Eto — vse o Rossii: k 100-letiiu so dnia rozhdeniia S. V. Rakhmaninova', *Krasnaia zvezda*, 1 April 1973; Boris Primerov, 'Vesennie vody', *Literaturnaia Rossiia*, 13(533), 30 March 1973, p. 15; Igor´ Belza, 'Genial´nyi russkii muzykant', *Sovetskaia kul´tura*, 26, 30 March 1973, p. 4; V. Renert, 'Moia muzyka — russkaia', *Kavkazskaia zdravnitsa*, 93, 15 May 1973, p. 2. V. Brosalin, 'V pamiat´ o vydaiushchemsia kompozitore', *Tambov*, 30 March 1973; A. Petrenko, 'K iubileinoi date S. V. Rakhmaninova', *Muzykal´naia zhizn´*, 5, 1973. For an example of the emphasis on the physicality of experiencing Rakhmaninov's former estate, see Dmitrii Kalashnikov, *Shkol´nikam o S. V. Rakhmaninove*, Voronezh, 1969.

[123] M. Aldanov [no title], in *Pamiati Rakhmaninova*, ed. M. V. Dobuzhinskii, New York, 1946, pp. 1–5 (p. 5).

he said: "I love my Russia, I adore it, but still I think I could never live there now."[124] Similarly, writing for *Novoe russkoe slovo*, Mikhail Gol′dstein emphasized that in America Rakhmaninov 'found a second homeland, and here he was buried. American earth gave Rakhmaninov the ability for his creative inspiration, for his amazing activity. And he gave Americans the fruit of his high talent. These fruits belong to the entire world, to all peoples'.[125] Nonetheless, both Soviet and émigré communities embraced Rakhmaninov as a site of memory of eternal cultural 'Russianness', even while their interpretations reflected the political demands of the era: a Cold War conflict between two world superpowers, in which Rakhmaninov's personal and creative choices had immediate political significance.

Conclusion: Soviet and post-Soviet spatializations of memory
In 1974, an article appeared in a local Tambov newspaper, describing in loving detail V. Bragin's recent trip to Rakhmaninov's former estate Ivanovka. Wandering through the old park and noticing the muddy remnants of a pond, Bragin sought to imagine Rakhmaninov beside him, drawing creative inspiration from the surrounding 'Russian nature'. Suddenly, as Bragin strolled through the park, 'the sounds of the amazingly light and emotional "Polka" of Rakhmaninov reach our ears. What is it?' Breathless, the author sped up, and turned a corner to find 'the very building in which Rakhmaninov lived and worked'. Destroyed in 1918, yet somehow magically rebuilt, Bragin's description of the sudden manifestation of the former residence of Rakhmaninov blurred the lines between memory and reality.[126] The reconstruction of Ivanovka appeared to physically recapture Rakhmaninov's lost world and symbolize his reintegration into Soviet collective memory. While émigré memories of the composer had been accompanied by a gradual spiritualization and decoupling of his significance from the physical space of Russia, in the Soviet context, collective memory of the composer became ever more tied to physical space. Ultimately, this Soviet narrative had the effect of physicalizing collective memory of Rakhmaninov, as it eschewed the spiritualized interpretation of the émigrés, and linked the composer explicitly to the physical space of Russia itself. This transformation of a national symbol into a physical relic, commemorated in spatialized terms, reflects a broader tendency in

---

[124] Swan, 'Rachmaninoff', p. 3. Emphasis added.
[125] Mikhail Gol′dstein, 'Slovo o S. V. Rakhmaninove: k stoletiiu so dnia rozhdeniia velikogo muzykanta', *Novoe russkoe slovo*, 22, 1 April 1973, pp. 4–6.
[126] V. Bragin, 'Vozvrashchenie v Ivanovku', [Unknown newspaper], 107, 6 September 1974, LCRA 88/12.

Soviet culture: an obsession with identifying, preserving (and recreating) material traces in apartment museums, sculptures and buildings that has found new impetus in the post-Soviet context.

Through the interaction of émigré and Soviet discourse, Rakhmaninov and his music were effectively forged into a site of memory, a nostalgic construction in which genuine cultural 'Russianness' was eternally inscribed, preserved and expressed. Whether in Harbin, Berlin, Paris, New York, Dresden, Riga, Prague or Moscow, Rakhmaninov's music came to be regularly heard as expressing a quintessential Russian truth, uniting its Russian listeners into a single imagined community that transcended political divisions: Rakhmaninov's politics might remain a topic of debate, but 'Russianness' itself could be experienced simply by listening to his music.

This shared construct emerged gradually, as the political divisions between émigré and Soviet understandings of Russianness were transformed in the cauldron of the Great Patriotic War. Rakhmaninov's own social background, political views and decision to emigrate made him a questionable symbol of Soviet values in the early years after the revolution, while making him a more natural embodiment of the values of those who, like the composer himself, had entered into exile. However, after official state policy in the USSR shifted to favour national categories of artistic expression in the 1930s, Rakhmaninov's music gradually found traction as a quintessential embodiment of 'Russian' national character, a development aided greatly by the composer's own display of patriotic support of the Soviet Union in its struggle against Nazi Germany immediately before his death.

While political differences remained between post-war Soviet and émigré interpretations of Rakhmaninov, a nostalgic image of Rakhmaninov as the embodiment of 'old Russia' took root in the Soviet Union thanks to interwar émigré discourses over 'Russianness'. Well before the late Soviet and early post-Soviet attempts to reintegrate émigré culture into a broader 'Russian' narrative in realms such as philosophy, literature and history, the reintegration of Rakhmaninov had begun. In contrast to Mark Raeff's claim that Russian émigré music 'rapidly merged into the international scene', music was not only a space in which Russian identity could be preserved, but, at least in the case of Rakhmaninov, was a space in which a unified site of memory of cultural 'Russianness' emerged.[127]

---

[127] See Raeff, *Russia Abroad*, p. 99. For a critique of this comment, see Christoph Flamm, '"My love, forgive me this apostasy": Some Thoughts on Russian Émigré Culture',

In the post-Soviet period, Medinskii's call for the physical return of the composer to his homeland highlights a continued spatialization of collective memory surrounding the composer, and it threatens the iteration of a selective national narrative of Russian identity. However, Rakhmaninov inhabits a curious space amid the archival treasures and physical remains of the first wave of Russian emigration. While other national symbols have been successfully readopted by a country seeking to reintegrate émigré and internal experience into a single national narrative,[128] Rakhmaninov's musical legacy and tragic fate have found common love and appeal outside of Russian circles (however defined), and his compositions are standard parts of the classical music repertory around the world. For better or worse, Rakhmaninov has come to embody both 'Russianness' and 'nostalgia' for music lovers around the world, and his symbolic meaning cannot be exclusively defined by any one community.[129] A 2013 Conference on 'S. V. Rakhmaninov and World Culture' held at the Rakhmaninov Museum in Ivanovka demonstrates that current Russian scholarship is aware of the broader narratives into which the composer fits, and it is to be hoped that the multiple meanings of Rakhmaninov, both for Russia and for world culture, will continue to be explored in the future.[130]

---

in Christoph Flamm, Henry Keazor and Roland Marti (eds), *Russian Émigré Culture: Conservatism or Evolution?*, Newcastle upon Tyne, 2013, pp. 1–18.

[128] Steven Lee Myers, 'For a New Russia, New Relics', *New York Times*, 9 October 2005 <http://www.nytimes.com/2005/10/09/weekinreview/09myers.html> [accessed 14 July 2018].

[129] On Rakhmaninov as a symbol of nostalgia outside of the context of Russia, see George Rousseau, *Rachmaninoff's Cape: A Nostalgia Memoir*, Middletown, DE, 2015.

[130] I. N. Vanovskaia (ed.), *S. V. Rakhmaninov i mirovaia kul´tura: materialy v mezhdunarodnoi nauchno-prakticheskoi konferentsii*, Ivanovka, 2014.

6

To What End *Rusalka*? Pushkin's Folk Tragedy and Dargomyzhskii's Opera

CARYL EMERSON

IN Russian folklore, a *rusalka* (water-nymph) is an ambivalent boundary creature. Capricious, enticing, linked with spring and summer rituals honouring the dead, she is equally at home underwater and on shore, and in liminal zones between life and death.¹ In Ukraine the rusalka is a lovely light-hearted prankster, but as she moves north she becomes more dreaded than beautiful, and often more feared as a witch than as a seductress.² The northern rusalka, who roams forest and field, is both protector and prophetess. The southern rusalka is more aquatic after the manner of Lorelei and mermaids — but her native element, water, is also ambivalent.³ While Damp Mother Earth is a stable reassuring presence, her soil permeated with life-giving moisture that promises good harvests, the unreliable depths of Russia's vast rivers and lakes could never be trusted. It was widely believed that the rusalki who dwelt there were the souls of unbaptized or stillborn infants or of drowned maidens, and thus part of the unclean force. They crawl up in trees, where the dead live, hydrating themselves by combing their long dripping hair and singing

I am grateful to *SEER*'s two anonymous outside readers, and to Simon Morrison and Michael Wachtel of Princeton University for their meticulous commentary and helpful suggestions, which greatly improved the final shape of this article.

¹ For a survey of rusalka types, see N. A. Borisova, 'Liricheskaia drama A. S. Pushkina o Rusalke. Istochniki, tvorcheskaia istoriia, poetika', in *Pushkin na poroge XXI veka: Provintsial'nyi kontekst*, vol. 8. Arzamas, 2007, pp. 16–20.
² Linda J. Ivanits, *Russian Folk Belief*, Armonk, NY and London, 1989, pp. 75–81. For the prophetic and protective powers of the fate-weaving and spinning rusalki, see Joanna Hubbs, *Mother Russia: The Feminine Myth in Russian Culture*, Bloomington IN, 1988, pp. 27–36.
³ For more on water imagery in the context of male anxieties over female power (both elemental and political) during and after the reign of Catherine the Great, see Inna Naroditskaya, 'Russian *Rusalkas* and Nationalism: Water, Power, and Women', in Linda Phyllis Austern and Inna Naroditskaya (eds), *Music of the Sirens*, Bloomington and Indianapolis IN, 2006, pp. 216–49.

as they swing in the branches. Rusalki live without men. At dawn and dusk, they often leave their watery home to slip ashore and mesmerize lost travellers, dragging them down to their crystal palaces through whirlpools and rapids. This unmotivated naughtiness is not necessarily gender-based or marked as erotic.[4] It is simply how water behaves. Unsurprisingly, among the pagan spirits presiding over the Russian landscape, the male water spirit (*vodianoi*) is nasty and ill-intentioned. Millers and fishermen, because they use water in their work, are obliged to pacify the water spirit with gifts. Morally compromised by these bribes, millers are often assumed to be sorcerers.

When Aleksandr Pushkin (arguably a Russian northerner with southern fantasies) began to sketch out a rusalka-and-miller play in the mid-1820s, such a panoptic vision of this potent female figure was not available to him. His interest in native Russian folklore was very recent, sparked by the pan-European Romantic fascination with *narodnost'*.[5] Working on his rusalka play between 1826 and 1832, he referred to it as 'Mel'nik' (The Miller), and like most of his folkloric creativity its plot and principals were borrowed from the West, in this case from magical Viennese operetta. But Pushkin's play observes a terse, sober psychological economy alien to its Austro-German musical sources. It was this severe economy and moral complexity that Aleksandr Dargomyzhskii (1813–69) set out to honour, amplify and return to music in 1856, when, acting as his own librettist, he recast Pushkin's play as his opera *Rusalka*. It would become the first of Pushkin's six dramas to be set to music.

This article considers some curious debates that erupted over the shape, meaning and closing scenes of Pushkin's *Rusalka*, after it had gained visibility and cultural traction through Dargomyzhskii's musicalization of it at mid-century. One debate took place near the end of the tsarist era (the 1890s); another near the end of the Soviet one (1970s–90s). In the post-

---

[4] For the prophetic powers of the fate-weaving, spinning, shape-shifting rusalki, see Hubbs, *Mother Russia*, pp. 27–36. The wise, powerful, grotesque rusalki of the north, ugly and hairy like Baba Yaga, are beyond child-bearing age and residents more of fields than of water.

[5] The poet did not absorb folk themes as a child from his serf nanny (a Soviet-era invention) but, beginning rather abruptly in 1824, from the pan-European literary fad for *narodnost'*, or 'folkness', an interest he then reflected in the changing image of Tat'iana in *Evgenii Onegin* from a reader of French novels to a young girl adept at folk divination. See Michael Wachtel, 'Pushkin's Turn to Folklore', July 2018, research in progress, cited by permission. Wachtel refines and strengthens the argument made by Mark Azadovskii in 1938, but long latent in Pushkin scholarship: M. K. Azadovskii, *Literatura i fol'klor: ocherki i etiudy*, Leningrad, 1938.

Soviet period, after the fad for all things Western had passed, the relation of opera to play was revisited and the work of establishment Party-line musicologists partially redeemed. Controversy has been kept alive by the fact that the play is, or is considered to be, 'unfinished'.

Pushkin never attempted to publish his folk tragedy, and his final draft breaks off on a question in mid-line. As tempting as it is to read *Rusalka* as a designed fragment (ending abruptly on an unanswered question appeals to the modern reader), Pushkin did leave a skeletal plan for the play's completion in keeping with his more neoclassical sense of a rounded poetic whole. It cannot be ignored. The unfinishedness of a literary work, especially by a nation's greatest writer, is always a prompt to its creative continuation by subsequent poets and composers. But in this case an eerie wholeness, a capaciousness, inheres at the very point where Pushkin — for whatever reason — stopped and went no further. The question he poses puts a moral choice on the table. If any participant in the play had dared to answer it, the plot would unravel, its awful unhappiness at last attached to a concrete acknowledged cause. Inevitably, any single resolution forces the choice, which in some sense thins out the drama. And thus the recurrent fascination with the 'unfinished' end of *Rusalka*: the poet leaves us dreaming at the edge of the water, that medium of justice, madness and the unconscious.

It is my hypothesis that Dargomyzhskii furthered Pushkin's poetic and ethical aims for his play by his prolongation of that sense of open moral choice inherent in Pushkin's final, truncated line. His compositional vehicle for this openness is the vocal ensemble, at which Dargomyzhskii was a great master. Only an opera libretto can accommodate and transcribe the simultaneities of ensemble thinking. The astonishing potency of the libretto as a narrative-musical form, competent to extend dramatic poetry into psychological realms it could not otherwise go, is everywhere apparent in this opera, especially in its trios, quartets and peasant choruses. The composer's compact, multi-layered librettistic solutions to unfolding dramatic conflict — alternately helpless, repressed, horrific — in turn fed into further dramaturgical attempts to complete Pushkin's play.

Dargomyzhskii's gift for psychological musical portraiture had ripened in a 'realistic' decade very distant from the aristocratic Age of Pushkin a mere quarter-century earlier. But the composer, like the poet and also like his predecessor Mikhail Glinka, had been raised and trained in West European idioms. 'Realistic', for the 1850s, refers to a style, not an ethnography. The lyrical songs and folk epos of the Russian *narod* had been adapted for popular anthologies by aristocratic Russian connoisseurs in the eighteenth century.⁶ But the rusalka art-narratives of Pushkin and Dargomyzhskii were concerned with 'psychological truth', a category of Romantic aesthetics rather than of folklore practice. On this score, over the next century and a half, poet and composer rendered each other valuable mutual service. One recent study, by the music historian Anatolii Tsuker (2010), begins with the oft-noted failure of Pushkin on the nineteenth-century dramatic stage. He acknowledges that Pushkin was not a librettist; the poet openly disdained such subservience to another medium. But, Tsuker argues, Pushkin's dramas in fact resemble libretti; they are so clean, compact, well-paced and symmetrically balanced that they require the modernist temperament of a Meierkhol'd to be properly presented on stage. In the absence of that twentieth-century option in the Russian imperial theatres, opera composers of genius fulfilled a 'directorial function' in relation to Pushkin the playwright. Their initiative then served to expand the resources of opera, first for Russia and then for the world. Tsuker considers Dargomyzhskii's *Rusalka* to be the pioneering work that 'opened the path for Russian psychological musical drama'.⁷ That path, as we shall see, was very far from the genre of the 'magical-fantastical comic opera', the home of European water-maidens and their russified imitators. But first to review the story as Pushkin wrote it.

Pushkin's drama, a terse little blank-verse folk tragedy in six scenes, opens on the banks of the Dnepr River.⁸ There are no proper names: only professions, ranks and family-clan relationships. The Miller is warning his daughter, one year into her liaison with a Prince, not to sell herself too cheaply. The father has looked the other way during these amorous visits and could now use some money. When the Prince belatedly turns up — to inform the daughter, gently but firmly, of his impending marriage to a highborn lady — that most terrible triangle is realized: a girl betrayed first by her father and then by her beloved. Horrified, she informs the Prince of her pregnancy, casts away his sumptuous gifts in disgust, and throws herself into the river. The scene shifts to the Prince's palace during his royal marriage. A wedding song performed by a choir of maidens is interrupted by a solo voice singing of a drowned girl who, while sinking

---

⁶ Richard Taruskin, 'N. A. Lvov and the Folk', in *Defining Russia Musically*, Princeton, NJ, 1997, pp. 3–24.

⁷ Anatolii Tsuker, *Dramaturgiia Pushkina v russkoi opernoi klassike*, Moscow, 2010, pp. 8–25.

⁸ A. S. Pushkin 'Rusalka', in *Polnoe sobranie sochinenii*, 19 vols, Moscow, 1995, 7, pp. 187–212 and 319–47 (for deleted scenes and drafts).

to her death, curses her faithless lover. The Prince is irritated: who let her in? When he kisses his bride and a faint cry is heard in the chamber, he orders his horseman to seek her out — but no one is found. Several years pass. The Princess, now seven years into a barren marriage, laments that her husband no longer loves her, that he is never home, that God has not sent her a child. Suddenly huntsmen arrive from the Dnepr, but without the Prince. He is lingering on the riverbank by the ruined mill, at the site of his earlier innocent love. Green-haired rusalki sing in the trees.

At this point in the plot the dramatic action, like the rhymes of a well-made poem, circles round to echo its origins, but in an insane and fantastic manner. The Miller, now identified as an Old Man (Starik), totally mad and calling himself a raven, appears in rags, addressing the Prince familiarly as 'son-in-law'.[9] Before his transformation into a scavenger bird, an eater of carrion, the Miller had renewed his relations with the unclean force and sold the mill to 'devils and woodsprites behind the stove'. The awful sight of this madness against the background of paternal tragedy moves the Prince to remorse and the stirrings of conscience. Come live in my palace, the Prince coaxes the Miller — but no, the Raven will not, he fears he will be strangled by a necklace of pearls. In the forest he is free. The penultimate scene takes place at the bottom of the Dnepr. The Miller's daughter, now queen of a sisterhood of rusalki, instructs her daughter Rusalochka to greet her father on the riverbank, tell him their story, assure him of her enduring love and invite him home. Seventeen lines into scene six, 'The Bank', this second-generation rusalka born of a drowned mother scampers up on shore to greet her astonished father the Prince, who asks her: 'Where did you come from, you marvellous child?'[10] Nothing follows this question, not even a stage direction. As noted above, it is assumed that Pushkin intended something further; a six-line plan for the play from April 1832 lists a final entry, 'huntsmen'.[11] Pushkin died in a duel in 1837 without having titled his play or definitively ordered its scenes.

In both dramatic and operatic versions of *Rusalka*, the life-death boundary is crossed with minimal fuss and no loss of acting or singing bodies. Each blends the fantastical world of a folk fabulate with psychological realism, downplaying the merely magical and elevating the heroine to imperial stature. Elements of southern and northern rusalki combine to

---

[9] Ibid., p. 205.
[10] Ibid., p. 212.
[11] 'Plan "Rusalki"', in ibid., p. 336. The six segments of the plot, in order, are 'Miller and his daughter', 'Wedding', 'Princess and Nurse', 'Rusalki', 'Prince, old man and Rusalochka', 'Huntsmen'.

create an image both helpless and imperious, emotionally unconstrained and utterly disciplined: in Andrei Siniavskii's formulation, this is the interrelated symbol-system of *water — woman — death — hair — spinning — fate*.[12] In both versions, the compromised Miller combines love for his daughter with love for money (each of these passions is genuine); when he realizes that permitting one to facilitate the other has resulted in the loss of both, he goes mad. The Miller's madness, together with the bewitchment and subsequent repentance of his daughter's rich and highborn seducer, complicates the question of evil in the drama, on the pagan as well as the Christian plane.

In rusalka narratives, as in the myth of the saved sunken city of Kitezh, transcendental justice is linked with a watery (rather than a heavenly) domain. For all its disagreeable spirits and very real dangers, water is the preferred elemental medium for moral growth. To unite with water can be empowering. From Chaikovskii's *Queen of Spades* to Shostakovich's *Lady Macbeth of Mtsensk District*, unhappy Russian operatic heroines drown themselves — some as victims, others as victimizers. But in those famous resolutions, the heroine's fate is wholly contained inside her own story-space, that of the desperate suicide of a deceived woman. In *Rusalka*, suicide is the *pre*-story. If reborn as rusalki, these women form a potent sisterhood. Although their moon-lit excursions to dry land are the stuff of erotic comedy, their underwater kingdom is a stern, rule-governed place. As we learn from Pushkin's scene set at the bottom of the Dnepr, the Rusalka-tsaritsa keeps her subordinate sisters hard at work over their distaffs and spindles. Although not hags (as are the Greek Fates), Rusalki are the Moirai, spinning the thread of life that connects a person's past deeds with a larger Destiny.

Thus the rusalki share some behavioural traits with traditional Western European water maidens — sirens, naiads, undines, Lorelei, mermaids — and depart radically from them in others. Rusalki have legs, not fish-tails and fins. And the rusalka's role is not merely to test the sexual appetite and self-discipline of an erring male hero, after the manner of sirens in Homeric epic.[13] As part of the matriarchal folk cosmos of the Eastern Slavs,

---

[12] Andrei Sinyavsky, *Ivan the Fool. Russian Folk Belief: A Cultural History*, trans. Joanne Turnbull and Nikolai Formozov, Moscow, 2007, p. 123.

[13] For rusalka symbolism in Russian culture, see Helena Goscilo, 'Watery Maidens: Rusalki as Sirens and Slippery Signs', in Catherine O'Neil, Nicole Boudreau, and Sarah Krive (eds), *Poetics. Self. Place: Essays in Honor of Anna Lisa Crone*, Bloomington IN, 2007, pp. 50–70. Goscilo argues that Homer had reduced the prototypical symbolism of the siren from hieratic initiation to 'facile sexual enslavement' (and Western culture followed

she is associated with patience, prophecy, self-control, constancy, fertility and knowledge. These virtues enrich and complicate the conventional Romantic-era emphasis on the water maiden's victimization, sexual jealousy and vengeance, none of which was obligatory for pre-nineteenth century representations of her image.[14]

'Where did you come from, you marvellous child?' So tantalizingly does the Prince's question hang in the air that several first-class artists lent their hand to completing Pushkin's play, among them A. F. Vel′tman, Valerii Briusov and, in 1942, Vladimir Nabokov.[15] Indisputably the most successful of these completions is Dargomyzhskii's libretto (and opera), which prolongs the final, fleeting 'Rusalochka' moment into a morally devastating finale. Writing of Pushkin's water-nymph as precursor to Nabokov's nymphet, the American Slavist Ksana Blank comments that 'Russian literature knows how to turn suspended endings into new beginnings, thus creating a whole web of literary plots'.[16] From the start, this web of rusalka plots included musical as well as literary strands, burlesque as well as transcendent tragedy. The rusalka motif could shift easily from vengeance to empathy, from agitated memory to moral enlightenment.[17] The whole spectrum, incidentally, is present in Pushkin. A rejected girl who ultimately presides dispassionately over a larger prestigious social unit, into which her now penitent former love is drawn only to be told that he must reconcile himself

---

suit); but a more complex image survives in Russian folklore, which 'splits the sirenic image, elevating one half to the transcendent (the tree of paradise), and situating the other half in the chthonic — the aquatic underworld, of which the rusalka is the multivalent representative' (p. 50).

[14] In pre-Romantic water-maiden tales, love interest and sexual misconduct were often altogether absent. See N. I. Verba, 'Ocherk pervyi. Drama Pushkina i "rusaloch′ia" tematika v kul′ture XIX veka', in N. I. Verba, *Arkhetipicheskie obrazy siuzhetov o morskikh devakh v drame 'Rusalka' A. S. Pushkina i odnoimennoi opere A. S. Dargomyzhskogo*, St Petersburg, 2015, pp. 8–11.

[15] V. Nabokov-Sirin, "Rusalka. Zakliuchitel′naia stsena k pushkinskoi "Rusalke"', *Novyi Zhurnal*, 2, 1942, pp. 181–84, and Jane Grayson, '*Rusalka* and the Person from Porlock', in *Symbolism and After: Essays on Russian Poetry in Honour of Georgette Donchin*, ed. Arnold McMillin, Bristol, 1992, pp. 162–85. Nabokov presents a sceptical Prince who tries to bribe Rusalochka into leaving him alone, but the little girl insists he will die unless he follows her into her underwater kingdom. The most famous part of this undistinguished continuation is its final stage direction: 'They disappear. Pushkin shrugs his shoulders' (p. 184). For a survey of the most important literary 'completions' of *Rusalka* that includes Dargomyzhskii, see Borisova, 'Liricheskaia drama', pp. 6–10.

[16] Ksana Blank, 'Nabokov's Nymphet and Pushkin's *Water-Nymph*', in *Spaces of Creativity: Essays on Russian Literature and the Arts*, Boston, MA, 2017, p. 106.

[17] Blank (ibid., p. 113) notes just such anguish in Chekhov's 1888 story, 'The Nervous Breakdown' ('Pripadok'), in which several young men on their way to a brothel hum the Prince's aria from Dargomyzhskii's *Rusalka*.

to loss, is, after all, the mature image of Tat´iana. Unwittingly perhaps, by not finishing his *Rusalka*, Pushkin left us a thought process floating in mid-air, perhaps only to work it out in other creative contexts. He wrote the second half of *Evgenii Onegin* during the years of gestation for *Rusalka*. As this article will suggest, those two heroines share an uneasy sisterhood, coexisting alongside earlier, more conventional variants by Pushkin on the water-maiden theme.

Contexts, sources and precursors of Pushkin's 'little folk tragedy'
By the early 1830s, while still sporadically returning to *Rusalka*, Pushkin had completed four 'Little Tragedies' (1830). These tiny playlets dramatized the denouements of familiar European themes: the Don Juan myth in *The Stone Guest*, avarice and negligent parenting in *The Miserly Knight*, musical genius and envy in *Mozart and Salieri*, reconciliation with death in *Feast during the Plague*. Since *Rusalka* too elaborated on a pan-European plot, some early readers welcomed it as a fifth tragedy (albeit longer and more ambitious) in Pushkin's sequence. The unfinished play was first published in Pushkin's journal, *Sovremennik* (6, 1837). Presented as a 'fragment' (*otryvok*) and titled *Rusalka*, it was staged, although without success, in April 1838. Its composition history has been a challenge for textologists: Pushkin left behind two chaotic notebooks filled with almost ten years of undated drafts and scenic fragments.[18] Earlier, the poet had also tried his hand at rusalka imitations, or faked imitations, in non-dramatic poetry.

Pushkin's earliest treatment of the theme, his ballad 'Rusalka' (1819), is a thoroughly Romantic tale of erotic hallucination inspired by the undines of Goethe and Zhukovskii. A water maiden entices an elderly hermit to his watery death. Pushkin, with his cool Voltairian mind, might well have been parodying the sentimental contours of this received plot.[19] Fifteen years later Pushkin included a more ambitious rusalka tale in the fifteenth entry in his *Songs of the Western Slavs* (1834), titled 'Ianysh Korolevich' (purportedly a partial translation from old Czech, although no original has

---

[18] The chronology of the *Rusalka* manuscripts (1826–32) can only be guessed at, often solely from colours of ink. See L. M. Lotman, 'Ob al´ternativnykh putiakh resheniia tekstologicheskoi "zadadki" "Rusalki" Pushkina', *Russkaia literatura*, 2001, pp. 129–51 (p. 132).

[19] Goethe's ballad (and Zhukovskii's variant on it) features a fisherman as the tempted male. Pushkin's substitution of a monk reflects an ancient Russian tradition of the errant or sinful hermit-ascetic. For a full account, see Borisova, 'Liricheskaia drama', pp. 33–39. Borisova suggests that Pushkin's early poem is a 'stylization at the edge of parody' (ibid., p. 39).

been found).²⁰ Prince Ianysh, intending to marry a Princess, abandons his lowborn lover Elitsa, who throws herself into the Morava river. There she gives birth to a daughter and eventually sends the child up on shore to grab the Prince's bridle as he gallops by. The Prince, thrilled by this unexpected trace of his earlier love, requests a meeting with Elitsa. She appears above the waves to interrogate him on his failed marriage, but prudently declines to meet the Prince on dry land: 'we won't kiss any more sweetly than we did in the past, you won't love me more intensely than you did in the past.'²¹ In this truncated stretch of plot we detect Pushkin's mature image of the rusalka: reconciled, patient, cautious, unmovable in her recollection of a precious past, and insistent (as is Tat'iana to the love-struck Onegin) that although love can last indefinitely, time and experience flow only one way. Opportunities when missed are missed forever, and decisions have consequences.

The third and most important precursor to the play — not an earlier work by the poet, but an influence on his creative imagination — is a serialized water-maiden musical in four parts, *Dneprovskaia rusalka* (The Rusalka of the Dnepr, 1803–07), which played to wildly enthusiastic houses in Petersburg and Moscow throughout the 1810s–20s.²² Pushkin, a passionate fan of musical theatre, surely saw it. *Dneprovskaia rusalka* was a russification by Nikolai Krasnopol'skii of two Viennese Singspiele, *Das Donauweibchen* (1798) by the composer Ferdinand Kauer, and *Die Nymphe der Donau* (1803), by the theatre director and composer Karl Friedrich Hensler (1759–1825). Russian sequels and imitations proliferated, becoming known as *Rusalka* parts 2, 3 and 4, which continued to the played on Russian stages well into the 1840s. Russian drama historian Simon Karlinsky calls it the 'biggest theatrical hit of the decade, perhaps even of the half-century', largely for its elaborate stage tricks — adding: 'It took all of Pushkin's genius to strip *The Water Sprite* of its excesses and absurdities and to convert it into his hauntingly poetic unfinished drama *Rusalka*.'²³ The absurdities Pushkin stripped away became subtexts elsewhere. In

---

²⁰ Michael Wachtel, *A Commentary to Pushkin's Lyric Poetry, 1926–1836*, Madison, WI, 2011, pp. 307–08. Wachtel suggests that the 'Czech original' might be Pushkin's mystification.

²¹ 'Yanysh Korolevich', in Pushkin, *Polnoe sobranie sochinenii*, 3, pp. 360–63 (p. 363).

²² The full text of the first part of Krasnopol'skii's 1804 libretto 'reworked from the German' has been reprinted as *Rusalka. Opera komicheskaia v trekh deistviiakh, Chast' I. Peredelannaia s nemetskogo N. Krasnopol'skim, muzyka G-d Kauer i Davydova* as an appendix to Borisova, 'Liricheskaia drama', pp. 109–94.

²³ Simon Karlinsky, *Russian Drama from Its Beginnings to the Age of Pushkin*, Berkeley, CA, 1985, pp. 186–88.

the second canto (line 12) of *Evgenii Onegin*, as an example of dreary rural courtship rituals, the poet puts a guitar into the hands of a hapless provincial miss and has her squawk out one of the musical's most popular songs: 'Pridi v chertog ko mne zlatoi' ('Come into my golden chamber'), an aria that Krasnopol'skii's rusalka Lesta sings to her Prince.[24] Nabokov, in his commentary to his *Evgenii Onegin*, further suggests that some of the horrors in Tat'iana's over-the-top gothic dream were imported from the musical's spectacular special effects: a tree becoming a windmill, dancing bags of flour.[25]

Whether Pushkin was parodying *The Rusalka of the Dnepr* or paying affectionate tribute to it, the parallels between this russified Austrian tetralogy and his own Rusalka are striking.[26] Krasnopol'skii's cast includes a Prince, his wife the Princess, her Father, the abandoned mistress Lesta, and a lovechild Lida born underwater. Pushkin's mill by the river and the ancient tree, site of the love-trysts, are taken directly from Krasnopol'skii's stage directions, as are the suddenly wilting, falling leaves during the Prince's sojourn to the riverbank. Lesta announces herself as the 'daughter of a local miller'. But that's not all she is, and here the differences between Pushkin and Krasnopol'skii are profound. Lesta is a rusalka from the start and a shape-shifter throughout. The *dramatis personae* of the play lists twelve roles for her, including an old woman, peasant girl, wanderer, female hermit, young knight and Gypsy singer.[27] Even amid these routinely exotic personnel of Viennese magic-folk comic opera, however, we sense a side of Lesta that will contribute to Pushkin's more disciplined and didactic heroine. Lesta is a siren with a moral sense. She sympathizes with the

[24] For the full text and contemporary reception of this aria, sung by the rusalka to her faithless Prince and promising him undying love if he only join her underwater in her golden chambers, see Borisova, 'Liricheskaia drama', pp. 25–29.

[25] Aleksandr Pushkin, *Eugene Onegin: A Novel in Verse*, trans. Vladimir Nabokov, 2 vols, Princeton, NJ, 1964, 2, p. 508. Noting that Pushkin's library contained a copy of a three-part Krasnopol'skii adaptation, with music by Kauer, Cavos, and Davydov (St Petersburg, 1804), Nabokov remarks: 'Pushkin had a strange leaning toward borrowing from ludicrous sources' (p. 247).

[26] See I. N. Zhdanov, '*Rusalka* Pushkina i *Das Donauweibchen* Genslera', *Pamiati A. S. Pushkina, Zapiski istoriko-filologicheskogo fakul'teta Imp. S-Peterburgskogo universiteta*, 57 (1900), pp. 139–78 (for specific parallels, pp.145–59). In Hensler, knight Albrecht marries Berta and is then visited by an earlier love, Hulda (suicided and transformed into a water maiden) and their daughter, Lilly. 'You may marry', says Hulda, 'but three days a year you must spend in these underwater chambers'. She gives Albrecht and his estranged wife Berta her daughter to raise; when the wife dies, Hulda revives her. She brings Berta to her watery kingdom for as long as is required for Albrecht to repent.

[27] See Borisova, 'Liricheskaia drama', p. 111. Slavomysl is a prince of Chernigov and the father of Miloslava, the unfortunate woman whom Prince Vidostan marries. In his folk tragedy, Pushkin replaces a focus on the high-born family with the residents of the Mill.

Princess, who suffers from her husband's neglect, and she tries to return the Prince to his conscience and his conjugal duties. (Dargomyzhskii too, in his own musicalized variant, will expand sympathetically on the neglected Princess, thus further isolating the opera's errant male.) There are limits to Lesta's counsel, however. Although she can fall in love with humans and become a mother through intercourse with one, her non-human nature is fixed. Thus the plot remains that of a wonder-tale, governed by whimsy and magic, and thus is at base comedic.

When Pushkin conceived his *Rusalka* in a tragic mode, he insisted on the human pre-history and therefore began with a fundamentally different set of options.[28] He replaced the special effects of magical operetta by paradoxes of Shakespearean texture and depth, a condition recognized by scholars of the Pushkin-Shakespeare interface, such as Catherine O'Neil.[29] In the play's lyrical and elegiac moments we detect echoes of a mad King Lear and Gloucester, of Macbeth, Ophelia, Cleopatra. As O'Neil writes, in his dealings with Shakespeare Pushkin tended to disregard the macabre and supernatural vocabulary of the Elizabethan stage, preferring to emphasize the moral situation.[30] She notes that in an early deleted episode from *Rusalka*, the drowned Miller's Daughter turns up as a ghost at the Prince's wedding, dripping water and leaving wet footprints (a member of the Prince's entourage thinks the apparition might be a holy fool). By the most complete draft, however, the drowned girl has been distilled into pure lyrical voice — a detail that must have delighted Dargomyzhskii as he worked over his libretto.

The mill by the river remains the privileged site of Pushkin's play. He eliminates the royal father of the Princess, a major role in Krasnopol'skii, and adds the Miller, peasant father to the heroine — carefully removing all proper names so that only relationships matter: Miller, Miller's Daughter, Prince, Princess, Matchmaker, Nurse, Rusalka, Huntsmen. Except for the fact that drowning brings not death but transfiguration, all traces of the magic-tale are removed. Everyone is human, and everyday human experience (its passions, exploitations, habitual cruelties and potential for repentance) is the backdrop. In post-Soviet Pushkin scholarship, the quest for Christian subtexts has yielded up multiple possible biblical motifs in *Rusalka*, from the Book of Revelation to the suddenly wilted 'Accursed

---

[28] For a discussion of differences between the rusalka plots of Krasnopol'skii and Pushkin, see Verba, 'Ocherk pervyi', pp. 22–28.
[29] Catherine O'Neil, *With Shakespeare's Eyes: Pushkin's Creative Appropriation of Shakespeare*, Newark, DE, 2003, pp. 143–46.
[30] Ibid., p. 245.

Tree'.³¹ But the supra-natural here is everywhere symbolic, it is not a special effect. As Natal´ia Verba has suggested, Pushkin shifts the genre of his tale from magic-comic to sacral by means of the symbolism of the mill.³² Its rotating water-wheel is the watershed between life and death, proof of the rule-governed interaction of earth and cosmos. Since mills are equally a home to unclean pagan forces and a sign of Christ's presence (grains of wheat that die to be reborn), humans at a mill-site, unlike the more rigidly defined royalty in palaces, are also liminal creatures. They can — and must — make moral choices. Doomed to exercise their freedom in keeping with Pushkin's activist understanding of fate, they contribute to a proper realization of their own destiny. Thus irreversible and extreme acts in Pushkin (like the duel between Onegin and Lenskii) take place near mills.

The space of Pushkin's *Rusalka*, then, is *dvoeverie*, the 'dual faith' of Russian folk life. In the first scene, a potent blend of Christian and pagan motifs near a riverside mill is played out as the demonic inversion of a peasant wedding.³³ Gifts to the bride and the bride's father are revealed as bribes. The father gives his daughter away, not once at the altar but over an entire year, and for profit. Her bridal garland becomes a snake. Instead of songs, dances and a goblet of mead moistening the way to the bridal bed, there is abandonment, flight, the desolate riverbed. The theme of travestied weddings at a mill-site was familiar to Russian theatregoers through Mikhail Sokolovskii's popular comic opera, *The Miller-Sorcerer, the Deceiver and the Matchmaker* (*Mel´nik-koldun, obmanshchik i svat*), libretto by Aleksandr Ablesimov (1779), still a staple of the stage in the 1830s. This comic opera was probably another stimulus for Pushkin's play, this time from the world of Russian folklore rather than Viennese *Zauberoper*. To develop Ablesimov's plot in a tragic direction, however, Pushkin had to amplify the Miller's role, invest it with the shape-shifting power usually reserved for the rusalka. The conscience of the Miller is 'literalized' as a raven, a bird that feeds on carrion, but a raven stubbornly retaining the human capacity to feel guilt and remorse. In Pushkin, regardless of label, location or outer bodily shape, everything important remains human. Thus the magical plot devices of comedy are transformed by the poet into the fully reasonable madness of parental grief; the insanity of the play's second half reinforces and mirrors the pragmatic realism of

---

[31] V. Iu. Kozmin, 'Khristianskie motivy v drame A. S. Pushkina "Rusalka"', *Al´bom-Katalog Vystavki 'Pushkin i Filaret, Mitropolit Moskovskii i Kolomenskii' v Gosudarstvennom muzee A. S. Pushkina, 20 dekabria 2000 g. – 28 fevralia 2001 g.*, Moscow, 2000, pp. 205–09.

[32] Verba, 'Ocherk pervyi', p. 22–25.

[33] Ibid., pp. 26–28.

the first. What does it matter that rusalki might not be 'real'? What is real is what triggers awareness of responsibility.

For this reason, creative writers and researchers alike have been fascinated by possible autobiographical resonances in Pushkin's *Rusalka*. Among biographical critics, much attention is paid to the fact that in 1826, the year he jotted down his first ideas about *Rusalka*, Pushkin learned that his peasant mistress Ol'ga Kalashnikova (from the mill-village of Bugrovo) was pregnant.[34] The poet was embarrassed, enlisted his friend Petr Viazemskii to arrange for the infant (if a boy) not to be sent to a foundling home, and promised to compensate the family. Ol'ga, according to her Russian biographer, was a practical, matter-of-fact girl. Even though their baby son Pavel died within three months, she made sure that the *barin*, the nobleman responsible, 'remembered' her family on the eve of his own wedding. Did Pushkin write some of the Kalashnikov clan's monetary calculation into the Miller, and his own remorse into the Prince? In 1924, the poet Vladislav Khodasevich claimed that he had.[35] Likewise Sergei Geichenko, legendary curator of Pushkin's estate-museum at Mikhailovskoe during the late Soviet period, long assured visitors that *Rusalka* was autobiographical: Pushkin, as befits the people's poet, had ardently loved his 'rusalka from Bugrovo' and the memory of that love burdened his heart and mind until the end of his days.[36]

Academic Pushkinists overwhelmingly disagree, and not only because Ol'ga had fallen short of drowning herself in despair. It is true that Pushkin's literary plots were often prompted by reminiscences and shaped by his understanding of superstition and fate. By the norms of Pushkin's time and place, however, the sexual indiscretion with Kalashnikova would not have generated any deep-seated guilt. More important to Pushkin, again, was 'psychological truth'. In the terminology of the time, this meant a dispassionate examination of consequences — which, stealthily, begin to

---

[34] For more on the Kalashnikova subtext to *Rusalka*, including the girl's practical and mercenary kin, see O. G. Zgurskaia, 'Mifologicheskii i real'nyi mir v drame A. S. Pushkina "Rusalka"', *Voprosy kognitivnoi lingvistiki*, 2014, 4, pp. 85–91 (pp. 86–88). Zgurskaia argues (in my view correctly) against an autobiographical reading of the play. In English, see Walter N. Vickery, '"The Water-Nymph" and "...Again I Visited...": Notes on an Old Controversy', *Russian Language Triquarterly*, 3, 1972, pp. 195–205, esp. pp. 195–98.

[35] See ibid., pp. 194–96. Sergei Bondi, in his commentary to volume 7 of the Academy Pushkin (1935), sensibly takes issue with Khodasevich (ibid., pp. 196 and 204). David Bethea, in his study of the later poet, calls the Kalashnikova-*Rusalka* hypothesis (which includes the fanciful detail that Pushkin's peasant mistress drowned herself) one of Khodasevich's 'brilliant errors'. David M. Bethea, *Khodasevich: His Life and Art*, Princeton, NJ, 1983, p. 132.

[36] Zgurskaia, 'Mifologicheskii i real'nyi mir', pp. 86–87.

make themselves felt as our choices, more or less perceived by us as 'free', become webbed into our fate. These choices have results: beneficiaries and casualties. How does consciousness cope with them? For this we must focus on the interactions between Miller and Rusalka (father and betrayed transformed daughter), and between Miller and Prince (collaborators in the girl's entrapment), in the play's drafts and projected final plan. These texts, together with Pushkin's posthumously published play, were available to Dargomyzhskii when he set out on his opera.

1856: Dargomyzhskii completes 'Rusalka'
Dargomyzhskii's *Rusalka* has never enjoyed the international fame of other works of Pushkin adapted for the operatic stage: *Boris Godunov*, *Evgenii Onegin*, *Queen of Spades*, even one or two of the musicalized 'Little Tragedies'. Pushkin's *Rusalka* premiered in English in concert performance only in 2015.[37] Far better known is the 1901 Czech opera of the same name by Antonin Dvořák. In the spirit of Hans Christian Andersen, Czech fairy-tales, and Hensler's *Das Donauweibchen* from the Viennese stage, Dvořák tells the Swan-Lake-like story of a mermaid's love for a Prince, a union facilitated by evil spirits and obstructed by the jealousy of a rival bride. Some themes in it appear to be pan-European. The Czech Prince also wanders back enchanted to the watery site of his first love; the water maiden redeems him (and forgives him) with a death-dealing kiss. Absent from Dvořák, however, are the signature motifs of Pushkin's Russian fantastic, whether urban (as in *The Queen of Spades*) or folkloric. These include transformation from the mortally-human realm to some other condition that is equally real (which is to say: still governed by the ethics of this world); a learning curve for the male made possible by the supra-natural but not wholly dependent on it (uncanny events permit also of a material explanation); and ultimately a moral victory for the female, in body or beyond the body. This article will argue that Dargomyzhskii eventually preserved precisely these 'psychologically truthful' Pushkinian motifs, amplifying them through the resources of music.

The composer's work on the opera (both music and libretto) began in the mid-1840s, and was very slow. Four variants of a verbal text are extant among Dargomyzhskii's papers; one of them is a fully finished libretto,

---

[37] The concert premiere of Dargomyzhskii's *Rusalka* took place on 22 November 2015 at the Aaron Copland School of Music at Queens College CUNY, New York City. Conducted from the piano by Leonard Lehrman, English translation of libretto by Emily R. Lehrman and Leonard Lehrman. Materials on this premiere, including texts and photographs, can be accessed at <http://helenewilliamsspierman.homestead.com/Rusalka_Index.html>.

but it differs substantially from the text the composer set to music and premiered. The other three variants are plans, more or less worked-out, and none in Dargomyzhskii's hand.[38] The earliest versions of the opera featured endings quite distant from Pushkin's play. (In the 1850s there was a revival of the box-office hit *Rusalka of the Dnepr*, and similarities can be noted between Krasnopol'skii's plot and Dargomyzhskii's early drafts.) Suggestively, the Miller's Daughter was originally called Tat'iana, not Natasha. In two of the variants, the Prince becomes a water god, the underwater marriage with Rusalka is sanctified, and life in the afterlife goes on. In the fourth variant, Dargomyzhskii tinkers even with the drowning: the Daughter stays alive to turn up at the Prince's wedding, flings her headdress in his face, and throws herself into the river only at some undisclosed later moment.

In these draft libretti, the Miller's Daughter as Rusalka-tsaritsa is also not free. In thrall to her sisters' vengeful ethos, she promises to drag the Prince down (a detail probably indebted to the ballet *Giselle*, hugely popular across Europe since its premiere in 1841 — although rusalki, of course, drown rather than dance the targeted man to death).[39] When the Rusalka queen sees her repentant beloved, however, she, like Giselle, forgives him. Since the other rusalki insist on a victim, the mad Miller offers himself up in place of the Prince: 'I should perish first, for I am guilty of my daughter's unhappiness.' In the early plans, then, the focus is on betrayed love among adults, not on the shame and potential of creating new family. There is no Rusalochka.

At some point in these experiments with the play text, Dargomyzhskii decided to return, as faithfully as possible with an unfinished source text, to Pushkin. The composer made that fidelity a priority, noting in his title that he had fashioned his libretto 'after Pushkin's dramatic *poema*, with the preservation of many of his verses'. Some technical adjustments were necessary. For example, Dargomyzhskii broke down Pushkin's long iambic pentameter lines, not convenient for singing, into shorter syntactic periods.[40] Some lines repeat as refrains. But Pushkin's words, as concise in this play as in his 'Little Tragedies' and thus almost a ready-made libretto, remain largely intact.[41]

---

[38] See M. Pekelis, 'Libretto *Rusalki*', in *Dargomyzhskii i narodnaia muzyka*, Moscow and Leningrad, 1951, pp. 65–67.

[39] For this and other musical-theatrical influences, see A. Gozenpud, *Russkii opernyi teatr XIX veka (1836–1856)*, Leningrad, 1969, pp. 404–34 (on *Giselle*, p. 423).

[40] See Gozenpud, on the adjusted metrics, p. 417.

[41] Russia's founding literary critic Vissarion Belinskii was the first to claim: 'People say that *Rusalka* was written by Pushkin as if it were a libretto for an opera' (in his Eleventh

The first half of the libretto musicalizes Pushkin's plot, ornaments it, but does not fundamentally alter the psychology of the characters. The Miller's Daughter is still stubborn and naive, dazzled by her prince and unwilling to see his shortcomings, both of personality and rank. Like her more bookish predecessor, Tat′iana Larina, she is living in a fairytale of her own. Waking up from this fairytale will be life-shattering. Her father and lover are more pragmatic. Importantly, their behaviour has been in place for a long time, over a year; its pleasures and profits are already a matter of habit. In Act I ('The bank of the Dnepr. Nearby a mill and an oak') the Miller, in his opening aria, literally 'dances' his greed, interlacing money with paternal advice about setting a price on one's favours. (Early audiences were startled by the absence of a chorus to open the scenic action, confronted instead with an imitation of Pushkin's abrupt *in medias res* soliloquy by the calculating but comic Miller.) The daughter, hemmed in by two self-serving men, gets no developed aria of her own while in human form. In the first scene, her voice is woven into two duets and a terzetto, but so firm is her true-love fantasy that she neither listens to others nor is heard by them. The operatic Natasha comes into her own vocally only when she assumes control of her underwater kingdom. As a mortal human girl, it appears, she is free only to react, and she is subject to an agonizing prolongation of her beloved's betrayal. The Miller quickly grasps the situation, the Prince procrastinates. To cheer him up, the Miller summons peasant choruses and round-dances. These opera-friendly insertions in Act I increase the folk element and provide colourful spectacle, but more importantly they mimic the rituals of a real wedding — or rather, as suggested above, an anti-wedding, the wedding that should have been but was not.[42] In their duets and trios, both Prince and Miller insist that time will heal all grief. Natasha, however, fighting for her own voice, becomes increasingly wrathful. She is already outside human time as she will soon be outside human space. Thus these tuneful choral and choreographed numbers do not divert us (as divertissements are supposed to do) from the dilemma of Natasha's entrapment by her mercenary father and his ally the profligate Prince. Quite the opposite. Like the chorus in Greek tragedy, they darken the tone rather than lighten it, commenting on the action and forecasting doom.

Article on Pushkin, 1846). Editors routinely claim that this statement has no base in fact, but it had become canonical and Dargomyzhskii surely knew it. See 'Stat′ia odinnadtsataia i posledniaia', in V. G. Belinskii, *Sochineniia Aleksandra Pushkina*, Moscow, 1961, p. 443.

[42] For a discussion of these mirrored scenes in terms of plot and musical themes, see 'Ocherk vtoroi. *Rusalka* ot Pushkina k Dargomyzhskomu. Opyt analiza arkhetipicheskikh obrazov opery', in Verba, 'Ocherk pervyi', pp. 41–44.

Dargomyzhskii's Act II, the royal wedding, generously expands Pushkin's laconic text. The Princess in the opera (a mezzo-soprano) is not just the female rival triggering the catastrophe but a serious deep figure, who takes ritual leave of her girlfriends and pledges eternal love to the Prince. He responds rapturously. After the drowned-maiden lament rises up from the chorus in Natasha's voice, the Prince is angry — but also conscience-stricken; the Princess too is full of dread. They are a caring couple who wish to make a fresh start, but it turns out that the past is not easily shrugged off. Foreboding is everywhere. To brighten this texture both psychologically and in terms of song-worthy tessitura, Dargomyzhskii replaces Pushkin's aged Nurse with a young orphan, Ol'ga (soprano), confidante to the Princess. Similar to the Miller in Act I, Ol'ga is a pragmatist and high-spirited comic. She fobs the ill-starred drowned-maiden lament off on some capricious 'unclean force' and requests happier songs from the chorus. Act III takes place twelve years later. The Princess has had time to be confirmed in her childlessness, Rusalochka has had time to grow up and is now dangerously close to the age when she can be herself seduced. Still, the irrepressible Ol'ga assures the grieving Princess that matters can be put right, that 'all men are like that', restless, inconstant, easily distracted — and she sings her a ditty to cheer her up. At that moment in the libretto, the huntsman arrives with news that the Prince has stayed back alone on the shore. The Princess, frantic, sets out with Ol'ga for the Dnepr. The opera now mobilizes for the group finale ('Huntsmen') that Pushkin designated but did not write.

The second scene of Act III, where the mad Miller confronts an increasingly desperate Prince, is the most famous part in the opera, both for its own excellence and because of its distinguished performance history. In 1856, Aleksandr Serov, St Petersburg opera composer and music critic, wrote a long and ecstatic ten-part review on *Rusalka* in *Muzykal'nyi i teatral'nyi vestnik* that singled out for special praise the Miller-Prince duet, emphasizing the 'full triumph' of its dramatism fused with 'musical truth'.[43] For Musorgskii and his fellow *kuchkist* composers, the mad

---

[43] See Aleksandr Serov, 'Rusalka', in *Muzykal'ny i teatral'nyi vestnik*, 1856, pp. 24, 26, 28, 32–34, 36–39 (reprinted in A. N. Serov, *Stat'i o muzyke, Vypusk vtoroi B*, Moscow, 1986, pp. 42–137. The Mad Miller-Prince duet in Act III is discussed in meticulous detail in his 'Ninth article', pp. 120–26. Serov, a foe of the 'Italianists' who held sway in Russian opera houses, was convinced that the 'musical truth' of this scene would 'act profoundly, irresistibly, even on those who for many reasons cannot sympathize with the beauties of this style' (p. 120). For an overview in English of *Rusalka* reception concentrating on Serov's ten-part review from 1856, see Richard Taruskin, 'The Stone Guest and Its Progeny', in *Opera and Drama in Russian As Preached and Practiced in the 1860s*, Ann

Miller was the paradigm of musical realism. In 1897, almost two decades after the imperial government had ended its monopoly over all theatre repertory, the Moscow Private Russian Opera mounted *Rusalka*, with Sergei Rakhmaninov conducting and the young Fedor Shaliapin in the role of the Miller. It became the opera's touchstone aria and one of Shaliapin's signature roles. There was justice in this new focus on the role of the men. Pushkin, we recall, had referred to his tragedy-in-progress not as *Rusalka* but as *The Miller*.

What is so startling about the Mad Miller scene? To begin, the two men are not singing *about* a feeling or an event (as happens in the lyric mode). They are experiencing an event in the present, hearing each other, trying to protect themselves from what they hear, failing to do so, and being changed during the singing. Their extraordinary duet, following hard upon the Prince's repentant Cavatina, serves to return responsible memory to each. As the Prince looks on in horror, the Raven-Miller becomes suddenly sober ('Yes, I'm now old and naughty [...] I wander alone like a wild beast. I once had a daughter, the joy of my life [...]'). But the Miller cannot bear to be lucid for long; madness is kinder. In that condition he can act out his agony. As a scavenger-bird he attacks the Prince physically, demanding the return of his daughter. The terrified Prince calls out for help, and the huntsmen arrive. The distraught Prince prepares to leave with his retinue and the Miller collapses unconscious on the shore — the discarded outer shell of that confident, sly, comic and calculating figure who had opened Act I with a ditty and dance-tune. He has moved back in time from Raven to Miller to Father, acknowledging the continuity by realizing that he had preyed on his own daughter.[44]

By the end of Act III, the opera has moved into a static realm. It is devoid of new events, no longer concerned with love, betrayal, or profits, but focuses solely on payments due. This implacable balance-sheet breaks upon the principals in staggered fashion but in coterminous realms, according to the ability of each to absorb it and remain sane enough to sing. Only a multi-layered musicalized text could realize accurately this psychology. For this, again, we must thank the sophisticated dramatic-verbal genre of the libretto. Literary masterpieces adjusted for singing are often dismissed as bowdlerized, and opera certainly knows its share of crude, caricatured simplifications. But as a blanket judgment it is unjust — and especially in the case of the complex maturations we witness in

Arbor, MI, 1981, pp. 250–62.

[44] For a demonstration of this psychological trajectory with precise musical examples, see Verba, 'Ocherk pervyi', pp. 47–53.

Rusalka. Only a libretto could permit the simultaneous expression of several ripening, contradictory, mutually interacting psychologies, each with its own emotional and logical arc. The audience must be literate enough to distinguish the voices, of course, and to intuit who on stage hears what (some musical lines are intended as arias, sung as private 'asides' to the hall and not heard on stage, whereas other lines speak to one another like recitative). In any event this librettistic complexity is wholly beyond the communicative devices available to the ordinary stage play, which, in linear fashion, is limited (if it is to avoid cacophony) to presenting one voice at a time. Dargomyzhskii, like Mozart and Chaikovskii, was superbly gifted in the psychology and developmental ethics of the ensemble.

Act IV of the opera opens on dancing, spinning rusalki at the bottom of the Dnepr. Their tsaritsa-Rusalka calls in her daughter and instructs her about her father on shore. Rusalochka, seven years old in Pushkin, is twelve in the opera, a speaking role with harp arpeggios. What is her mother? A harpy? A siren? Natasha's extravagant bel canto 'revenge aria' that ends Act IV, scene 1 — her most virtuosic, vitriolic stretch of singing — suggests that as a rusalka she has joined those other punitive mythical female creatures. Operatic psychology and coloratura part-writing underlie this melodramatic showpiece, which met with a mixed reception at the 1856 premiere. The music critic F. M. Tolstoi praised Dargomyzhskii for not allowing 'Russian peasants to bawl out Italian arias', while also acknowledging the composer's desire for greater 'universality' of musical form — perhaps only attainable with that Italianate aria in an underwater realm; still, Tolstoi considered the final union of the Prince and the Rusalka 'utterly contrary to the poem's moral aim'.[45] In his massive retrospective on the opera, Serov (who considered it his duty to provide detailed music-writing advice to the composers whose works he reviewed) criticized Dargomyzhskii for 'excesses' such as the revenge aria, insisting that the composer was not at his best with the operatic-fantastic.[46] But this aria, although the heroine's set piece, is only her penultimate voice.

Dargomyzhskii's final scene on the banks of the Dnepr (Act IV, scene 2) prolongs the 'Rusalochka moment' beyond the operatic commonplaces of the vengeful, the exotic and the erotic that govern Rusalka's bel canto aria. More women arrive on the shore (Ol'ga and the Princess), but the focus inexorably turns toward the traumatized Prince, who is mesmerized by

---

[45] F. M. Tolstoy, 'Analysis of A. S. Dargomyzhsky's *Rusalka*', *The Northern Bee*, 1856, no. 118, May–June, translation cited from *Russians on Russian Music, 1830–1880*, ed. Stuart Campbell, Cambridge, 1994, pp. 53–57.

[46] Serov, 'Rusalka', p. 142.

Rusalochka, his child. The Princess — loving, deceived, hurt and proud — looks on in disbelief. Although an archetype of the 'rival', in her grief the Princess is not opposed to, but fused with, the Miller's Daughter.[47] Ol′ga tries to intervene. But the Prince, as his culpability becomes ever clearer, is pulled inexorably toward the river's bottom. Like so much else in the opera, this guilt is doubled, even tripled: guilt not only for the mad Miller and his drowned Daughter but also for his own abandoned wife, who has tracked him down in this distant place, accuses him of betrayal, and begs for the return of his love. As in the royal Wedding of Act I, a woman's voice from nowhere rises up — this time not to punish him with stories of her drowning, but to call him home ('I wait for you as before [...] We will be inseparable'). As the Prince begins to follow Rusalka's voice, the Princess begs him ever more frantically to leave with her. But the Raven-Miller, fantastical patriarch of the first abused family, appears on the bank to protect the 'bridegroom' from these interlopers from the palace. Everywhere the Prince looks, he sees someone he has betrayed. The banks of the Dnepr are the banks of the Real.

Part of that reality is the Wedding, which can only happen once and is happening now. Rusalki whisper and laugh above the waves. As the Prince is led to the river, the Princess falls unconscious on the shore. Just before the curtain falls, the corpse of the Prince is deposited silently at the feet of the Rusalka-tsaritsa. But it is unclear whether real and fantastic worlds can coexist and both continue to live. The opera ends on a staggered chorus of rusalki and huntsmen, each defending its own realm. As in *Evgenii Onegin*, the woman might not get everything she wants, she too is bereft — but she does the right thing, and does not die. A woman either becomes a Muse (as does Tat′iana Larina), or like the abandoned Princess an innocent sacrifice, or like Rusalka a symbol of cosmic justice. The man, over and over again, does not do the right thing, cannot make amends, and loses all. This was the sombre pattern at the end of Dargomyzhskii's opera, and it would be reinforced in subsequent interpretations and continuations of Pushkin's play, to which we now turn.

The afterlife of the two Rusalkas: Two completions
In 1897, two years before the Pushkin Centennial, a flurry broke out in the Russian academic and journalistic world. The prestigious Petersburg scholarly periodical *Russkii arkhiv* published three hitherto unknown

---

[47] See Verba, 'Ocherk pervyi', pp. 58–60 for this painful conflation of two deceived women. Verba also draws an interesting parallel between Rusalochka and the child in Berg's *Wozzeck*.

concluding scenes to *Rusalka*: a continuation of scene six and three wholly new scenes seven through nine.[48] These 228 lines were presented by the editors as a literal transcript of Pushkin's own words, recited at the home of the poet and *Faust* translator Eduard Ivanovich Guber (1814–47), in November 1836, two months before Pushkin's death. These scenes, it was claimed, had been jotted down after the fact by a fourteen-year-old guest present at the reading, one Dmitrii Zuev, endowed with an astonishing memory.[49] No trace of these scenes had been found among Pushkin's posthumous papers. Inexplicably, Zuev chose to make his transcript (*zapis'*) public only sixty years later. This would seem to be a routine literary mystification — or simple fraud. But tantalizing hints from the memoirs of Pushkin's friends confirmed that in the months preceding the fatal duel, Pushkin was indeed telling his friends about his 'lyrical drama' *Rusalka* and especially about its end.[50] Just enough in the odd story seemed plausible to merit taking the 'addendum' seriously. Scenes six through nine contain the following events.

Zuev's transcript begins where Pushkin's final draft ends, the Prince's question: 'Where did you come from, you marvellous child?' Rusalochka has no problem answering. She is a chatty little girl who supplies pre-histories and motivations. She describes her mother's plight, enduring love and instructions to 'kiss and caress' the man on shore. The Prince, fascinated, takes the little girl's hand and kisses her. At that moment the mad Miller bursts in: 'are you thinking to ruin my granddaughter too? I'll pluck out your heart, peck out your eyes and bring them as a gift to my daughter'. He throws himself on the Prince. This aggressive detail became one item in the forgery case mounted against Zuev, so derivative is it of Dargomyzhskii's operatic drafts, all dating after Pushkin's death, and so absent from any of Pushkin's plans.

Scene seven: the frightened Rusalochka calls out to her mother for help. The Miller's Daughter (for thus is she identified, not as Rusalka) rises out of the water to curse her father the Miller and drive him off. Then she turns to the Prince, relating how for years she had thirsted for vengeance

---

[48] These three and a half scenes, under the title 'Zapis' g. Zueva', were reprinted in 1900 in a volume assembled by A. S. Suvorin, *Poddelka 'Rusalki' Pushkina. Sbornik statei i zametok*, St Petersburg, 1900, pp. 40–55.

[49] Eminent intellectuals such as the jurist and political philosopher Boris Chicherin were persuaded by Zuev. See Chicherin's letter to the editor of *Russkie vedomosti*, 20, 29 January 1897 (Suvorin, *Poddelka 'Rusalki' Pushkina*, pp. 36–38).

[50] See P. Bartenev's defense of Zuev in Suvorin, *Poddelka 'Rusalki' Pushkina*, pp. 56–57. He argued that the scenes might have been confiscated by the Third Section before Pushkin's archive was turned over to Zhukovskii.

but now, seeing him, she forgives him everything, loves him as before, and desires his embrace. 'But my kiss is death', she adds. 'Farewell, flee, be happy with your young wife, forget me.' The Prince refuses to leave: 'I haven't the strength to live without you, without our child.' *Scene eight* opens on the huntsmen and a chorus of rusalki. The Prince has vanished. Rusalki sing in the trees. A new character, 'The Favourite of the Prince' ('Liubimets kniazia'), appears among the hunters sent by the Princess. His purpose is to elicit, and then to discredit as a pagan fairy-tale, the story of the drowning and surviving of the Miller's Daughter. One of the hunters hears from the river the distant voice of the Prince, then of a child, then an old man's threat, then a woman's voice. The Favourite is fed up with these stunts. Little Rusalochka again appears on shore, this time bringing a wedding ring that the Prince wished returned to the Princess (with a request to pray for him — but, says Rusalochka, 'I don't know what praying is'). The favourite, sensing the presence of the unclean force everywhere, orders the little girl seized. But Rusalochka slips back under the waves, as the Miller's corpse washes up on shore. The huntsmen flee. In the final *scene nine*, the royal chambers, the Princess relates to her Nurse a terrible dream. She was dressing herself in rich jewels for her wedding, then entered the church where choirs sang and candles and gold glistened, when at the sanctifying moment, the floor beneath her turned translucent and through its icy mirror she saw her Prince marrying another woman, a beautiful water creature: 'I uttered a cry! [...] and awoke.' At that moment the huntsmen rush in with the ring. Seeing it, the Princess collapses dead in the arms of her Nurse. The Nurse's final plea: 'Accept her into the angelic host, Almighty!'

This Zuev transcript polarized Pushkin-lovers. Remarkably, academics and textologists tended to credit it, either as 'possibly belonging to Pushkin' or as an imperfect paraphrase of one of his rough (not yet publishable) drafts. Thematically, much in it did suggest Pushkin's tragic vision. The symbolism and sanctity of a wedding was now central to every scene, for every social class, and in both the real and the fantastic realm (the inversion of scene 1 is at last set right). Huntsmen turn up in the final scene, as per Pushkin's 1832 plan. The moral growth of the hero in the second half of the play is now explicit, as is the stubbornly persistent love of the Miller's Daughter, who in the end desires not vengeance against the Prince but his acceptance of her and their shared past. She wins her case through love. (In the transcript, it is not clear whether the underwater kingdom is of the living or the dead; that boundary is not significant.) And then there is the Princess's Dream, structurally comparable to other prophetic dreams in Pushkin (Grigorii Otrepiev's nightmare in scene 5 of *Boris Godunov*, Grinev's dream in *The Captain's Daughter*, Tat´iana's dream in *Evgenii Onegin*).

The literary-journalistic community remained sceptical, however. Insisting that the Zuev transcript was a forgery, critics pointed out that many of its lines did not scan (impossible for Pushkin, even in a working draft). Rusalochka and the Prince's Favourite talk too much, and without motivation; Pushkin does not put backstories in the mouths of his characters for the convenience of the audience.[51] Children in Pushkin — not to mention children born and raised underwater — do not babble about themselves to adults. No Russian nanny in the Pushkin era would commend her charge to the 'Almighty host' in the style of Gretchen from *Faust*. What is more, the simplest scholarly procedures for authenticating a manuscript had not been observed before its publication (dating by paper, colour of ink, vintage of writing instrument). When had the writing-down of this 'completion' actually occurred? Zuev (very suspiciously) had 'transcribed' by memory only the three-and-a-half scenes that happened to be missing from Pushkin's posthumous papers. The death knell of this controversial episode, which revealed it as more about the ownership of Russian culture than the authenticity of Pushkin's literary corpus, was sounded by the respected philologist and professor Fedor Korsh (1843–1915), who analysed the additional scenes and concluded that they *might* have belonged to Pushkin. Korsh declared that true scholarship (that is, his method) had nothing in common with 'newspaper criticism'. In response to this insult to his profession, the distinguished publisher Aleksei Suvorin assembled a compendium of the debates as of 1900, titled it *The forgery of Pushkin's 'Rusalka'* (*Poddelka 'Rusalki' Pushkina*) — and framed the anthology with a definitive exposure of Zuev. Suvorin demonstrated handily that Zuev had cobbled together ('pilfered and compiled') his scenes from over a thousand lines of previous '*Rusalka* completions' by other hands, of varying and questionable quality.[52]

---

[51] K. Medvedskii in *Moskovskie vedomosti*, 20 February 1897, in Suvorin, *Poddelka 'Rusalki' Pushkina*, pp. 70–79 (p. 76). Medvedskii acknowledged moments of Pushkin-like genius in Zuev, such as the Princess's dream, but insists that the 'transcript', if not an outright forgery, was an extremely imprecise paraphrase of anything Pushkin could have uttered.

[52] See Suvorin, *Poddelka 'Rusalki' Pushkina*, pp. 3–24 and 261–84. By the 1890s, 1,225 lines of spurious *Rusalka* completions had been published, which are selectively reflected in Zuev's text. In his final pages Suvorin turns very nasty toward Korsh and the 'academicians'.

After the episode, no pages of text had been added to Pushkin's corpus. In 1919 Boris Tomashevskii, the great Russian Formalist verse scholar, invoked this controversy (thereby confirming Suvorin's verdict) at the end of his rigorous statistical analysis of Pushkin's iambic pentameter. He showed how the amateur Zuev had modelled his forgery on the rhythmic profile of the early Pushkin, not the Pushkin of the 1830s. 'To fake words is easy', Tomashevskii cautioned. 'To fake rhythm is impossible.'[53] But the 1900 compendium, for all its mix of rumour and passionate hypothesis, is an absorbing document of *Rusalka* reception. Perhaps, as one contributor suggested, Pushkin had halted precisely on the Prince's question because he realized he had gone too far. His mesh of realistic and fantastic could not be acted out in a single shared space. Attempts to guess out the whole of *Rusalka* continued in the Soviet period.

The most sustained of these attempts was by the actor and director of the State Pushkin Theatre Centre in St Petersburg, Vladimir Retsepter.[54] His

---

[53] With ingenious charts, Tomashevskii shows how his analytic method could have unmasked the forgery. Zuev placed a caesura after the second foot far more frequently than Pushkin did (Pushkin had used the caesura throughout *Boris Godunov*, but not in the blank verse of the 'Little Tragedies' and *Rusalka*). Moreover, Zuev's lines had a much higher percentage of word breaks after the seventh syllable than did Pushkin. 'Much paper has been wasted on whether or not Zuev's "The Conclusion of Rusalka" belongs to Pushkin', Tomashevskii writes. 'Every line in this "Conclusion" has been analysed, but as a whole [*v masse*] the verse was not researched. Of course there can be endless doubts over each line, just as over each word: did Pushkin use it or not? But rhythm is inertia created by a chain of lines of verse. And this inertia is individual for each poet. To fake words is easy. To fake rhythm is impossible. One can carry out a successful forgery of rhythm only after the most painstaking study of a poet, which clearly Zuev had not undertaken.' V. V. Tomashevskii, ch. 13 of 'Piatistopnyi iam Pushkina', *O Stikhe*, Leningrad 1929; repr. Munich, 1970, pp. 138–253 (p. 249). The essay was initially presented in a lecture at the Moscow Linguistic Circle on 8 June 1919, written up in November of that year and first published in Berlin in 1923. Bibliographical details in ibid., p. 327. I thank Michael Wachtel for alerting me to this essay.

[54] These publications, covering much the same ground, are: Vladimir Retsepter, 'Nad rukopis'iu "Rusalki"', *Voprosy literatury*, 2, 1976, pp. 218–62 (hereafter, Retsepter, 1976); V. E. Retsepter, 'O kompozitsii "Rusalki"', *Russkaia literatura*, 3, 1978, pp. 90–105 (hereafter, Retsepter, 1978); V. E. Retsepter, '"Vysokaia tragediia" ("Rusalka" i dramaticheskaia reforma Pushkina)', *Moskovskii Pushkinist*, 4, 1997, pp. 233–77 (hereafter, Retsepter, 1997), and finally a gala bilingual publication sponsored by Retsepter's Pushkin Theatre Centre, *Vozvrashchenie pushkinskoi Rusalki / The Return of Pushkin's Rusalka*, St Petersburg, 1998, with a photo-reproduction of Pushkin's manuscript and illustrations by the contemporary artist Mikhail Chemiakin. (Those fascinating pen drawings show a rusalka-mermaid mother and a Rusalochka daughter who is fish and fins all the way to her shoulders: a startling interpretation of the helplessness and vulnerability of these female creatures, but not in accordance with the legged and footed Russian rusalki.) This volume contains a new essay by Retsepter, 'The History of Readers' Delusions (the last tragedy)', a translation by Antony Wood of Retsepter's version of the play, and a translation of Retsepter, 1978, 'On

strategy, arrived at through a re-examination of the markings in Pushkin's manuscripts, was to impersonate Pushkin as self-editor. Respecting the poet's impulse toward ever greater concision in his revisions, Retsepter did not add new material to the play. Instead he took some away. He deleted seven lines at the end, transposed several passages to eliminate repeats, and re-ordered the three final scenes. Over two decades and four major publications (1976–98), Retsepter argued that Pushkin *did* finish his play (only he failed to create a new fair copy before his death). The Prince's famous final question 'Where did you come from, you marvellous child?' should not be answered (by Rusalochka or anyone else), nor should it hang in the air for the audience to ponder, but rather should be altogether struck from the play.[55] It was important for the mature Pushkin's sense of tragic denouement that the real and fantastic worlds never intersect. Echoing F. M. Tolstoi's criticism after Dargomyzhskii's premiere, Retsepter argued that Pushkin had never intended to bring the Prince together with Rusalka. But the poet was unsure about the proper dramatic closure, and postponed completing his play.

Retsepter, a theatre professional, considered Pushkin a reformer of the stage as radical as Chekhov and Ibsen. And in Retsepter's view, authentic vengeance of the sort prepared by the impersonal spinning Fates could not be realized in the familiar melodramatic modes of dire punishment, spectacular death and otherworldly release. Much as twentieth-century theatre directors, beginning with Meierkhol'd in 1936, have striven to 'return Pushkin to Pushkin' in de-operatized productions of *Boris Godunov*, so the operatic finale must be resisted in our attempt to complete Pushkin's *Rusalka*. Retribution according to Pushkin is accomplished when all parties succumb to necessity and continue to live, fully conscious of their past choices and aware that they are now defined by them. With this understanding of fate as a texture of life rather than as a dramatic end-point, judgments of right or wrong are muted. Redemption and forgiveness become largely irrelevant. The choices that were made back then created the terms of our reality now. 'In the second part of *Rusalka*', Retsepter writes, 'the Miller's Daughter, the Prince, and the Miller all appear in a qualitatively new light, all three (even the mad Miller) feel and acknowledge the changes that have occurred within them, and these

the Composition of *Rusalka*' (hereafter, Retsepter, *Return*).

[55] The lovechild confronting (and delighting) her father on shore was a cliché from the Krasnopol'skii libretto that Retsepter was convinced Pushkin rethought and meant to delete. See its origin in Borisova, 'Liricheskaia drama', p. 116, when Lesta appears to Vidostan with Lida in her arms ('What do I see? Who are you, you charming singer?').

changes must be grasped by the reader or spectator as the *main content of the tragedy*'.[56]

The fanciful Zuev addendum to *Rusalka* had shared this purpose too, up to a point. With its dutiful longwinded Rusalochka, its verbose huntsmen and death-dealing Princess's dream, it too aimed for a heightened moral atmosphere, a deepening of the play as the consequences of irresponsible acts radiate outward in time and space. But Retsepter is against addenda. He insists that Pushkin as tragic dramatist always sought the most efficient and stripped-down way. He would perfect a work by cutting it back and mirroring its major acts in the minds of the characters, never by inflating it, repeating or retelling known material, or adding new speaking parts. How, then, to deal with those 'huntsmen' sent by the Princess in the final line of Pushkin's plan, and does this minimalist version of *Rusalka* succeed in rounding itself off?

As Pushkin's most updated plan, Retsepter proposed a new, lucidly symmetrical order of scenes.[57] No changes are made in the first half of the play. 'Bank of the Dnepr. The Mill' remains one long scene where the girl is betrayed by father and lover and chooses suicide. It is followed by the royal Wedding in the Prince's palace, where the betrayed girl, reduced to pure voice, might be visiting from another realm, or (like the ghosts seen by Macbeth) might be a projection of the Prince's uneasy conscience. The second half of the tragedy takes place seven years later, in those sites where the various principals continue to live: Bottom of the Dnepr, the Princess's anteroom, Dnepr-Night-Huntsmen. If the first half plays out the Prince's abandonment of the Miller's Daughter and their unborn child, thus guaranteeing the sterility of his 'legal and public' marriage, the second half, which opens on rusalki spinning their thread, introduces the Tsaritsa-Rusalka and her diminutive assistant Rusalochka, an irresistible pair whose 'hour has come'. Choice rules the first half, Destiny the second. We then shift to the Princess, for whom time has stopped. She frets to her nurse about her husband's neglect and her childlessness until interrupted by huntsmen, who confess that the Prince had sent them home while he stayed on alone. Horrified, the Princess sends them back to the riverbank. Huntsmen in the real world are like rusalki in the realm of the fantastic: middlemen, mediators, bearers of fate and servitors to a higher power.

Finally: the Dnepr at Night. Rusalki are singing in the moonlight, primed for mischief, when they sense the arrival of the Prince. Since

[56] Retsepter, 1997, pp. 274–76.
[57] Retsepter, 1976, p. 246.

the two worlds cannot mix, the rusalki must hide. The Prince sinks into reverie; suddenly the leaves wilt, the tree blackens, and the Old Man (Miller-Raven) appears, muttering madly. By the time the huntsmen arrive from the Princess, the Prince is in the grip of remorse and horror. Here Retsepter begs us to attend to Pushkin's stage direction: 'he leaves' (*ukhodit*). The Prince not only 'exits', he goes home. Irritated, of course, depressed, angry at being pursued by his nagging wife — but obedient. His life has been 'saved'. With the Prince's departure the rusalki again rise up. They regret the loss of their prey. They would like to frolic further in the trees and fields. But it is late and the moon has set. Their 'stern sister' the Rusalka-Queen is waiting for them below. Like the Prince, they are resigned to follow a higher order, an unseen unknown force. In keeping with Pushkin's modesty in the metaphysical realm, this force is not labelled clean or unclean, sacred or demonic. It simply *is* and exercises its awesome gravitational pull. Retsepter alerts us to the stage direction that ends the play: 'They vanish' [*Skryvaiutsia*]. We must ask: had these water-creatures ever existed, outside the minds of the Prince and the mad Miller? Rusalka too had waited for her Prince, but in accordance with the spinning Fates she must learn to live without. As Retsepter defends this sequence of events: 'The meeting with Rusalochka did not happen, "vengeance" did not happen. The Prince did not catch a glimpse of his daughter, he obediently returns to an unloved and infertile wife, tormented by pangs of conscience and the consciousness of happiness forever lost. Is that not the most terrible retribution?'[58]

One of Pushkin's trademark devices is an ending that cycles back to the beginning, revealing everything to be as it has always been. Onegin and Tat'iana are both alive at the end of the novel but do not touch each other and share no future. Germann in 'Queen of Spades' is again without a fortune and indefinitely in a madhouse. At the end of *Boris Godunov* Russia once again has no ruler — or perhaps another false ruler. In the non-canonical arrangement of scenes suggested by Retsepter, *Rusalka* too ends on open-ended survival, with all parties wiser and more resigned. But in terms of events, the text is anti-climactic. Composers who adapt Pushkin

---

[58] Ibid., p. 249. Consciously or not, Retsepter enters a debate here with Vladimir Nabokov. When Edmund Wilson suggested that the hapless Prince should return to his wife rather than perish with his Rusalka (as in Nabokov's completion), Nabokov insisted that this was 'utterly wrong [...] The end I tagged on is in perfect keeping with the general ending of all legends connected with mermaids and fairies in Russia. [...] Pushkin never broke the skeleton of tradition — he merely rearranged its inner organs, — with less showy but more vital results'. Letter from Nabokov to Wilson, 16 June 1942. See Grayson, '*Rusalka* and the Person from Porlock', pp. 165–66.

to the stage routinely desire stronger dramatic closure. Chaikovskii throws Tati′ana into Onegin's arms and the distraught Liza into the Winter Canal; Germann stabs himself (or shoots himself). Only Musorgskii dared to suspend time with the dark babblings of a Holy Fool, as if to say: there is no plot to end this opera that the human mind can grasp. It could go on like this forever.

For Musorgskii's group of nationalist composers known as the 'Mighty Handful', Dargomyzhskii was a revered role model in musical naturalism. Especially precious for them was the radical experiment Dargomyzhskii conducted near the end of his life: a word-for-word setting of Pushkin's 'Little Tragedy', *The Stone Guest* (1869). His earlier *Rusalka* is musically more conventional but its moral psychology, if anything, is more unsettling. By the end of Act III, Dargomyzhskii had anticipated Retsepter's denouement for Pushkin's play, proposed over a century later. Central to both endings is trauma for the two responsible males. The Prince is 'saved' by being sent back to live in his past, chosen world — what might be called closure in the open-ended Onegin mode. But like Zuev in 1897, Dargomyzhskii had not sacrificed the provocative 'Rusalochka moment' where natural meets supernatural; in fact, he had expanded this moment into an entire fourth act. All victims of the Prince's initial casual seduction come together in an ensemble of sorrow and condemnation. Some can sing and love their way out; others cannot.

'Singing one's way out': to explore this possibility, we return to and extend some recent commentary on *Rusalka* by the music historian Anatolii Tsuker, whose 2010 study, *Dramaturgiia Pushkina v russkoi opernoi klassike* (Pushkin's Dramas in Classic Russian Opera Repertory) was invoked at the beginning of this article. Its second chapter discusses Dargomyzhskii's *Rusalka*, and Tsuker makes a point of 'consciously concentrating attention on the social nature of the conflict'.[59] He admits that this emphasis is in part his irritated response to post-Soviet scholarship that dismisses out of hand the great scholars of the Soviet musical establishment — Gozenpud, Keldysh, Pekelis, Solovtsov — because, for ideological reasons, they were obliged to reflect the class nature of the conflict between Miller, Daughter and Prince.[60] In focusing on the social (rather than on the intimate or metaphysical), these Stalin-era critics had gotten a great deal right. For the genre of Dargomyzhskii's opera is not magical-mystical-everyday-folk-romantic (Tsuker considers such monstrously conflated labels largely meaningless), but a 'musical tragedy of the Shakespearean type' — by

---

[59] Tsuker, *Dramaturgiia Pushkina*, pp. 73–74
[60] Ibid.

which he means, its major heroes pass through grief to enlightenment. There is nothing sentimental, supernatural, or simple about the progress of its events. It stays true to the personal even though every person in it is dependent on extra-personal circumstances. None of the easy binaries work in it: not good-evil, victim-scoundrel, unhappy-happy, innocent-guilty, life-death. The otherworldly is simply a projection of this world, and its continuation: one can walk into it and out of it. The only opposition sustained in the opera, Tsuker claims, is that between free and unfree.

The Daughter is ever constant, on land and under water. She loves absolutely and unrestrainedly, acts in accordance with that love, and thus is free. She prays to the mighty river, because only the Dnepr can understand this sort of uncompromising elemental purity. The Miller and Prince are not evil — but they are compromisers, enslaved and blindsided by their social class and rank. They love Natasha earnestly but according to their means. There is no way the Prince could marry a miller's daughter. There is no hope that the Princess will retain her husband's affection. Of happiness for any party there is none. Tsuker analyses the 'intonational profiles' of the leading roles. Natasha is anxious and frightened from the start (unlike her naively trusting counterpart in Pushkin). The Prince is no villain; his image, cruel and cynical in Pushkin, is 'softened and ennobled' in the libretto.[61] Their love duet is sincere. But he too is trapped, his singing lines are lyrical and elegiac. The Miller also is no villain; he introduces himself and his pragmatic philosophy of life in a brisk polka, good-naturedly and inoffensively comedic. The 'deformation' of this dance theme into the tragic grotesque (the mad Raven) after the daughter's drowning is a Gogolian literalization of one legitimate trait, taken to appalling and hallucinatory extreme.[62] Tsuker agrees with Serov and F. M. Tolstoi that the ending of Dargomyzhskii's opera is weak. To lay the dead body of the Prince at feet of the Rusalka in her underwater kingdom is an 'external' special effect, a banal 'opera cliché' (*opernaia vampuka*).[63] The psychological truth of the opera, Tsuker insists, is in its real-life social backdrop, where the powerless prove the most free and the powerful are rendered utterly impotent by acts of freedom.

Tsuker's analysis of the opera's 'realistic' value system is refreshing and convincingly Shakespearean. But it is remarkable, given its focus on the social, that it avoids discussion of Natasha's pregnancy. The Miller's Daughter might act freely, but surely out of desperation and a projection of

[61] Ibid., p. 74
[62] Ibid., pp. 76–77.
[63] Ibid., pp. 79–80.

her dismal and shameful fate. No singing principal has the right to ignore this condition, nor to conflate it with the mood and melodies of unburdened (even if unreciprocated) erotic love. It is this belated realization that breaks upon both Prince and Raven-Miller in their haunting duet in Act III, scene 2. The site is precisely that of the opening scene, the Mill by the River, but now in ruins. We learn that when Natasha cast herself into the Dnepr, her father tried to follow her. But while the Daughter was granted rusalka-hood (she had female life to protect), the Miller was turned into a scavenger bird. Horrifyingly for both Prince and Miller, their consciences awaken during this duet, enabling them to sense the past not only as nostalgia but as long-term failure in the moral sphere. True, neither was (or is) ever free. Their unfreedom might create the tragedy, but cannot resolve or forgive it. Dargomyzhskii's Rusalka-tsaritsa is kinder to her parent than Pushkin had been. To her daughter Rusalochka she calls the Miller on shore an 'unfortunate old man' (*Starik neschastnyi*), not, as in the play, a 'crazy miser' (*bezumnyi skryaga*). The men are exposed and isolated, and yet everyone comes on stage to witness destiny at work. Tsuker is correct: the relentless sociality of the final scene 'polyphonizes' and humanizes it. To what end *Rusalka*?

Dargomyzhskii, conventionally for opera, slows down the crisp pace of Pushkin's plot with a large number of choruses and round-dances. These episodes interrupt and deepen the intonational profiles of the principals. As we noted, these collective choral inserts are not ornamental diversions. Or rather, as diversions they might delight the audience in the hall but do not have the desired effect on the singers on stage; after the round-dance in Act I, the Prince admits that none of this jollity is cheering up anyone. Father, Daughter and Prince dimly sense that these 'inserts' are equivalent to a Greek chorus, the voice of Fate anchored outside the story-space, questioning and commenting on the action of the opera in a folk version of choral antiphony. In Act II the Princess, whose role in the opera is to grieve non-stop, senses this immediately, for all that Ol'ga exists to brighten her mood. The Prince's 'Where did you come from, you marvellous child?' and her piping reply in the second scene of Act IV trigger an explosion of ensemble singing, which prepares us for the appearance of the Huntsmen at the opera's final moment. They too are a Greek chorus; they interrupt a (similarly fateful and fatal) 'Chorus of rusalki' singing their ha-ha-ha from the watery depths. Like Prince Andrei Khovanskii at the end of Musorgskii's *Khovanshchina*, drawn into elemental fire by the woman he has abandoned to the sound of a celestial chorus, so is the hapless Prince in *Rusalka* drawn by an 'unknown force' (*nevedomaia sila*) toward that lower element, water, and then into it. Individuals are literally being absorbed by their collectively determined fates. Should we still wonder why the jocular, pragmatic, self-confident Miller dances his opening number solo to launch the opera, disdaining the expected welcoming chorus, one answer is because the presence of a chorus, or of complex ensemble singing, is proof that your voice cannot control anything by itself. It is wise only when heard together with others, and obliged to harmonize with them. This lesson the Miller learns only deep into his own fate.

Tsuker grasps these ethical functions of the ensemble, potentially healing because inevitably contextualizing. But he perhaps overestimates the degree to which each voice within the ensemble is free. His neglect of the pregnancy in pursuit of the 'social' is symptomatic. The *Rusalka* endings discussed in this essay do not make that error. They reflect archetypical Pushkinian anxieties about one-way acts in delicate suspension: unreciprocated love (Tat´iana in *Evgenii Onegin*), nostalgia for the departed spontaneous desires of youth, madness understood not merely as the loss of one's grip on reality but as an unwillingness to *accept* reality, that is, to accept responsibility for actions that cannot be undone.[64] It is very much in the spirit of the mature Pushkin to consider his Rusalka, this 'stern, cold tsarina' of the Dnepr, a complex enabling figure whose primary role is not, as with the classical sirens, to drive men mad. Again, her task — like Princess Tat´iana's when Onegin comes abjectly courting in the final scene — is the reverse: to call the beloved man soberly to his senses, to summon up his better self and compel it to confront its past. The woman puts a halt to the pain of this past by confirming her love while herself agreeing to remain bereft.

There is a larger mythopoetic pattern in Pushkin's *Rusalka* that is found throughout the poet's work in all genres. When a bond of love, family, or pledged loyalty is broken out of a calculated desire for money or power (or out of carelessness, for convenience), the punishment is barrenness and the loss of one's line.[65] Recall *Boris Godunov*, or again *Evgenii Onegin*. In

---

[64] Scholars routinely note parallels between *Evgenii Onegin* and *Rusalka*, down to identical adjectives for Tat´iana and the water maiden, and between the lovestruck Prince returning to the riverbank and Onegin circling around the Petersburg balls. For a summary of the parallels (and charts), see Verba, 'Ocherk pervyi', pp. 15–19.

[65] For a fine discussion of this side of Pushkin's genius, see Andrei Sinyavsky, *Strolls with Pushkin*, trans. Catharine Theimer Nepomnyashchy and Slava I. Yastremski, New York, 2017, p. 23: 'The calculating man in Pushkin is a despot, a rebel [...]. The calculating man, having calculated everything, stumbles and falls, never understanding why [...]. It's hard to say what many of Pushkin's works are for or what they are about — to such an extent are they about nothing and to no end but the roundedness of fate and the plot.'

Dargomyzhskii's musical parable on *Rusalka*, responsibility for a broken bond can be accessed best through the vocal ensemble, a sobering device to tune up and contextualize one's conscience. The Prince and the Miller, losing their minds before losing their lives, are never as honest, real, or clear-sighted as in their Act III duet. When the Prince sings alone, he is full of self-pity. When Natasha-Rusalka sings alone, 'vengeance boils in her blood'. But when she sees and hears her Prince, vistas open out and her lyrical voice returns. Pushkin, I believe, would have agreed that the rhyme had come home, the circle had closed in the correct way.

NOTES ON CONTRIBUTORS

Philip Ross Bullock is Professor of Russian Literature and Music at the University of Oxford, Fellow and Tutor in Russian at Wadham College, Oxford and Director of TORCH | The Oxford Research Centre in the Humanities. His most recent book is *Pyotr Tchaikovsky* (London, 2016).

Caryl Emerson is A. Watson Armour III University Professor Emeritus of Slavic Languages and Literatures at Princeton University. Her scholarship has focused on the Russian classics (Pushkin, Tolstoi, Dostoevskii), Mikhail Bakhtin, and Russian music, opera and theatre. Current projects include the Russian modernist Sigizmund Krzhizhanovskii, Bakhtin and the performing arts, neoThomist aesthetics, and the great Russian novelists approached as religious thinkers.

Pauline Fairclough is Professor of Music at the University of Bristol and a specialist in Soviet musical culture, especially during the Stalin period. Her last book, *Classics for the Masses: Shaping Soviet Musical Identity Under Lenin and Stalin* (New Haven, CT, 2016) was co-winner of the BASEES Women's Forum Book Prize (2017). Her biography of the composer Dmitrii Shostakovich will be published by Reaktion Books in their 'Critical Lives' series in 2019.

Rebecca Mitchell is Assistant Professor of History at Middlebury College. Her first book, *Nietzsche's Orphans: Music, Metaphysics and the Twilight of the Russian Empire* (New Haven, CT, 2016), won the W. Bruce Lincoln Book Award of the American Association of Slavonic, East European and Eurasian Studies in 2016.

Olga Panteleeva is Lecturer in Musicology at Utrecht University, specializing in the history of musicology, music during the Cold War, and contemporary politics of music. In 2017–18 she was a Fung Global Fellow at Princeton University.

James Taylor completed a PhD in Musicology at the University of Bristol in January 2018. His thesis, 'The Culture Doctors: Music, Health and Identity in Revolutionary Russia', examines the critical role music played in building Soviet society after 1917. He is currently researching Soviet radio and the senses in the interwar period.

www.ingramcontent.com/pod-product-compliance
Lightning Source LLC
Chambersburg PA
CBHW051053160426
43193CB00010B/1167